P9-DUQ-729

The Cowgirls

THE Cowgirls

by Joyce Gibson Roach

UNIVERSITY OF NORTH TEXAS PRESS

Manufactured in the United States of America

Second Edition, revised and enlarged

10 9 8 7 6 5 4

The cover art, "A Helping Hand" by H. Dunton, is used by the permission of
The Rockwell Museum, Corning, NY.
Photography by James Milmoe.

The paper used in this book meets the minimum requirements of the American National Standard for Permanence of Paper for Printed Library Materials, Z39.48.1984.

Library of Congress
Cataloging-in-Publication Data

Roach, Joyce Gibson.
The cowgirls / by Joyce Gibson Roach. — updated and rev. ed.
p. cm.
Includes bibliographical references and index.
ISBN 0-929398-15-7 : $15.95
1. Cowgirls—West (U.S.) 2. West (U.S.)—Social life and customs.
I. Title.
F596.R65 1990
978'.02'0922—dc20

90-39339
CIP

For Ada Worthington Womack,
the only real cowgirl left—at least the only one I know.

Jackie, Mary, and Ada Worthington

CONTENTS

Preface

Cowmen—and cowwomen—are a breed apart. People who live with and by cows have always been a little farther out—geographically speaking— than the rest of the population. They pioneered in new country, lived hard and often dangerously, called no man master and occupied land that nobody else wanted. Some of them still do. As a result we like to think of them as more independent, more stable, more themselves than other men. They wear their own uniforms, live as they always have lived and keep some of the flavor of an earlier, braver, simpler, kinder America.

Some years ago, when I was on the road looking into the situation of the contemporary cattleman, I stopped at a place at the end of the trail in a remote part of Colorado. A friendly, weather-worn human being greeted me: "Come in, Stranger! All we've got here is a lot of brush and a few good neighbors, but you're welcome!"

This, we like to believe, is still the spirit of the cattleman in spite of airplanes, oil wells and politics. His business is dependent on weather and the market and his life is never secure. This keeps him from becoming a fat cat unless he is a fat cat already and is using the ranch for a tax write-off. In such cases the boots and the big hat are a disguise, but everybody in the cow business knows the difference.

He has his faults, of course. Cowboys were once considered wild and some still are. A few cattlemen are crooked. Admitting these things, we still feel that out on the range it is harder to be dishonest than in Washington.

I asked Farrington Carpenter, a top cattleman, one time what percentage of cattlemen he considered honest. "They are about two percent sons of bitches, like everybody else," he replied. This figure gives them a considerable edge over other American groups, including teachers and preachers.

It seems obvious that the cattle person, past and present, is well worth knowing, and indeed we do know a good deal about him. We do not, however, know as much as we should. Most of the books have been written by writers who are not in the cattle business or by people in the business who can't write. Then too, the mythical cowboy of the movies and romantic novels is always getting in the way of the facts, and the changes which have come with time confuse us even more. The idea of a ranchman rounding up steers in a jeep seems somehow sacrilegious, and such equipment as the walking boot and the foam-rubber-padded saddle come close to obscenity. Life in the country and in the cow business keeps much of the old lifestyle going, however, and we can still talk about cowmen and cowgirls with some certainty that we know what we mean.

The cowgirls have had less attention than their male counterparts and this is to be regretted, for they are just as varied and just as interesting a group as the men. Ace Reid's bedraggled ranchwomen are at the bottom. Edna Ferber's rich bitches are at the top. And there are thousands in between. They are all interesting, and their tale should be told.

Joyce Roach is the one to tell it. She lives in the country at Crosswinds, north of Fort Worth. She and her husband, Claude, have cows and horses. Their children were involved. She has known ranch people from her childhood and has come to know them better through years of correspondence and interviewing. She is close enough to being a cowgirl herself to speak with knowledge, and she can write.

Her book is timely. The women's movement is in full swing and housewives all over the country are clamoring to be "liberated." Joyce contributes by showing that cowgirls are already liberated. And she can prove it!

C. L. Sonnichsen
Tucson, Arizona
1977

Acknowledgements

I am first and foremost still indebted to Dr. C. L. Sonnichsen of Tucson, Arizona, for critically reading my manuscript, making suggestions, leading me to dozens of helpful people, giving me ideas, and holding the reins or applying the quirt. His generosity has made him a legend in his own time. He made me feel, as he has made dozens of others feel, that I was absolutely his favorite and most loved friend and that no research was as important as mine.

If I could I would thank the late Dr. Mabel Major who led me through the classics of English literature only to show me that nowhere was the grass greener than in my own Southwestern backyard and the late Mody C. Boatright who agreed with me that the cowgirls were more interesting than the cowboys and who graciously loaned me his file on frontier women.

My thanks sincerely go to others who made this book possible:

Tad Lucas, Ruth Roach Salmon and Velda and Charlie Smith who spent leisurely afternoons remembering about their participation in the early days of rodeo.

Mabel Strickland Woodward, Mildred Chrisman, Vera McGinnis Farra who patiently answered questions by mail.

Don Russell who searched old rodeo programs many times in my behalf.

Edward T. LeBlanc for reading the chapter on Dime Novels and for lending me his personal copies of some of the novels.

Deolece Parmelee for some true facts about Sally Skull.

Joe Rosa who had to come all the way from England to point out a lady drover.

Eugene Briscoe for research help and friendly encouragement.

Alys Freeze and Hazel Lundburg of the Western History Section of the Denver Public Library for never batting an eye over my many requests.

Alice Marriott, Frances Gillmor and Dorothy Johnson for searching their files and the memories of their friends for names worth looking into.

The staff of the Arizona Historical Society Library.

The staff of the Panhandle-Plains museum and in particular Joni Scott.

Doris Foster of the Keller Public Library who obtained material through interlibrary loan.

Nora Ramirez whose acquaintance I made in the Arizona Historical Society Library and who took time from her own research to lead me to *The Little Lady of the Triangle Bar.*

James Bratcher for a good story and many helpful suggestions.

John Kelt, Lacy Simms, Clara Snow and Roy Harman for remembering about Susan McSween.

Robert Mullin for responding to an inquiry about Susan McSween with a long letter and his personal notes taken while editing Fulton's *History of the Lincoln County War.*

Mary Haughian for information about Susan Haughian.

Hallie Stillwell for information about Alice Stillwell Henderson.

Stella Polk for some delightful stories about ranch women.

Anabelle Jones of San Angelo, Texas, for leading me to Mabel Day and the Fence cutters.

Eve Ball for information about Susan McSween.

Harwood Hinton for a conversation on an August afternoon in 1973 about ranch women and about Uncle John Chisum.

Carl Hartman for leading me to Mollie Monroe.

Beverly Stoeltje who keeps up with women and folklore.

And, in the revised edition of *The Cowgirls*, I add my thanks to:

Ann, my mother, who makes all the good things in my life possible.

Darrell and Delight, who are now old enough to read *The Cowgirls* and to understand their mother.

Ron Tyler of the Texas State Historical Association, for asking that *The Cowgirls* be revised and reprinted.

Suzanne Comer, for suggestions and help.

Judy Alter, who encourages and teaches in large doses, along with friendship.

Members of the Texas Folklore Society, who have inspired and nurtured me for twenty-five years.

Introduction

"Life used to be so simple," said a cowgirl who, along with her two sisters, knew what it was to work a large ranch roping, riding, branding, herding, castrating, birthing, breeding, slaughtering, vaccinating, cooking, washing, living with danger every day, and riding the bus for miles back and forth to school. She lived that uncomplicated life during the 1930s and 1940s when hard times were multiplied three-fold if you lived on an isolated ranch in Jack County, Texas.

I pointed out to Ada Worthington Womack that times right now ought to seem better, easier for her. Things should be more convenient and less complicated than in her childhood. Ada did not agree. She confessed that she did not understand the modern world, that words didn't even have the same meaning anymore.

In the past, life may have seemed more simple because folks had a better handle on labels—we knew what to call things. "Cowgirls" is such a label, difficult to get a grip on today. No one can agree on the meaning of the label, yet it is a descriptive word—it says what it means. Since a cowgirl seems the feminine counterpart of a cowboy, I suggest this definition: A cowgirl is a female whose life is or was for a significant part influenced by cattle, horses, and men who dealt with either or both. The men are a part of the cowgirl's environment, often as dominant figures but not always.

This book, however, does not seek to bury the cowgirl in a narrow grave by defining her. Rather, this study seeks to point out the many types of women who might even loosely be described as cowgirls, as well as those who ride squarely under the banner.

In the volumes detailing the rise and fall of the American West, cowgirls have been neglected, generally lumped with pioneer women and thus too narrowly hemmed in. If noticed, they are disparaged. In his [1968] collection of essays titled *In a Narrow Grave*, Larry McMurtry called them "that awful phenomena."[1] More recently, a survey in *Texas Monthly* warned: "Think twice before you call them cowgirls. They do not necessarily warm to the term, since it is a word that managed to diminish both cattle and women. But what are we supposed to call them? Women with a Professional or Recreational Interest in Livestock?"[2] Even when cowgirls first appeared, in the middle of the 1800s, those early women would not have recognized that label and any man who knew it being attached to his female relative would have demanded an explanation, with a hand on his holster or with his fists clenched and ready.

Still, when Susan B. Anthony and her hoop-skirted friends were declaring that females, too, were created equal, a woman named Sally Skull was riding and roping and marking her cattle with the Circle S brand on the western frontier of Texas. Wearing rawhide bloomers and riding astride, she thought nothing of crossing the border into Mexico, unchaperoned, to pursue her career as a horse trader. She asked no man's leave and needed no man's escort. Sally was one of many.

In Colorado, Cassie Redwine rounded up her cowboys and ambushed a group of desperadoes. Ann Bassett, also of Colorado, backed down a group of men who tried to force her off the open range. In Montana, Susan Haughian took on the United States government in a dispute over some grazing rights and the government got the short end of the stick. Susan McSween, the "Cattle Queen of New Mexico," carried on an armed dispute between ranchers, the U.S. Army and other interested citizens. In Arizona, Annette Taylor experimented with new grasses and found cures for the diseases that plagued her stock.

These women had more in common than their free but not easy life. They were part of a revolution in the affairs of women which was taking place, unheralded and unnoticed, throughout the United States. They were, in fact, the advance guards of the movement, for the trend toward equality for women was most apparent in the cattle country where some of the manliest, most stubborn men ever to grace myth and legend were riding tall in the saddle. Quite naturally, since these women spent their lives in the company of cattle and of the men who took care of cattle, they came to be known to the rest of the world as cowgirls. But it bears repeating that on the range anyone calling a ranch woman a cowgirl was living recklessly.

For one thing, many of the women weren't girls, but mature women. For another, the term cowgirl smelled of commercial enterprises such as Wild West shows which sometimes had little to do with ranch life. Nevertheless, cowgirl is the term by which an international following came to identify ranch women in the American West. These women probably never heard of Susan B. Anthony and the rebellious ladies who wished to have the right to do exactly what the cowgirls were doing, but they rode down the same road, some distance in advance of the theoretical feminists.

How women on the cattle frontier took their place as equal partners with men is an important chapter in the history and folklore of the West. The cowboy may be our most authentic folk hero, but the cowgirl is right on his heels. Other frontier women were more or less forgotten with the passing of the frontier. The life of the farm woman, for instance, was never heroic, just miserable at least according to many factual and fictional accounts and she disappeared from our consciousness. But the cattlewomen, like cowboys, stayed in the saddle and survived. Nothing short of a woman bound for outer space aboard a rocket would seem a likely candidate to replace the cowgirl. It's an interesting coincidence that the first female rocket rider's name should be Sally Ride, a name that draws our thoughts to others who ride or have ridden before her.

The cowgirl's unique history begins when she left the trees and faced the pains and perils of the Plains, enduring hard weather, drought, loneliness, primitive living, and a lack of spiritual and medical comforts in the vast, treeless expanse. Everything was against her, just as it was against all the women who came to the frontier West. The difference is that women of the cattle frontier, from this point on known as cowgirls without apology, encountered the hardships in a special place known as a cattle ranch.

Historian Dixon Wecter has noted that the War between the States shattered "the decorum of the sentimental years."[3] Women were called upon to do many things which would have been unheard of in peacetime. When people moved west after the war, women were obliged to keep doing these things if the family was to survive. The last traces of the southern Camelot had been kicked over. Historians for a long time have compared knights in armor to cowboys on horseback, and they have known that it wasn't far from Camelot to the cowlot, but the cowgirl was no Guinevere. She did not stay at home weaving the events of her life into a tapestry and awaiting the hero's return.

Nor were all the women who went west from genteel backgrounds or even from the South. Rich or poor, refined or rough, high born and low found that the frontier experience was a great leveller. But for women on cattle ranches, the experience was different.

Men have often found women helpful wherever they were and have generally praised women for their roles as helpmates. For women on cattle ranches helping required hard work. Frontier cattlemen were away from home much of the time, and women found themselves with new responsibilities. One woman had to take charge of a cattle ranch when her husband deserted her.[4] The obligation of ten children and a crippled husband caused a Montana woman to drive a team for the local stage line, in addition to managing the ranch.[5] Sometimes a lady pitched in because she realized there was extra profit if she helped—orphan calves became the particular project of Mrs. H. J. Ficke, who added 150 animals to the family herd in six years.[6] Occasionally, a woman discovered she did not necessarily need to help a man but that she could wear the britches all by herself and do a man's job because she found it profitable. The most striking example was Lizzie Johnson who, after making a considerable amount of money writing under a pen name and investing the money in cattle, registered her own brand in 1871.[7]

Still another group of women did a man's job because they were good at it, liked it, and grew up with it. Some of these women, usually from the second generation born on ranches or in cattle country and growing up in the last years of the frontier, at the turn of the century, participated in Wild West shows, thereby popularizing what women were doing in the West. Lucille Mulhall grew up on an Oklahoma ranch and exhibited her skill at roping, riding, and tying steers with the Miller's 101 Show and with her father's show. After she impressed a future president by roping a wolf from horseback, so the story goes, the term cowgirl was coined for her. Tad Lucas used to ride races with the Sioux on her father's Nebraska ranch and made a reputation for herself in rodeo as a trick and bronc rider.

Because cowgirls' lives were lived on ranches, three factors were significant in the formation of the myth and legend surrounding these women: clothes, horses and guns. Interestingly, these same items are central to a cowboy's life, too.

If there were dangers and hardships for women on ranches, there were also compensations. For one thing, they could dress as they pleased. When a woman began to deal point-blank with cattle, clothing adjustments had to be made. Long full skirts and petticoats were not appropriate. Divided skirts stitched up the middle to form what are called culottes today were early but unsatisfactory changes. Shortened versions worn with knee-high boots came next. Women in men's trousers and overalls must have come fairly early on the cattle frontier, even if the pants were worn under long skirts. Nobody was around keeping tally sheets on ranch fashion, but it seems logical that women who led such isolated lives reached independent but identical conclusions about clothing and found themselves a pair of britches when they needed to.

The adaptation of masculine clothing had less to do with cattle than it did with horses. Some of the genteel ladies from the South had no doubt mastered the art of clinging to a side-saddle atop a long-legged Thoroughbred, but the duties of ranch life were pursued riding a different kind of beast entirely. Cowponies and cowhorses eventually came to be a breed unto themselves, and if horses helped make heroes, they also made heroines.

Texas folklorist J. Frank Dobie noted in *The Mustangs* that "no man by taking thought can add to his stature, but by taking a horse he can."[8] The same statement applied to cattlewomen. The emancipation of women may have begun not with the vote, nor in the cities where women marched and carried signs and protested but rather when they mounted a good cowhorse and realized how different and fine the view. Farm wives walked behind a plow, where horizons were blocked by a horse's rump and days were spent trying to keep from stepping in something. But from the back of a horse, the world looked wider. Cowgirls discovered more than transportation in horses, and the almost spiritual communication between women and horses, a theme in world literature, is particularly evident in Western literature.

Guns were the third important element in the adjustment made by women on the cattle frontier. Women naturally had to protect themselves from obvious dangers, and they could use guns when necessary as well as ropes, knives, whips, and whatever they could lay hands to. In their original and imaginative use of the weapon, the ladies may have outdone the menfolk. When journalists first brought cowgirls to the attention of the nation and the world early in the twentieth century, the reporters mentioned guns along with horses and wardrobes. It might seem easy to accuse those early journalists of sensationalism and sheer fabrication but in truth what they reported was based on fact.

Cowgirls had some influence on law throughout the nation. In Wyoming in 1890 cattlemen wished their country to remain a territory unless women were given the right to vote in the new state.[9] A study by T. A. Larson indicates that the Wyoming Legislature, mainly bachelors, voted in favor of women's suffrage to get publicity for the state, to encourage more women to move there, and to embarrass the governor who was against the plan.[10] For whatever reasons, the bill was enacted, and the women, who had already been voting for twenty-one years in the territory, were able to continue the process. In 1916, the first congresswoman, Jeannette Rankin, was elected from Montana.[11]

Accepted by the men of the cattle country, who had themselves become the cowboy-folk hero, it was natural that the cowgirl should become a folk heroine. The circumstances of the cowgirl's usefulness to cattlemen and her adaptations of traditional roles to the needs of the frontier were particularly right for western legend and myth. When women rode, roped, fought, rustled, went up the trail and managed ranches like men, they took on some of the heroic qualities ascribed to males.

When the frontier became civilized, the cowgirl legend was kept alive in dime novels, folk stories, Wild West shows and rodeos, movies, songs and western humor. The clothes, horses and guns were translated into gaudily embroidered garments, silver and pearl-plated weapons, and fantastic beasts. The women and their animals became gigantic and brilliantly-enough colored to appear on the western stage. As C. L. Sonnichsen said about the West, "What people choose to believe about the facts is a fact in itself and just as important."[12] Those who would imitate the West often looked no further back then the dime novel era, and why not? The view is grand.

As long as the cowboy rides, the cowgirl rides with him, sometimes by his side, sometimes just ahead, but never far behind. The cowgirl in all her roles from the frontier to the footlights, in fact and folklore, is what this book is all about.

For scholars, historians, and interpreters of life in the West, I hope this study will serve by displaying a rich variety of women. For those who write creatively, I offer examples enough to fill dozens, yea, hundreds of novels. But it is for a third group that I write—ranchers, cowboys, cowgirls, Westerners, teachers, country people, and students who read *The Cowgirls* in its first printing and kept it alive for some eight years. Each of the three groups, however, will find it easy to draw their own conclusions, make their own connections, champion their own interpretations.

I asked Ada Worthington Womack if she minded being called a cowgirl. "No," she replied. "It's what I was. I don't mind being called one today." She continued with a grin, "Anybody who wants to can be a cowgirl today. How about you? Aren't you a cowgirl?"

I told her cowgirl was a name someone else must bestow. I couldn't do it for myself. She said I was old-fashioned, and I accused her of the same thing.

Joyce Gibson Roach
Keller, Texas
September 1989

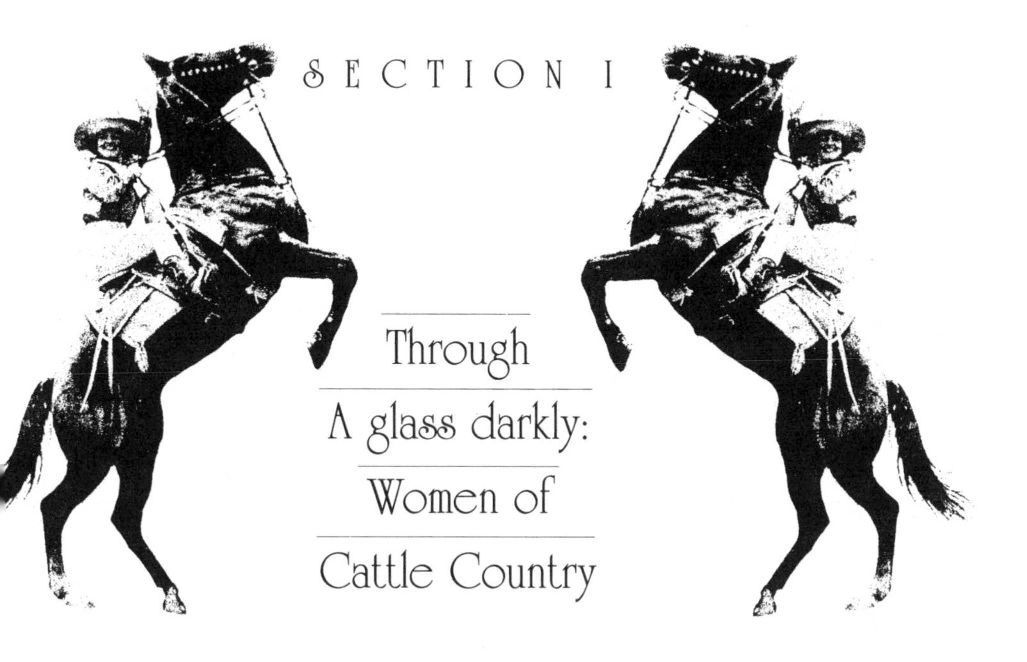

SECTION I

Through A glass darkly: Women of Cattle Country

Who were the original cowgirls? They were first flesh and blood—real persons who lived on ranches during a period in history when cattle and ranching was important. How the women responded to the environment was often memorable. No matter how far from the truth folklore might later take them, no matter how dimly we perceive them, cowgirls were from the beginning vital, interesting creatures. Whatever the cowboys were doing, the women of the cattle range were doing, too. If polite society considered roping, herding and branding a man's work, then the women were busy shattering the old standards. Up the trail with the herd and out on the range, women were on hand. Housekeeping arrangements in conjunction with ranch duties did undergo unique changes and adaptations but females kept the cattle kingdom in order. The fusion of domestic and working responsibilities created, from the very beginning, a different female environment in the West.

At home and away, articles such as whips and ropes helped the cowgirls keep their occupational life in order and in the use of guns—rifles and pistols—they were formidable. Women often had to protect themselves and they found interesting ways to do it with firearms. Bluffing, for example, was not a game they often played. Some even took up arms in larger battles such as cattle wars and in skirmishes and quarrels with neighbors if necessary. A few discovered what some of the men already knew: Somebody else's stock was easier to round up and brand, unless you got caught.

1

Hairpins on the Trail

Nowhere are cowboys, both real and imaginary, more noticeable than on cattle drives. From journals and diaries to the silver screen, the drama of stampede, crossing the herd, prairie fire, storm, bandits, Indians, gunplay and death is clearly a man's province. The few women in the fictional treatments are generally at the end of the trail waiting to offer comfort. Some go so far as to say that there were no women on cattle drives, just as there were no women on board sailing ships, period. The thought of women going up the trail with wild animals and rough men offended the sensibilities of polite society, or it might have if polite society had known such a state of affairs was going on in a remote part of the continent where even neighbors did not see each other once a year.

Women, of course, did go up the trail. They shattered old standards and left behind evidence that they were there with the first herds. But they weren't called cowgirls.

The mountains of Colorado provided a properly rugged setting for a drive where a new hand took breakfast with the crew and then mounted up to help gather a thousand Long-horns scattered in the canyons and valleys around Long's Peak. Back and forth, over fallen rocks and snags of dead pine trees, through the dense undergrowth and across slippery streams, the new hand managed to gather a hundred head alone. The small bay horse, keeping stride with the other cow ponies, spun away from the thrust of horns time and time again, and rider and horse stood their ground with the others as the great herd milled and began to surge against the drovers. The new hand recalled:

> It seemed like infantry awaiting the shock of cavalry as we stood as still as our excited horses would allow. I almost quailed as the surge came on, but when it got close to us my comrades hooted fearfully, and we dashed forward with the dogs, and, with bellowing, roaring, and thunder of hoofs, the wave receded as it came.[1]

The year was 1873 and the new hand was an English woman, Isabella Bird, who had come to see the elephant and hear the owl hoot. Dismissed as a dude and tourist by some, Isabella nevertheless caught the spirit of the cattle drive.

In order to tour the rugged regions of Colorado, Isabella got rid of her dress and rode in long pantaloons. She sometimes traveled in the company of a guide, Mountain Jim, who was considered dangerous by some. During the course of Isabella's tour she was chased by a bear, pierced by thorns, dashed against rocks and timber, worn down by many hardships. She was thrown from a bronc, and, although she received serious cuts and bruises, Isabella came to love cowponies that exercise "their intelligence for your advantage, and do their work rather as friends than as machines."

While many outsiders found grave fault with the cattle industry as a cruel enterprise, Isabella understood the necessity of the branding corral and slaughter pen. She worked briefly as a hand and not only was she admired by the men with whom she rode the trail, but she also gave an accurate and early account of a woman in the saddle.

While Isabella Bird passed a pleasant vacation in Colorado, there were other women, usually the wives of the owners of the herd, who spent time on the cattle trails of the Great Plains.

It would be pleasant to think that the women melted in with the crew, made hands, and never got in the way. Truth to tell there seem to have been a good many scattered hairpins, trunks of clothes, and even children to keep up with. Sometimes the women got lost. Sometimes they did awful things such as setting prairie fires—unintentionally of course. They were afraid some of the time and spent a good deal more time wondering where everyone else was. One man's job on the trail with some outfits probably was not to chase cows but to try to keep the bosses' wife headed north. It is not recorded that the men complained. Cowboys don't talk much. But the women did talk later and left records of what they knew of life on the cattle drive.

Mrs. A. P. Belcher of Del Rio, Texas, remembered trailing behind the chuck wagon and eating son-of-a-gun stew from a tin plate in the 1870s. Mrs. W. B. Slaughter remembered heading out with her husband from Fort Sumner, New Mexico, in 1896 with a herd of fifteen hundred. It was her job to hunt watering holes, rustle wood and help the horse wrangler on the trail to Liberal, Kansas. Neither Mrs. Belcher nor Mrs. Slaughter had much to say about going up the trail but Mrs. Amanda Burks of Cotulla, Texas, knew plenty and she told about it in *The Trail Drivers of Texas.*

Amanda generally stayed home during Mr. Burks's drives up the Kansas trail, but when he was only one day out from home on one of his drives, Mr. Burks sent word that Amanda was needed. Amanda never explained just how she was needed, but, taking Nick, her Negro servant, and hitching her ponies to the buggy, she started out on an adventure which earned her the title "Cattle Queen of Cotulla."

The early part of the drive must have seemed a pleasant diversion—camping out in new country. Amanda slept in a tent and had her meals prepared separately from the crew's by Nick. She stayed near the horse herd, and, since they generally followed the cattle, Amanda found opportunities to catnap. It is probably just as well that she rested when she could because soon her narrative livens up as she recounts events which have always made cattle drives dramatic.

Amanda describes how cattle had to be rushed through stretches of timber in order to keep them from scattering, and how during electrical storms "lightning seemed to settle on the ground and creep along like something alive." She survived a hail storm during which she had to tie her horses to keep them from running away with her, and then found herself lost from the group. When she was with the crew, Amanda often was left alone in camp at night while the men stood alert for stampede. Sometimes her tent fell in.

Amanda saw the great spectacle of fifteen herds lined out waiting to cross the Trinity River and of a stampede caused by Indians in which the Burks's herd was mixed with another.

While many women must have seen prairie fires, probably few ever saw one which started with their own two little hands. Amanda, thinking she would be helpful, decided to build a fire in a dry gully attached to the prairie on either side. It did not take long to set the entire countryside ablaze. Mrs. Burks was impressed that the cowboys did not fuss at her about the fire. In fact she noted that along the trail the men were attentive to her and made a point of hunting surprises of wild fruit and prairie chickens for her.

Mrs. Burks knew what it was to suffer through winter on the Plains, but of each of her hardships she said that it helped break the monotony. Some felt sorry for Amanda but her reply was:

> . . .what woman, youthful and full of spirit and the love of living, needs sympathy because of availing herself of the opportunity of being with her husband while at his chosen work in the great out-of-door world?[2]

Mary Taylor Bunton was another who found pleasure on the trail. Mary was a refined and educated young woman when she married and went to live on her husband's Cross S ranch near Sweetwater, Texas. When her husband was forced to boss his own herd up the Chisholm Trail to Kansas in 1886, Mary, a bride of two months, persuaded him with tears that she ought to go, too. Wearing a dark green wool riding dress and taking along other dresses and one ball gown for the social affairs of civilization, Mary climbed in her Concord buggy and started up the trail. Claiming a cream-colored Spanish pony for her own, the new bride often rode ahead of the herd. She wrote:

> Riding ahead of the herd I would turn in my saddle and look back, and it would look as if the entire face of the earth was just a moving mass of heads and horns.[3]

Mary was taken with the wildflowers, buffalo, fowl, and other things which graced the prairie. She also had her share of storms, Indians, and rattlesnakes, and she had to listen to the cowboys sing "Bury me not on the lone prairie" until, it was said, "she was ready to scream."

It was not all fun and frolic with cows, and there was more hiding in the landscape than wildflowers, game and singing cowboys. In 1871, Harriet Cluck gathered her three children up and along with George, her husband, and one thousand head of cattle, headed north from Texas up the Chisholm Trail. The family packed their belongings in an old hack, but Mrs. Cluck kept her spy glass and shotgun always with her.

The journey went smoothly until the herd hit the Red River. The river was flooded and Mrs. Cluck handed her children over to trusted riders while she climbed on behind her husband on his horse to make the crossing.

Mrs. Cluck made it a point to scan the horizon for trouble and one day she found it—rustlers. Helping to load the shotguns, Mrs. Cluck bolstered the courage of younger cowboys by calling out, "If any of you boys are afraid to fight, come here and drive the hack and give me your gun and horse." When the rustlers approached the herd and asked for a tribute, George Cluck replied, "I have sixteen as good fighters under me as ever crossed the Red River and they are all crack shots. When you get ready, open the ball, but us Texans will dance the first set." No doubt Harriet felt the same way.[4]

Even when there were dangers to be faced and problems to be solved, the women later remembered it all as a great adventure. In the early 1870s, Mrs. Minta Holmsley accompanied her husband, James, and a herd to Abilene, Kansas. She rode in a handsome carriage which had set Mr. Holmsley back seventeen hundred dollars. Not only did Mrs. Holmsley travel in style, but during the trip she also made the acquaintance of

John Wesley Hardin, contributed a cure of cream of tartar, sulphur and salts for poison oak, chased a buffalo herd, and got thrown on her head. After the group arrived in Kansas, Mrs. Holmsley's husband and his partner were out of town when a telegram arrived saying to ship the steers immediately. Minta took matters in her own hands, shipped the steers and got top price. Two days later the bottom dropped out of the market.[5]

While Minta Holmsley was a great asset to her husband, other women were not as helpful. Lizzie Johnson Williams went up the Chisholm Trail to Kansas with her husband Hezekiah between 1879 and 1889, but she did not entertain any notions about being a helpmate. Lizzie took her own herd up the trail. Hezekiah took his own herd up the trail. Lizzie let Hezekiah ride in the buggy, and that is about as much help as she was prepared to give him.

Lizzie was the embodiment of an idea whose time had not yet come—she was emancipated in every sense of the word. Lizzie had other interests before cattle claimed her attention. Her father established Johnson Institute, one of the first institutions of higher learning in Texas, near Austin. In the family school she taught such subjects as French, arithmetic, bookkeeping, music, and spelling. Later her bookkeeping skills enabled her to add to her income by keeping books for St. Louis cattlemen.

Still another ability helped Lizzie to get her start in the cattle business. Under a nom de plume, she wrote magazine and newspaper articles and stories which she sold to *Frank Leslie's Magazine*, later renamed *Judge*. She kept her ventures a secret, but with the money she made from her writing she began to invest in cattle.[6] The following statement attests to her success in these early business investments:

> At one time she bought $2500 of stock in the Evans, Snider, Bewell Cattle Company of Chicago; this paid her 100 percent dividends for three years straight, and she sold it at the crucial time for $20,000.[7]

Although Lizzie registered her own brand in Travis County in 1871, she did not give up school teaching or writing. The aftermath of the Civil War provided Lizzie with an opportunity for expanding her cattle enterprises. Because so many men were away at war and because there were no fences, large numbers of unbranded cattle multiplied in the brush of South Texas. The maverick cattle belonged to anyone with means and energy to round them up and to get them to the northern market. Combing the thickets for cattle was known as "brushpopping," and Lizzie expanded her holdings by that method.

When Lizzie was thirty-six years old she took time away from her cows to take a husband. Hezekiah Williams—a preacher, a widower, a poor businessman, and a hard drinker—needed a woman like Lizzie to keep him on the straight and narrow. Lizzie was not about to turn over her business operations, but neither was she going to usurp his place in his own affairs. To her thinking, there was only one reasonable solution: she would manage her affairs, he would attend to his. To be sure of retaining her holdings, Lizzie made Hezekiah sign an agreement saying that after their marriage all her property would remain hers and that all future profits made by her, would be hers alone. Selfish as the practice appeared, it proved beneficial to Hezekiah. He was such a poor manager that Lizzie often had to get him out of a bad deal with her own money.

Until Lizzie's marriage to Hezekiah, there is no evidence that she physically took part in her cattle business. It may be that she hired others to do her brushpopping, branding and shipping. Her special gifts were a shrewd judgment and a good business head. After her marriage to Hezekiah, however, Lizzie personally supervised the choosing of steers. It was said that when she was buying cattle she was willing to stand all day in order to use her excellent judgment and to point out the steers she wanted. When Lizzie and her husband went jointly to the pens, it was Hezekiah who got the short end of the stick. She would tell her hand to put the best steers in her herd. The couple used the same foreman for their spreads, and he was not a man to be envied. There is an undocumented story that Lizzie instructed the foreman to steal all of Hezekiah's unbranded calves and to mark them with her brand. Hezekiah instructed the foreman to return the favor by stealing all of Lizzie's unmarked stock and burning his mark on them. Those who know say that Lizzie still got off with the most stock.

Lizzie's high-handed treatment of her husband would lead one to believe that she did not care for him. Yet when Hezekiah went broke on some business fling, Lizzie would lend him as much as $50,000 to re-establish him in business. When he was solvent, she made him pay back the money. From all reports she was actually very fond of Hezekiah in her own way. It was rumored that she gladly paid $50,000 ransom for him when he was kidnapped by bandits in Cuba during a stay there. When Hezekiah died in El Paso and Lizzie brought him back to Austin for burial, she spent $600 for his coffin—a high price in those times. When she returned the bill with payment, she wrote across it, "I loved this old buzzard this much."

Lizzie's personality did not endear her to everyone. Her students remember her as "austere and firm." Some considered her odd and sometimes mean, but she was friendly to a few, such as her cowhands. She once told her niece that "the cowhands would do anything for her and thought lots of her but that . . . bankers admired her only because they wanted her business." The fact that Lizzie succeeded at a man's occupation and went up the trail with her own herd indicates that she enjoyed her place in a man's world:

> She preferred the company of men and came to think and talk as cattlemen did, while still retaining the manners of a Southern lady. Later actions in Lizzie's life indicate a strange mixture of the cattleman and the lady.[8]

Sometimes Lizzie showed herself to be more cattleman than lady. On trips to Austin, Lizzie would occasionally see Major George W. Littlefield—an important cattleman of Austin, president of a bank, and a gracious gentleman from the Old South. Lizzie's greeting was usually, "Hello, you old cattle thief!" In response the Major would smile and bow.

If Lizzie's personality caused people to dislike her, she had other ways of making society pay attention to her. She used her money:

> She kept churches, schools, and even the University of Texas hopeful of donations which she gave them to understand she was considering. In this way she made people be nice to her, keeping them anticipating money which, from the beginning, she had no intention of giving.[9]

Lizzie did not give up feminine dress as some frontier women did. She was fond of silks, satins, and laces and only when she went up the trail with her herd did she settle for calicos, cottons, a bonnet and a gray shawl. Lizzie was described as striking in appearance, tall and stately, if not beautiful. On one trip to New York Lizzie bought diamonds valued at ten thousand dollars. She dressed beautifully and expensively on trips and for church and social affairs, but at home in Austin she affected a more simple style.

The frontier abounded with people who, to Easterners, appeared unusual. Compared with other pioneer lives, Lizzie's existence was not really so peculiar. She died, however, an eccentric. In spite of wealth, Lizzie allowed herself only the bare necessities during the last years of her life. She dressed so pitifully that people on the street gave her money, and she often subsisted on crackers and cheese. Lizzie spent the last year of her life, 1923, in the home of a niece where she admired the electric lights and relished the "custard" made of eggnog and whiskey. She left a vast estate when she died, but the family found other things, too, such as twenty-eight hundred dollars worth of five-dollar bills hidden about her room. Her diamonds were located in the basement in an unlocked box. Locked boxes concealed such treasures as parrot feathers and flowers from her husband's funeral wreath. But who can say what is important and what is not when you have driven your own herds up the Chisholm trail?

While many drives took herds to Kansas, Mrs. George Reynolds accompanied her husband farther west. The summer of 1868 saw George and his wife and his brother Ben trailing a thousand head wearing the Long X from Texas to Colorado.

Mrs. Reynolds rode in a hack, and while she endured the hardships of any woman on the trail, there was one overpowering presence on her journeys—Indians. The trail to Kansas was relatively safe from Indians compared to the routes the Reynolds' herds followed to Denver, Cheyenne and Salt Lake City. Mrs. Reynolds remembered vividly the Horsehead Crossing of the Pecos River where Indians attempted to encircle the herd. The night before, the Reynolds' horses had been stampeded, and the Indians had followed the herd to the Pecos, hoping to stampede it again before they crossed. Mr. Reynolds posted his men and climbed in the hack with his bride, ready to make his last stand. Mrs. Reynolds made her husband promise that if worse came to worse he would save one last bullet for her. It was the kind of statement fictional literature would put to dramatic use many times in the years to follow. Fortunately, because of help from another herd, Mr. Reynolds crossed safely and didn't have to shoot his wife or anybody else.

There were times when Mrs. Reynolds did not see another woman for months, but still she insisted that she "would not have traded those days for any since."[10]

At the end of the Civil War, Texas was without a good market for a time and some cattle drives headed west, especially to California where the drought was serious.[11] For really hair-raising drives the route to California by way of Apacheria in New Mexico and Arizona was the one to take. Kate Medlin, a widow, helped trail a herd all the way to California, and her narrative illustrates that while the journey was a long one, it was made more quickly when the Apaches helped things move right along.

Kate was no stranger to hard work or tragedy. Some years before, her mother, Mary Ellen Malone, had died in her arms. Mary Ellen had refused to let a German man in Denton County, Texas, have her daughter for a wife. The man promptly shot Mary Ellen. Kate's father, Perry Malone, just as promptly took the gun away and broke the man's neck with it. Kate later married but her husband was killed during the Civil War.

It was probably not an easy thing to decide to take four children on a cattle drive to California, but she did it. Kate, along with others in seven ox-drawn wagons, set out from Hays County, Texas, in 1868 with a herd of fifteen hundred. They were in good spirits for they expected to get rich from the sale of the cattle. On the advice of the trail captain, who considered the journey quite safe, the group failed to provide themselves with adequate ammunition and supplies, and the rest is right out of an action-packed western scenario.

Trouble first interrupted the idyll of pleasant camping grounds and plenty of water in the form of illness. Kate's brother-in-law, Joseph Bradford, began to suffer from peritonitis. As his condition worsened, the group discovered Indians watching them. The Indians did not watch long but quickly attacked.

Kate gathered her children and, while the other women sat down and sobbed, she put the children in a wagon and put feather beds around them because she had heard that bullets would not penetrate the feathers. Giving her female companions a stiff lecture that "crying would not keep them from killing us," Kate set to work molding bullets to fire at the Indians. The arrows fell thick until sunset, when the Apaches retreated to the mountains. Half of the herd had been run off. The next morning as the Indians gathered on all sides, Kate again saw the necessity of being practical and cooked breakfast. Nobody ate much. The men let the remaining cattle go, hoping that the Indians would let them pass on.

Then, in a gesture which seemed peculiar and completely out of keeping with what the pioneers expected, the Apaches performed a strange rite. Instead of attacking, they sent a young squaw riding on the trail captain's stolen horse. As Kate remembered, she carried "a long spear lying crosswise before her. She came riding directly for the wagons, singing an Indian war song." Someone in the party guessed that she was sent as a dare and that if they shot her, then the battle would be renewed. The day continued in a stand-off with the Indians coming closer and closer but with no shots fired. By evening the Indians' ferocity had cooled to curiosity and they told the group to go, that they were now friends, but that the Indians waiting at the next watering hole would not be friendly.

The remainder of the journey was haunted by death, loss of wagons and provisions, lack of water, injury to one of Kate's children, and the constant fear of rattlesnakes. Finally the party got back a portion of their herd picked up by another drive and traded some of the animals for provisions enough to get to California.[12]

Not all trail-driving stories about women had an ending half as happy. An item in the *Wichita Weekly Beacon* of June 4, 1873, announced that Mrs. T. M. Borland and her three children were stopping at the Planter House after accompanying a herd from Texas to Kansas. A follow-up item appeared in the July 9 edition saying that Mrs. Borland died from mania "superinduced by her long, tedious journey and over taxation of brain." Her remains were returned to her home in Victoria, Texas, and the reporter added that everything was "done by relatives and friends to smooth the rapid current of the dark rolling waters."[13]

Going up the trail was primarily a married woman's privilege, and the mode of travel generally was in a buggy. Some, however, made it alone and on horseback. Samuel Dunn Houston told of going into Clayton, New Mexico, to hire trail hands and coming back with Willie Matthews. The boy looked about nineteen and made a good hand with the horses and cattle. The boss declared that Willie got up on the "darkest stormy nights" and stayed with the cattle. Equally impressive was the fact that Willie did not drink, chew, or cuss.

After about four months, when the bunch reached the Colorado-Wyoming line, Willie said he was homesick, asked to draw his pay, and rode off. Later in the day, a well-dressed young lady rode in and addressed Mr. Houston, asking if he did not recognize her. Houston realized that it was really Willie and that Willie was not a boy after all. It was the one time the man could not think what to say, "for everything that had been said on the old cow trail in the last three or four days" came to his mind right then. When he demanded to know why the young woman had done such a thing, the maiden explained that her father had once been a drover and she wanted to know what it was like. Hearing that a drive was passing near, Willie had borrowed her brother's clothes and horse and headed for Clayton.[14]

Cowboy Jo Monaghan of Idaho was another girl who not only trailed herds but lived most of her life in a man's disguise. Jo was one of those wronged women who decided that since her life was ruined anyway, she might as well go west. She left her small son in the care of her sister and tried mining and sheepherding before she began trailing cows. Jo had problems from the beginning. When you are barely five feet tall in a pair of high-heeled boots, when you shun saloons and will not spend money on dance halls or gambling or liquor, and when your appearance is delicate and your voice high-pitched, folks notice. The fact that Jo was a superb horseman and bronc buster, a dependable drover, and an expert with the lariat was not peculiar. Nevertheless, Jo kept to herself, raised cattle, horses and chickens on a ranch and generally lived the life of a recluse. When she died and the secret was discovered, it gave the folks around Rockville, Idaho, something to talk about for a long time afterward.[15]

Compared to the number of men who trailed herds, women were few. But, stories about those who went show that they made up in grit what they lacked in numbers. And the stories show one thing more—the women seemed to enjoy going along for the ride, were willing to disguise themselves in order to go, and, in some cases, were beginning to look and act suspiciously like cowgirls even if no one was there to mark the occasion and tag them with a label.

2

Amazons on the Range: The Lady Ranchers

> There were a few ranches owned and capably operated by women. . . . Even these women obeyed the custom which Range femininity imposed on all its members, and fled to the kitchen the instant a visitor had received his welcome. The women of the Range all sacrificed themselves to competitive housewifery.[1]

Philip Ashton Rollins, who made that statement in *The Cowboy*, is considered an authority on men of the range. That is not to say, however, that he knew all there was to know about ranch women. Rollins must have forgotten how isolated ranches were and how few occasions occurred for feminine competition of any kind. Probably most ranch wives whose husbands were running the business did serve in traditional roles, primarily as homemakers. When cattle entered into the homemaking routine, life altered considerably. Some of the time, at least, the women were not even in the kitchen or anywhere in the house.

The care of children particularly created an area of special concern on the cattle frontier. Open fireplaces, uncovered cisterns and wells, snakes and lack of medical help were only a few of the hazards which caused mothers to be especially watchful. One mother, Mrs. Charlie Hart of New Mexico who helped her husband herd cattle, solved her problem by taking it with her. She carried her first baby on the front of her saddle. When she had to make room on her saddle for a new baby, she tied the first child to the porch to prevent his falling into the well. Every two or three hours Mrs. Hart would ride back to the house to check on the child. When they reached the age of four, the children were mounted on their own horses and joined mother on the range.[2]

In the early 1900s, Mr. and Mrs. Bob Crosby of New Mexico tried a similar solution when their daughter was born. With diapers in one pocket and a bottle in the other, Bob would carry six-month-old Roberta on a pillow in front of him on the saddle. As Mrs. Crosby tells it:

> When Bob had to work cattle or mend fence, he'd just hand the baby over to me. Every four hours we dismounted and fed her. If we found a fresh cow, we could replenish her bottle without returning to the house at the end of eight hours. If not, I went.[3]

In addition to children, however, or even without them, ranching dictated that a woman live a different kind of life. In Texas, no ranch-homemaker is better remembered than Mary Ann Goodnight, known affectionately as Molly. When she first came to the Palo Duro Canyon with her husband, her nearest neighbor was two hundred miles away. She rarely had the opportunity to compete with other ranch wives for cooking honors. There were, no doubt, more important things on Molly's mind.

Legend ascribes to almost every heroine a noble background. While few, in truth, could claim aristocratic origins, perhaps none came any closer than Molly. The daughter of an attorney-general of Tennessee, granddaughter of Robert Henry Dyer, hero in the battle of New Orleans under General Jackson, great-granddaughter of the first governor of Tennessee, sister of Confederate soldiers, Molly was to preside over a solitary cabin overlooking a canyon fifteen hundred feet deep, ten miles wide and almost one hundred miles long. She would be doctor, nurse, homemaker, spiritual comforter, sister and mother to the hands who worked for her husband, Charles, on the JA spread. She would take in trappers, hunters, and traders. There may have been Confederate heroes and statesmen in her ancestry, but it was Molly, "darling of the open range and mother of the Panhandle," who was remembered.[4]

Molly was fourteen years old when her mother and father, Joel Henry and Susan Dyer, came to Texas in 1854. The family halted near Waxahachie and settled down to a hard, frontier existence. In 1864, Mrs. Dyer died and Molly took her mother's place in caring for her father and younger brothers, Richard Lee, Samuel and Walter. Meanwhile the elder Dyer brothers were serving in the Confederacy and there made the acquaintance of Colonel Charles Goodnight. Charles and Molly met and fell in love, but they were unable to marry for nearly ten years because of family obligations. Finally in 1870, Molly and Charles were married and settled down to ranching near Pueblo, Colorado, where Charles and Richard Dyer had earlier begun ranching operations. For seven years the Goodnight-Dyer Cattle Company remained in Colorado. The need for more range caused the company to turn toward Texas, specifically to the vast Palo Duro Canyon on the High Plains. In 1877 the Goodnights and Mr. and Mrs. John Adair of England made the two-month trip to Texas. Molly drove one of the wagons while the men moved the cattle ahead. One can only imagine what Molly's thoughts were as she beheld the canyon where there was not another woman, as estimated, "from the Red to the Rio Grande on the south, Ft. Dodge, Kansas, on the north, Henrietta, Texas on the east, and Pueblo, Colorado, on the west . . . ."[5]

Mr. and Mrs. Adair returned to Colorado after a two-week stay, and Molly set up housekeeping with all the attendant hardships. The young wife found her time more than filled not only with household duties but also with the care of the JA hands. When none could be spared to stay near home with her, Molly went wherever her husband and the cowboys went—doctoring, cooking, mothering.

In addition to homeless cowboys and wandering hunters, Molly's care extended to starving Indians—Indians of whom she was afraid. They often came in bands to the Palo Duro Canyon and frequently Molly looked up to see the Indians peeping through her door. When Mrs. Goodnight asked the cowboys why the Indians came to her door to stare but never attempted to come inside, the boys told her that they had told the Indians that "the god who sent messages—the postoffice—was in the Goodnight home. This kept them from molesting her."[6]

Molly did find time to entertain, and on such occasions she probably did spend a lot of time in the kitchen. It was said that she claimed the Fourth of July as her party day. Colonel Goodnight claimed Christmas as his day and entertained the entire Panhandle. Often as many as 175 people attended. One of the Christmas parties was described thus:

> Long tables, in the form of a cross, were loaded with food, roast beef, wild turkey, antelope, cakes, pies and other delicacies of the day. At the point where the long tables met was a Star Navy tomato box decorated with pieces of colored glass and pretty pebbles and covered with a spotless white cloth. Upon this central table stood the Christmas tree, a spruce or other evergreen from the Palo Duro Canyon, ornamented with bunches of frosted raisins and strings of popcorn and cranberries. Each guest received at least one present.[7]

While Molly's life centered more on the traditional chores of ranch life, her interests and care extended to a unique job—the care of baby buffalo. Many of the motherless animals were left to starve when commercial hunters began extermination. According to one biographer, Mrs. Phebe Kerrick Warner:

> With the crack of the hunter's rifle and the pitiful wail of the starving calves ringing in her ears day and night, Mrs. Goodnight saw it was only a question of a few years when Texas would be robbed of her God-made emblem of strength and power.[8]

Molly asked her brothers and husband to bring some of the calves home and she raised them by hand in order to save some examples of the species for Texas.

Mrs. Goodnight was always aware of the beauty around her and in later life she paid an artist twelve hundred dollars to paint the scenes near her cabin. She had other interests as well. After the Panhandle became more thickly populated, churches, schools, and other philanthropic organizations always found Molly willing to help.

The lady of the Palo Duro has long since departed the canyon, yet her presence is felt in the tales left behind, in the cultural life of the Panhandle, and in the memory of cowboys who never knew her but claim her just the same. Could she be called a cowgirl? No, and yet in many respects those who came later might say she came close.

Another pioneer cattlewoman, Mrs. Viola Slaughter, tried to maintain a traditional home on the cattle frontier for a husband who not only ranched but was a famous sheriff of Cochise County, Arizona. There is evidence that she got out of the kitchen—often.

Mrs. Slaughter was born in Missouri in 1860 and came with her family to Montana in 1865. In 1869 the family moved to Nevada and then in 1879 on to New Mexico during the Lincoln County War. Mrs. Slaughter's family took sides with the small operators against John Chisum. While the family was in New Mexico, Viola met John Slaughter. She reminisced:

> He was on his way to meet a herd of cattle—his first herd of cattle—which his brother was sending out from Texas. He stayed with us three or four weeks waiting for the herd, meantime persuading my father to change his mind and come back to Arizona with him. So when the herd arrived, they threw in together and we all started west.[9]

Viola rode most of the way on horseback beside John. Although he was nineteen years older than she and had two small children by another marriage, it was love at first sight. The couple rode ahead on the trail to Tularosa and were married in spite of the objections of Viola's mother.

Mr. Slaughter planned to send the children away to live with his brother, but Viola became so attached to them that she could not bear to part with them.

The Slaughters and Viola's parents brought their herds to the Sulphur Springs in southern Arizona where Mr. Slaughter had a beef contract with the government to supply the San Carlos Indian reservation. A young lieutenant who, Mrs. Slaughter said, "hardly knew a cow from a bull," received the cattle. Anxious to show his authority, the lieutenant would point out this one or that one and reject it for no reason at all. Sitting on the fence watching, Viola thought of the money lost. Mr. Slaughter and his men accepted the rejections calmly. When another bunch was brought in, Slaughter would include some of the rejects. The rejected cattle usually made the count the second time around. By the time the herd was delivered, there were only a few rejected steers.

Viola often went with John to bring back herds from Mexico to their ranch in Arizona. She took her saddle and made the trip as far as Hermosillo by train. Then she would come back with the herd.

Around 1883, Mr. Slaughter sold out and took his family to Oregon, planning to start a ranch there. He carried his money in a belt around his waist. The family traveled by train to Salt Lake City and by stage from Boise City, Idaho, to Ogden, Utah. At one station the driver warned them of tough characters and suggested that John turn his money over to him. John assured him that he was man enough to take care of his own money. When the couple were alone, John made Viola put on the money belt.

After the couple reached their destination Mr. Slaughter had a lung hemorrhage, and they decided to go back to the dry air of the Southwest. At Silver City, New Mexico, Slaughter contracted to supply beef to the Santa Fe Railroad.

In 1887, John Slaughter was elected sheriff of Cochise County, Arizona. Mrs. Slaughter and the children accompanied him on many official duties. On one occasion Viola was along when John went looking for a murderer, Juan Lopez. John got his man and, along with a deputy and his family, started back home. At noon the group stopped for lunch and the handcuffs were taken off Lopez so that he could eat. During the meal the deputy, who was left-handed and carried his pistol on the left side, walked near Lopez' free right hand. Viola tried to get the deputy's attention. Finally she asked him if he didn't want another egg. Instead of turning around to take it, the deputy reached back his hand. Viola put the egg in the hand and held on. After she tugged a time or two, the deputy realized something was wrong and finally turned around.

In addition to Mr. Slaughter's children, Viola raised Apache Mae, an Indian child found in a teepee after a raid on her village by Arizona ranchers. The child died from burns when she was six years old. There were many others who benefitted from Viola Slaughter's kindness and her name ranks high among ranch women of the West.

Not as well known but equally helpful on a ranch was Mrs. Asenath Alkire of the Triangle Bar Ranch in Arizona. Her story is told in an unpublished manuscript entitled *The Little Lady of the Triangle Bar* written by Frank Alkire and given to the Pioneer Historical Society Library in Tucson, Arizona. While he had much to say about Asenath's life on the ranch, Frank did not comment much on her abilities as a housewife. He probably didn't care because she more than pulled her weight on the range.

Frank Alkire had a hardware store in Phoenix before he went into ranching. In 1889, when his business went under, he and his wife Asenath, who was the daughter of a New Orleans cotton broker, moved to the Triangle Bar Ranch on Black Canyon Road north of Phoenix. Asenath knew nothing of ranching and cattle. As they made the trip to the ranch for the first time, they stopped under a mesquite tree for the night. Frank asked his wife to gather wood but she had not been gone long when he heard her cries for help. She had tried to gather ocotillo cactus to burn and her hands were full of thorns.

Mrs. Alkire's house was better than some ranch homes of that day. It was built of adobe and lumber. Her kitchen boasted a "turkey red checked cloth" and napkins and china instead of the usual oil cloth and tin ware. Everyone ate at the same time and at the same table in her home. The house also boasted a five-foot bull snake which lived in the ceiling and caught rats.

Mr. Alkire once decided to redo the house for his wife. He called in a noted character, Billy the Painter, to do the wall papering. Billy's paper job was almost guaranteed varmint proof. He mixed cayenne pepper with the flour paste so that if mice decided to chew the paper they would not chew it for long.

Frank Alkire raised his own horses and when one cut himself badly, he decided to shoot it. Mrs. Alkire's grandfather had been a doctor and she knew something of medicine. She decided to see if she could save the horse. The wound was terrible to behold. She ordered hot water, a sponge, an antiseptic, and a long curved needle used to sew grain sacks. She put on a large apron, chose a skein of silk embroidery thread, blindfolded the horse, and went to work. Frank could not stand to watch her close the gaping wound.

After it was over Asenath went into the house, washed her hands, took off her bloody apron, changed her dress and went to her husband. "Hold me, please," she said. Frank took her in his arms and held her until a heavy chill left her.

Asenath rode sidesaddle and no horse on the place would put up with one. Frank solved the problem by giving her a Spanish mule who did not mind the sidesaddle. The mule had one bad trick. He tried to brush Asenath off whenever she rode near a mesquite bush.

When the Alkire's first baby was due, Asenath went to California to be with relatives and near a doctor. Frank received word that a telegram was waiting in town for him. Knowing it was about his wife, he packed his clothes, gave orders to his hands, and spent six hours trying to get to the telegraph office. When he got there the telegram read: "Can you furnish three hundred fat steers? What price?"

After the baby was born and the family was once again on the ranch, Mr. Alkire and a hand went to Mexico for horses. Mrs. Alkire announced that she and the baby were going, too. The next day they packed up baby clothes, bottles and other equipment needed for a baby on the trail. Asenath could not hold the baby on her side saddle so Frank put him on a pillow in a tomato box and carried him in front of his saddle. At the end of the day they discovered that the baby was sunburned. They doctored him and made him a sunbonnet.

The next morning Frank mounted his ginger-colored horse, ordinarily a steady, solid horse but known for his vinegar. When Frank took the baby, the "show started." The ginger horse bucked into a river bed full of big boulders. Finally the father took a good grip on the baby's neck clothing and held him at arm's length until the horse quit.

The Alkires discovered later in the day that they had left the canned Eagle Brand behind. Frank suggested that Asenath take a clean cloth, fill it with sugar and bread, dip it in water and let the baby suck on that. Asenath didn't like the idea. Frank decided he was not going to take them along anymore.

As the baby grew older, he got into things. Once they found him playing with a rattlesnake. Another time he got loose and went to the pen to play with the bull. Finally Frank tied a rope to one ankle and staked him out in the yard. His wife thought it was an awful thing to do to a baby, but Frank tied him until he was "halter broken."

Alkire wrote his tribute to his wife and gave it to the museum in Tucson in 1942. According to a letter found in the file, Asenath never knew that her husband had told on paper of her courage and loyalty and of his love for her.[10]

While many ranch wives divided their time between homemaking duties and helping on the ranch, there were other women who were able to wear the britches all by themselves. When the masculine force was absent for one reason or another, ranch women not only took to the saddle but proved they were at least as tough and smart as the men. Someone else could worry about Philip Ashton Rollin's "competitive housewifery."

Mrs. William Mannix of Montana was both smart and tough. At Christmas time in 1918, the Montana winter had covered the ground with ice and snow. Mrs. Mannix should have been thinking about a Christmas tree and presents for her large family, but she wasn't. Rather, her thoughts were on the thirteen of her family in bed with the flu, on twenty-seven cows waiting to be milked, and on a herd of cattle waiting for feed. Only one hired man helped her. No one was anxious to work on a ranch where flu was on the rampage. Nevertheless, on Christmas Day, Mrs. Mannix found much for which to be thankful. All of her family survived the epidemic and three of her sons were well enough to help feed the cattle.

That Christmas was not the first or the last time Mrs. Mannix faced hardship. Born in 1876, she spent her childhood on the frontier. In 1898, she married William Mannix, and when the couple began ranching between Helmville and Avon, Montana, tragedy was not far behind. Mr. Mannix became crippled from polio and, with ten children to support, Mrs. Mannix was forced to take over the management of the ranch. Often the baby rode the range with her in a one-horse cart.

When ranching did not provide enough income, Mrs. Mannix found another job. She drove the stage which carried passengers, mail, and express twice a week from Finn to Avon. For fifteen years the stage run supplemented the Mannix ranch income.

Before the Depression officially became a fact in 1929, Montana ranchers were already facing losses. Drought forced many to sell out, but Mrs. Mannix, on the advice of her banker, held on. All winter the cows ate forty-dollar hay only to sell in the spring for twenty dollars a head. In 1927, after her husband's death, Mrs. Mannix was forced to sell the home ranch. She immediately went to work to buy it back. It took her twenty years, but she did it.

When Mrs. Mannix reached seventy years of age, her sons decided that she ought to retire. She did not agree. She took to riding off at dawn and did not return until late at night. Finally deciding that when mother rode the range they at least knew where she was, the boys invited her out of retirement.[11]

Granny Jeffers was another who knew how to take over without a man's help. She insisted on staying in the saddle long after retirement on her ranch in northern Arizona. Granny was raised in New Mexico and married a cattleman. Their herd ranged in Chihuahua, Mexico and Texas. According to her daughter-in-law:

> She has driven cattle, flanked calves, run horse races, repaired windmills, pieced dozens of quilts, raised four children and was never too tired to dance all night to fiddle music.[12]

On one occasion Granny Jeffers, in spite of her eighty-one years and an artificial arm, leaped into the saddle and went after two unbranded calves which had been missed during roundup.

Sometimes a man had to find another job in order to make ends meet. He was fortunate if there was a good woman at home waiting to take off her apron and put on the chaps. When her husband had to run a freight wagon to make a living, Idella Smyers took over the ranch and did her cowboying on the High Plains of Texas. She looked after the cattle and the kids and was hard on both cows and children. Prairie fire and blizzard made Idella tough and practical. She once saved her starving herd by turning them into a maize field which was to have been used as a sale crop.

Idella was generous with her children. They were all given their own horses—unbroken. They could have the animals provided they broke them themselves. She claimed she bathed her large brood by running them through the tank. Her idea of raising children was to make them tough enough to meet any emergency.

Idella asked no more of her children than she herself was able to give. She roped, branded, bulldogged, charmed horses, dosed sick cows, and tailed up weak ones. She ran the ranch and made the business deals, and she used a brand of language that her neighbors understood.[13] Idella was a range woman in the best sense of the word, and so far as is known, nobody ever said whether she was a good cook or not.

Some women waited until late in life to discover careers on the range. Rosa Katherine "Grandma" Hilton was fifty-eight years old and going it on her own alone before she ever sat a saddle, but she made up for lost time in a hurry. Her ranch was back up in the New Mexico Rockies near Las Vegas, and, in addition to cattle, Rosa looked after rabbits and chickens and a bunch of saddle ponies. At the age of seventy-one, Grandma

Hilton continued to carry the mail to some seventeen mountain families and neither crippled horses nor personal injuries slowed her down.[14]

Some men left more than just the housekeeping to their wives. A horse wrangler and bronc buster should have been a great hand on a ranch but a Mr. Fox of Mangum, Oklahoma, left some things to his missus, Lillie. She was the one who had to break and train the work mules because her husband did not have the patience for the job.[15]

Sometimes a cattlewoman found herself alone and a long way from home when she had to manage her own ranch. In 1905, Dan Haughian returned to Ireland to court a girl. He had spent time working in the diamond mines of South Africa, and he had also worked on the plains of the western United States. It was to Miles City, Montana, in 1905 that he brought his bride Susan Quinn, who was eighteen years old. The couple began with forty acres and a two-room cabin. While Susan knew how to sew and crochet, she had never learned to cook. A brother-in-law helped her learn the kitchen arts. In 1931 Dan died and Susan and the ten children, five sons and five daughters, were left to cope with sheep, cattle, Montana weather and a livestock-market disaster. What she needed to know could not be found in the recipe book. By 1932 it was "Susan Haughian and Sons" and later it became "Haughian Livestock Company." Forty acres grew eventually to thousands of acres divided into two ranches north of the Yellowstone River.

The way up was not easy. In 1934, when the bottom dropped out of the market and ranchers were selling out to the government for twenty dollars a head, Susan had the boys move the herd over a hundred miles closer to the Missouri River near Jordan, where there was a little pasture. When that grass gave out, Susan found more land. Not knowing whether the owners would lease, she sent a check anyway and trailed the herd in only to find two strangers already there. Susan's boys insisted that they had already leased the land, and even without any paper to prove it, they bluffed their way through. When that water hole played out, Susan went into Jordan to mail money for another lease. Overhearing two men talking about the lease she wanted,

Susan hurried back to Miles City and the nearest telegraph office, where she sent a wire and sewed up the deal.

While moving her herds from one water hole to another, Susan was also beginning to buy up land, half a section at a time, for seventy-five cents to a dollar an acre. In time, Susan had dams constructed to catch the rainfall, and she dug artesian wells to insure that water would be there when she needed it.

Dry holes and drought were not Susan's only enemies. She had to fight the government, too. In the late thirties Congress passed the Bankhead-Jones Act under which a group of unsuccessful dry farmers were to be moved to an irrigation project near Miles City. Each family was to have 120 acres of irrigated land and grazing rights on pasture land where ranchers had been established for years. The Haughians dared them to come. The government and the settlers backed off.

Susan was always careful of her dress and she was a lady. Divided skirts were as much a concession as she was willing to make in spite of the fact that she always traveled horseback. And when she attended stockmen's conventions, she went not to the men's meetings but rather to the gathering of the ladies auxiliary.[16]

Tucson's *Arizona Weekly Citizen* of December 4, 1875, told of Mrs. Mary Ahart who built a ranching enterprise all alone. Mary lived in a tent with her seven-year-old daughter on the edge of Laramie, Wyoming. Her bed was made of straw, and boxes served as chairs and table. Her only source of income was two cows and two calves. Mary carried the spare milk around town in pails and sold it. When she got a few dollars ahead, she bought another calf or yearling. In less than seven years Mary possessed several hundred head of cattle, a farm, a comfortable, "even luxurious" home and property valued at forty to fifty thousand dollars. *The Citizen* concluded by saying that she had no government contracts, no outside help, and did not fall heir to any property.

Ranch wives both with and without husbands proved their worth on the range, but the daughters of ranching families took no back seat to their mothers.

Miss Amelia Dunn, known as Melie to her friends, did not set out to become the proprietress of an Arizona ranch. She came from Elmira, New York, to Holbrook, Arizona, with her father. He came in 1877, because he had consumption, and hoped the dry air and outdoor life of cattle raising would make him well. It didn't. When Mr. Dunn died, Melie was only seventeen years old. Hardship in the form of cattle-stealing Navajos, drought, and riding endless miles with her father had taught Melie to pay attention if she wanted to survive. It took her three or four years to get the hang of buying and selling, and of constantly moving her cattle as far as two hundred miles to grass and water, but she managed. She managed so well that she built up a herd of forty-six hundred head which she supervised with the aid of two faithful dogs.

Melie dressed like a cowboy, complete with guns at her waist. She rode broncs with ease, snagged bogged cows out of the mud, or hazed them on to greener pastures. When asked how she felt about her life, Melie replied that she regretted that she had had no time to develop any feminine accomplishments in literature or music. She added, however, that since she made good money at ranching, she might one day make up her deficits.[17]

Another Arizona girl who knew the life of a cowgirl was blonde-haired, blue-eyed Annette Taylor. At branding time Annette, mounted on a Thoroughbred horse, gave orders, instructed and made suggestions to her hands. She was twenty-three years old and already a successful rancher. Her father was a consumptive who had brought his family from Aurora, Illinois, in 1895, to the healing climate of Yavapai County in Arizona. After Indians and bandits stole most of the cattle, after weather had taken its toll, and after the ranch had been mortgaged nearly into bankruptcy, Mr. Taylor expired.

Annette had kept books for her father. She knew the paperwork end of cattle raising, but she knew more besides. She rode the range, held her herd together, and hired as few men as possible. She sometimes spent as much as thirty hours at a stretch in the saddle. What Annette did not know, she learned. She studied books on cattle diseases and learned to treat and doctor her own cows. She found the country around the ranch especially suitable for raising mules, which she sold to the government. Experimenting with grasses for permanent pasture, Annette planted an Australian variety which flourished in a land of scanty rainfall. By 1898, the mortgage was paid off and the enterprising young woman was able to buy up more land and cattle.

Annette's sister Alice often rode the range with her. They dressed like men, slept in tents many miles from home, and went armed during roundup.[18]

Norma Diorn and her two sisters helped their daddy on his ranch near Marble Falls, Texas. They bragged that no mustang ever unseated them. With a Winchester in the saddle boot, the young women rode fence, repaired windmills, killed wolves, and branded calves. And Norma did one thing more. She roped a Mexican lion and dragged him all the way home. It wasn't a smart thing to do, but since she did it, the Southern Texas Cattle Association saw fit to present her with a goldmounted revolver and a Mexican sidesaddle.[19]

Mary Stuart grew up on her father's Montana ranch in the 1870s. Her father was Granville Stuart, one of the first settlers in the state. Mary's mother was a Shoshone Indian. The DHS ranch was renown for its fine cattle and hospitality. Mary remembered such things as roller-skating on the dining room floor, parties at Fort Maginnis, living the life of a tomboy, and enjoying the pemmican made by neighboring Indians. Mary's ranch life continued when she married the colorful Teddy Blue Abbott.[20]

Records do not often tell the events of the social life of a rancher's daughter because there was very little social season. There were other things a rancher's daughter did to impress the boys. John Leakey's daughter, Mattie, rode sidesaddle to punch cattle near Uvalde, Texas. W. W. Hall's sister, Mary Lizzie, did, too. They hooked their knees under the sidesaddle horn and those who knew them said they never were unseated.[21]

A Mr. Casey found a willing and capable ranch hand in his daughter, Lily. Born in 1862 in Texas, Lily preferred walking to riding in the wagon when the family moved to New Mexico in

1877. She was an expert horsewoman and not afraid to use a gun. Because business kept her father away from home much of the time and because she was the healthiest and strongest of the children, Lily did most of the riding and herding. Even when Lily's father was home, he was busy planting and working at the mill which was operated on the ranch property. Lily continued to herd, rope, and brand. The cattle seemed determined to get into the cultivated fields and one of the major responsibilities of Mr. Casey's daughters was to keep them out. Lily's father died when she was thirteen and she continued to support her family by doing a man's job.[22]

"She's one of the best damned cowmen in Yavapai County." That's what they said about Fergus White's daughter, Kittie. Kittie's father came to Arizona in 1876. In 1883, the family bought a ranch at Minnehaha Flat. When Kittie's father died in 1893, Mrs. White at first tried to keep the ranch going with hired help. When that plan failed, Kittie, then fourteen, and her thirteen-year-old brother Jim took charge of the ranch. With some help the brother and sister butchered and sold meat to the mines near their home.

Kittie's mother at first made her daughter ride sidesaddle because she thought it immodest for young women to ride astride. One day Kittie was thrown from her horse and her foot caught in the stirrup. After the accident Kittie's mother let her wear divided skirts and use a regular stock saddle. To bring in extra income Jim later went to work in the Silver Bell mines and Kittie took full responsibility for the ranch. Kittie's sisters helped some but the hard riding, roping, branding, butchering and horseshoeing was left for Kittie to do. Her roping ability particularly was widely recognized. At a Fourth of July celebration in 1904, Kittie beat nine other cowboys' time in roping and tying steers.[23]

Some daughters of ranchers found time for pursuits which did not pertain either to ranch life or to homemaking on the range. Sharlot Hall of Arizona is best remembered as a writer and historian. Much of her inspiration came from her experience with Indians and cows on the Orchard Ranch near the town of Dewey. Sharlot once remarked: "I think that perhaps

Arizona was my best school—the old days were still very near when we came, and I had a long, long, pioneer inheritance far back of that. I could not help loving it all and trying to make others love it and understand it."[24]

Sharlot was born in 1870 in Lincoln County, Kansas. Her father was a buffalo hunter. The child's earliest memories were of being passed from one to another of her father's friends, of hearing tales of life on the Great Plains, and of fingering beaded shot-pouches and embroidered buckskin belts. The Sioux, Cheyenne and Comanches were still taking scalps, and Sharlot sometimes watched her mother wash the scalped heads of men who were victims of the Indians.

The Halls traded the grasshoppers and drought of Lincoln County for the cattle thieves and outlaws of Barbour County near the edge of the Indian Territory in 1879. The year 1881 found the family moving again, this time to Arizona by way of the Santa Fe Trail. Sharlot, riding sidesaddle, herded the horses. Once while she was herding, the child's horse bolted and threw her, injuring her spine seriously. Nevertheless she kept on herding.

The Halls branded their cattle with the wineglass brand and established their ranch about twenty miles from Prescott on Lynx Creek. Arizona dealt its own brand of misery, and the Hall ranch went under. The family tried mining for a while, but eventually they moved back to their ranch. They added an orchard and consequently the ranch was known as Orchard Ranch.

In 1890, Sharlot's spinal injury became a serious problem. For a year she was bedridden. It was during this period that she began to write and publish.

As Sharlot's strength returned, her family's health began to fail. Both her father and brother were unable to do ranch work and so the daughter took over not only the home ranch but also her own homestead of 160 acres.

In spite of the burdens of ranching Sharlot continued to write. When an article of hers appeared in *Land of Sunshine* in 1897, she became acquainted with editor Charles F. Lummis. He published more of her work and guided her writing career.

Sharlot worked for Lummis, eventually being promoted to associate editor of *Land of Sunshine*, which by then had changed its name to *Out West*.

In 1909, Sharlot accepted the first public office held by a woman in the Territory of Arizona—territorial historian. During the time she was working for *Out West* and as historian, Sharlot traveled back and forth to Orchard Ranch, which was still her responsibility.

In 1912, she returned to the ranch full-time. Her mother died in 1915, and, soon after, Sharlot's spinal injury put her in bed again. Poor health and an invalid father caused her to sell the ranch, but she was forced to take back ownership when the new owners could not pay.

Writing and ranching continued to occupy her time. In 1928, Sharlot's father died. They had never been very close and one of the great regrets of Sharlot's life was that her father never appreciated her talents as a writer. On the ranch Mr. Hall had valued his daughter for her physical strength, but it puzzled him, even when her mental skills earned wages and supported the ranch, that she set store by book learning.

Sharlot's later life was devoted to a museum which housed her personal collection of Indian and pioneer artifacts. Ten years after her death in 1943, a collection of Sharlot Hall's poems, *Poems of a Ranch Woman*, was published.[25]

Not all ranch women were wives and daughters of ranchers. A few made it on their own. Fanny Seabride of Chicago went west to be a governess on the Horseshoe XX in Texas. Apparently Fanny got in some riding practice after hours, because when one of the cowboys got hurt, Fanny forked a mustang before anybody could stop her and went to finish the cowboy's job of mending fence. When the cowboy quit, Fanny applied to Colonel Sansome, owner of the Horseshoe XX, for his job. The Colonel obliged her and Fanny went to it, quirt and spur. According to a newspaper item, killing wild animals for bounty became Fanny's thing. She bagged "531 coyotes, forty-nine lobo wolves, thirty-nine wildcats, two bear cubs and a Mexican leopard." With the accumulated bounty of $1,261 Fanny proceeded to buy land and cattle and established her own ranch. Fanny captured human outlaws with the same skill she applied to wild animals, and she was rewarded with many valuable gifts from her ranch neighbors—so they say.[26]

Another Texas story was told by Professor W. Zursna of Austin, Texas. He claimed that while it seemed improbable, it was nevertheless a fact that there were some fifty cowgirls operating a ranch in the Hill Country between San Marcos and San Antonio in the mid-1880s. Some supposedly came from the finest families in the state and some from the worst. They could, of course, ride and rope and do other appropriate cowgirl things. Their leader was a whip-cracking brunette from the Oklahoma territory whose boyfriend was an outlaw by the name of Payne.[27]

Maude Reed was a Swedish girl who gathered a herd in Colorado. According to a brief news item she "started with a few head of cattle, and by strict attention, economy and braving all the hardships of a frontier life, she is today one of the shrewdest and ablest cattle owners in Mesa County."[28]

One young woman had no intention of becoming a cowgirl. She did, however, manage admirably. Nadine Parmer was an orphan teaching music in a small Ohio town when the wife of a wealthy Toledo merchant asked her to become her companion. The woman, a Mrs. Payne, suffered bad health and wished to visit the healthful climate of Texas. Nadine accompanied the woman to San Antonio, where Mrs. Payne promptly expired, leaving Nadine stranded. The rest was right out of a melodrama.

Nadine did the only sensible thing. She sat down in the lobby of the Maverick hotel and wept—loudly. She kept it up until, lo and behold, she was discovered by a rich cattleman named Old Bill Ferguson. Old Bill inquired as to the source of her distress, and when he found out the reason for Nadine's tears, he begged her not to worry. He said, "I have three great, big girls, all of them just dyin' for some pretty, smart young lady about your size and grade to come and learn them to read, write and cipher and play the piano."

Without inquiring about her benefactor's reputation, Nadine accepted because "something in the fine old man's rugged features" made her trust him.

Nadine accompanied Mr. Ferguson when he set out to do some shopping for the family before they went to the ranch. There he assured her she would be received with open arms. Bill bought some dress patterns and then ordered three pianos, one for each daughter.

Act two: Nadine established herself on the ranch and imparted to her pupils all the learning at her command. At the end of six months Mr. Ferguson paid Nadine six hundred dollars for services rendered. Nadine threw up her hands, and probably said "I declare" at such a sum, and insisted that she couldn't take it. Her benefactor banked the money in her name anyway. In time, Mr. Ferguson offered to invest the money for her. Nadine readily complied. Bill kept on depositing and investing. When Nadine heard that she had a herd of seven hundred head of cattle, she decided it was time to take an interest in cows. The next year she added another bunch and branded them all with a key. She used the key because one of her friends had once remarked that she carried an "invisible key to all hearts."

Act three: After about four years of multiplying her herd, Old Bill Ferguson died, leaving his family in great distress. Nadine, never one to forget a kindness, bought Ferguson's Broad Ax Ranch and everything else in sight. Ranging her enormous herds from Texas to Mexico, Nadine became a regular cattle baroness. In her leisure hours she developed a fondness for hunting wolves. She imported a pack of greyhounds which eventually numbered one hundred fifty. With her vaqueros and dogs, Nadine cut quite a figure while she helped rid the plains of lobos which, no doubt, were a menace to her cattle.[29]

A Prescott, Arizona, newspaper article from *Hoof and Horn* dated April 28, 1887, reported that Miss Ellen Callahan from Sierra Valley was a capable rancher in her own right. Selling forty-six head of cattle to James Miller for eight and one-half cents a pound, Miss Callahan received the highest price paid for beef in the valley.

Ellen had inherited two ranches and cattle and horses from her brother some fifteen years before. She took over the management of the ranches, learning even to break horses, harness teams, and run ranch equipment. The capable woman was known to take young calves, colts, chickens, and ducks into her kitchen to protect them from the weather.

The newspaper suggested that Miss Callahan would make a good catch for a middle-aged bachelor. Dudes need not apply. Her age the paper tastefully declined to speculate about but the account did add that she weighed about one hundred thirty pounds, wore no false teeth or hair and had good eyes and complexion. More important, she owned property valued at ten thousand dollars, enjoyed herself both outdoors and in, and drove a pair of "unbeatable steeds" in "a manner peculiar to herself." Ellen carried her money from the bank in barley sacks, would not take checks or gold notes, and believed all bankers were swindlers.

Not all ranch women were as independent as Ellen Callahan but most of the ladies of the range proved in one way or another that they were able to rise to whatever the occasion demanded whether by the side of husbands or fathers or going it all alone. Maybe some did, as Rollins suggested, uphold the honor of the ranch by fleeing to the kitchen. Others, however, added to the reputation of the ranch by doing a man's job in a woman's way. And they are remembered more for their abilities in the saddle than for their apple pie.

3

Lay That Pistol Down, Babe

A ranch woman's ability with cows and horses and her methods of maintaining a ranch were unique, at least to outsiders. Whips and ropes helped cowgirls keep their kingdoms in order, but in the use of guns—rifles and pistols—cowgirls were formidable. Women had to protect themselves and what belonged to them, and they found interesting ways to do it with firearms. Bluffing was a game they did not often play. Some even took up arms outside the ranch in larger battles such as cattle wars or in skirmishes and quarrels with neighbors.

The cattlemen of the West adhered to an unwritten code in the use of guns. Eugene Manlove Rhodes in *Beyond The Desert* put it into words:

> It was not the custom to war without fresh offense, openly given. You must not smile and shoot. You must not shoot an unarmed man, and you must not shoot an unwarned man . . . .[1]

A few pistol-toting cattlewomen also observed a code, and while it had little in common with the ideas of fair play expressed by Rhodes, cowgirls added their own touches to the code. Briefly put, the women's gun rules advised:

1. Strange men will do to shoot.
2. Shoot first, ask questions later.
3. If you shoot a man in the back, he rarely returns fire.
4. Scare a man to death even if you do not intend to kill him.
5. If a man needs killing, do it.

The late Mody C. Boatright, Texas folklorist, picked up a story about Mrs. Frank Adams, a Texas woman who rode, drank, and shot expertly and was thought to have plugged a man in the back. No doubt she thought he needed killing and she was tough enough to let him have it without batting an eye.[2] An unnamed South Texas woman who ramrodded her own ranch and broke her own horses was reported to have blown the top off a cowboy's head with a forty-five slug when he got fresh and pinched her ankle in fun.[3] She probably felt justified in making an example of the stranger and nobody ever made the mistake of teasing her again.

One problem about women with guns was that a man never knew whether a woman might shoot first and ask questions later or whether she was bluffing. Bob Crabb remembered when someone stole his mother's oxen from their ranch in the Panhandle of Texas. Two men came riding up to the ranch and said they would hunt the oxen for a thirty-five dollar reward. Bob's mother replied that she did not have that much money. The men returned the next day with the oxen, but refused to give them to her until she paid them five dollars. As the men started to leave with the animals, Mrs. Crabb reached for her forty-five and said, "Go ahead, but I will kill both of you before you get away." One of the men tested her: "You would not kill a man would you?" When Mrs. Crabb replied that she would just as soon kill them as a snake, the men decided not to call her bluff. Bob added that his mother could "kill a bird on wing—she hardly ever missed."[4]

A woman known in New Mexico as Lady Castile had her methods of persuading a man that she was not bluffing. When Ed Hall, a herder, got smart with her and refused to leave, she pulled her gun from her belt, fired and just missed his ear. She explained: "I didn't try to hit you that time, but I just wanted to show that I mean what I say." Ed quit.[5]

Another unidentified but dangerous female made use of disguise and passed as a cowboy traveling over the cattle trails from one herd to another until she located her false lover. Part of her costume was a revolver. When the woman found her man, she called him aside and revealed her identity to him. She never did tell just what she did to him but she remarked: "I'll bet he won't trifle with another girl's affections."[6]

Mrs. Cassie Redwine of the Texas Panhandle practiced the code on outlaws. While she did not necessarily shoot men in the back, she did ambush a few. When robbers were terrorizing the upper Red and Canadian rivers, and when five hundred head of Cassie's stock disappeared, she decided to put a stop to it. For three days her cowboys pursued the thieves until they discovered three men in a secret camp. Cassie ordered some of her men to surround the desperadoes, capture them, and change into their clothes. Cassie's men then took positions on either side of the camp and when the rest of the robbers rode unsuspectingly into camp, Cassie picked off Black Pedro, the leader, and the rest fell soon after or were captured. Next morning the prisoners were shot or hanged but the reporter insisted that "Cassie had nothing to do with that part of it."[7]

A Mrs. Wheeler of Mobeetie, Texas, figured that two guns were better than one and that she would ask questions after she used her weapons. When she discovered that someone had stolen her daughter, Mrs. Wheeler armed herself with a six-shooter and a Winchester and prowled the streets of Mobeetie looking for the guilty party. Innocent bystanders hid behind a picket fence. The marshal hid with them until more law arrived. As Cap Arrington, the sheriff, came on the scene, the marshal threw down on Mrs. Wheeler. Both officers disarmed her, but before they could get her to jail, Mrs. Wheeler tripped them and drew a pistol from her bosom. After a scuffle the men finally got her to jail.[8]

Edie Fenley of Uvalde, Texas, was an expert with a rifle and thereby gained the admiration of most of the men in those parts. She also planned to shoot first and talk later when she got the news that a Mexican had hit her brother, Sol Holland, in the head and killed him, then pushed him into a vat of sheep dip. Mrs. Fenley picked up her rifle and went looking for a Mexican—any Mexican. When she found one, she leveled her rifle at him. Fortunately someone who knew the circumstances told her before she pulled the trigger that she was aiming at the wrong Latin.[9]

Some women did not always take justice into their own hands, but helped the men practice the code. When a hand for the Bassett ranch in Colorado was shot in the back by three strange men from Texas, Mrs. Bassett took her Winchester in hand and disarmed the gunmen. She marched the three over to the dying hand and asked for an explanation. The one who had done the shooting claimed that Rollas, the wounded man, had shot and killed his brother in Abilene, Kansas. The gunman claimed that this was the prescribed method of settling such a score. Mrs. Bassett informed the men that shooting a man in the back was not the custom in Colorado. She then proceeded to show them how it was done in Colorado. Lining up the three against the bunkhouse wall, Mrs. Bassett invited Rollas to shoot one or two or all three if it suited him. Rollas, however, was too weak to hold a pistol.[10]

Guns provided some women with the courage to shoot strangers who were also thieves. Ellen Casey of Lincoln County, New Mexico, became excited when Apaches robbed the pioneers of their cattle and ran off their horses. Realizing the importance of not being left afoot, Ellen went after the horses. "I'm not afraid," she declared. "I've got a gun." Paying no attention to her husband's advice against such a maneuver, Ellen grabbed her shotgun, loaded it, ran after the horses, and returned the animals to safety. When the excitement was over, Robert Casey pointed out to his wife that she had loaded her trusty shotgun with both charges of buckshot in one barrel, put all the powder in the other barrel, and had only one cap which was in the barrel of buckshot.[11]

Mrs. Molly Owens of Arizona never knew which stranger might need killing so she made it a point to put on her apron whenever a stranger rode up. The apron had a special pocket in which she concealed a gun. Coleman Evans, a pioneer cowboy who knew Molly, said, "She knew men and could read the signs."[12]

Often a woman had to use her wits and invoke the rule of scaring men to death with a gun even if she really meant them no harm. Mrs. Mary Nugent was accosted near her Tombstone, Arizona, ranch by Apaches. Knowing she could not get to her gun quickly enough, she decided on another course of action. Letting it be known that she saw them and was not afraid, Mary invited the Indians to a fine breakfast. They feasted and afterwards she said she needed some help. Mary put the Apaches to work hauling various items to a storeroom with a heavy door. When the visitors were off guard, Mary slammed the door and bolted it. Then she ran for her rifle, sent her son for help, and proceeded to shoot at the door and at other places where the Indians might think of coming out. There is no evidence that they tried. In time, the Indians were freed, but nobody ever thought to ask why they had come to the Nugent home in the first place.[13]

Mrs. Stevens who lived in Lonesome Valley, Arizona, believed in the part of the code which dictated that strangers would do to shoot—especially Indian strangers. When Lewis Stevens had to go to town thirty miles away, he left his wife at home to guard the ranch and children. Mrs. Stevens was going about her business when she looked out the window. She saw what looked like a rag on a bush outside, but since she did not remember hanging anything on a bush outside, she decided it was an Indian. Mrs. Stevens grabbed her gun, drew a bead on the rag, and plugged an Apache right between the eyes. After the Indian had fallen, the frightened woman discovered that the ranch was surrounded by Indians. What she did to one she could certainly do to the others. The lady held off the Indians until some cowboys chanced by and ran off the Apaches. When things settled down, the cowboys prepared to ride away. They asked Mrs. Stevens if she wanted to send a message to her husband. On a piece of paper she wrote:

> Dear Lewis,
> The Apaches came. I'm mighty nigh out of buckshot. Please send more.
> Your loving wife.[14]

Cattlewomen sometimes dealt out the justice of the code behind men's backs with weapons other than guns. There was Mrs. Victor Daniels who ranched with her husband in the upper Gila Valley of Arizona. Ordinarily, it was Mrs. Daniels's job to ride herd on the cattle for her husband, but a sick baby kept her at home one day. Looking up from her work, Mrs. Daniels observed two men driving the herd off. Springing into the saddle, she raced after them, built a loop and caught one by the neck, jerking him out of the saddle. As he fell strangling to death, Mrs. Daniels drew her pistol and invited the remaining desperado to drive the cattle back home. When his task was completed, Mrs. Daniels told him to clear out. When the other man was found later in the chaparral with his neck broken, there was no inquiry as to how such a thing happened. Those who knew figured he needed killing.[15]

Sally Skull was one of the most memorable gun women, skilled in the code of deciding who needed killing. She was described as "a merciless killer when aroused,"[16] and there were several who could testify that it did not take much to arouse her. A man once made an unkind remark about Sally behind her back, and when she found out about it, she called him out and shot bullets at his boots until he danced.[17] On another occasion a witness testified that Sally and some unidentified man faced each other and that the lady's six-shooter spoke first. What the cause for gunplay was, nobody ever said, but the witness speculated that the victim was somebody who was better off dead.[18]

In the 1850s, Sally was divorced in Refugio County, Texas, and left with a son and a daughter to support. Jobs for women were scarce on the frontier, and Sally apparently decided that if she was going to take over a man's responsibilities, she would do a man's job. It seems likely that Sally learned about horses from her first husband, Jesse Robinson, who raised race horses in Live Oak County, Texas.[19] Horse trading became her occupation.

The frontier of Texas and the Mexican border area were dangerous places to live in the 1850s. A woman traveling alone in daylight and dark across the border for the purpose of buying and trading horses was begging for trouble. And yet Sally often traveled south of the border and was, for the most part, left alone. Only once did she encounter difficulty when she ventured into the territory of Cortina, a bandit and self-proclaimed governor just south of the border. He put Sally in jail for a few days, but no doubt she looked upon the stay as more inconvenient than dangerous.[20]

There were several good reasons for Sally Skull's fearlessness. She spoke fluent Spanish, hired Mexicans to work for her, and thought well of the Mexican people in general. In addition, she used a vocabulary which would have scalded the hide off a dog—a talent which inspired a certain respect from the males even if it did not endear her to the ladies. But Sally's real talent was in handling firearms. She carried a rifle and was deadly with it. Her pistols, which always hung from a cartridge belt around her waist, she used with either hand and with equal skill. It is reported that she carried a whip with which she popped flowers off their stems for entertainment, or the hide off backs when she meant business.[21] She was an accomplished horsewoman and made her trips on her horse, Redbuck, a Spanish pony of almost unlimited endurance.[22]

There are conflicting reports about what Sally wore. One newspaper account says that she dressed in rawhide bloomers.[23] A Refugio County historian reports that she wore men's clothes and rode astride. Others say she rode sidesaddle and appeared in a long riding skirt, or in a dress and a bonnet.[24] It is likely, however, that Sally was remembered more for her guns and her uninhibited behavior than for the way she dressed.

According to legend, Sally realized that the frontier and her unusual occupation did not produce a wholesome atmosphere for her children. She had much stock branded with her Circle S, and her horse-trading provided the funds to give her daughter a better environment. Supposedly, the daughter was sent to New Orleans to a boarding school where she developed into a cultured and refined lady.[25] Another story claims that the daughter became so refined that she took to keeping a pet dog whose company she valued above the presence of human kind. The dog tried to bite Sally when she went to visit her daughter and Sally drew her gun and blew the pet to kingdom come. The act so enraged the daughter that she and Sally became estranged and never made up their differences.[26]

Sally's son, Alfred, apparently stayed with his father after his parents were divorced, but he must have had occasional contact with Sally. He mentions to his wife in a letter dated December 1, 1863: "I saw Mother at Kings Ranch but had not time to speak to her but a few minutes."[27]

Tall tales, whether based on fact or concocted, were bound to accompany such a person as Sally Skull, spelled Scull by some. It was reported that she was fond of Mexican fiestas. She also liked to gamble and played poker at Haynes' Saloon which another famous personality, John Wesley Hardin, was reputed to have frequented.

Another story concerns Sally's first husband, Jesse Robinson. Supposedly they, along with some Mexican hands, were on their way north on a business trip when Mr. Robinson was drowned in the San Antonio River. One of the hands asked if she wanted the body recovered from the river. Sally's reply was that she did not care about the body but she would like to have the money belt which Mr. Robinson had been wearing.[28] No doubt the story was fabricated since Mr. Robinson lived a long life in Live Oak County, Texas.

Sally had many friends who were quick to defend her reputation. One remarked that, considering the rough times and unsavory people with whom she dealt, it was necessary for Sally to meet circumstances in a firm, even if in an unladylike, way—sometimes with guns blazing. Other acquaintances insisted that she was loyal to friends and performed many acts of kindness for those she liked.[29]

Sally was married a second time to a man by the name of Skull and by whose name she was ever after remembered. She was married a third time to Bill Horsdoff,[30] but that venture proved to be a fatal mistake. Apparently Sally and Bill did not get along. There were rumors that a divorce was in the offing and that Bill wanted a share of Sally's property. The couple traveled to the border to buy and trade horses. Sally, as was her usual custom, may have carried a large sum of money. When the trip was concluded, Bill returned home alone. Some say he murdered Sally and threw her body in a brush pile in Mexico. Later he left the Refugio area.[31]

Stories about Sally Skull's methods of horse trading vary considerably depending on who is doing the remembering. Those who find fault with her behavior and dress tend to make her a notorious, even a villainous, character. Dressed in dirty men's clothes, she would steal away from her home in the middle of the night, either alone or accompanied by her hired Mexican toughs. When she arrived in Mexico, Sally contacted certain men whose corrals were known to be filled with stolen horses. She paid from the money belt strapped around her waist, and, her business concluded, made her way to a cantina. She may have passed the night gambling and drinking and making a spectacle of herself, using her pistols and whip. At dawn Sally and her compañeros rode out of town in a mood of drunken playfulness, guns blazing, to collect their horses.

Mrs. Skull's friends leave a different impression. Sally did wear women's clothes but rarely since she was either coming or going with horses. Probably her method of trading involved contacts in Mexico who knew she would come at fairly regular intervals. It is likely that Sally was a welcome guest in many of Mexico's haciendas. No doubt she was called upon to display her skill with whip and firearms. People along the way were sure to be impressed with her magnificent Redbuck, blanketed in bright colors and under a fine Mexican saddle trimmed in silver. It would have been no more than good business to dress flamboyantly, to be splendidly mounted, to enter fully into the life of fiesta or hacienda, and to give an account of herself in such a way as to show how comfortably she fitted into and admired the Mexican way of life. Clearly, Sally was a woman to be trusted, and the large amount of money strapped to her waist must have been assurance that she would deal squarely.

Whatever else people remembered about Sally, they never forgot her guns. Ben Kinchlow remembered seeing Sally Skull put her finger through the trigger guard of a pistol, whirl it around, and then catch it and fire. And she could do it with either hand.[32]

Men respected Sally's vocabulary almost as much as they respected her pistols. Once even a preacher had reason to be grateful for the Refugio woman's inspired exhortations. Sally was hauling freight to Mexico when she encountered a two-horse buggy mired down in the road. The driver of the buggy, a preacher, tried to coax his team out of the mud by shaking his lines up and down on the animals' backs. The animals refused to pull. Sally watched for as long as she could stand it. Suddenly she rode forward and yelled: "Get out of here you blankety blank blank blank ______! Get the hell out of here!" The horses dragged the buggy and the startled preacher out of the way and proceeded hastily down the road. It was not long, however, before the preacher was stuck again. Not wasting any time with any more of his own feeble efforts, the preacher went back and got Sally. "Lady," he said, "will you please speak to these horses again?"[33]

Sally Skull's behavior and appearance must have indeed caused comment and alarm during an era which valued traditional femininity and gentility. She, out of necessity, released herself from notions about where and what a woman's place was and got on with her business. It appears likely that Sally Skull was a mixture of good things and bad in a place that required both unless you liked the idea of dying too soon.[34]

On the intersection of U. S. Highway 183 and State Highway 202 two miles north of Refugio, a marker has been erected which reads:

> SALLY SCULL
>
> Woman rancher, horse trader, champion "Cusser." Ranched NW of here. In civil war Texas, Sally Scull (or Skull) freightwagons took cotton to Mexico to swap for guns, ammunition, medicines, coffee, shoes, clothing and other goods vital to the Confederacy.
>
> Dressed in trousers, Mrs. Scull bossed armed employees. Was sure shot with the rifle carried on her saddle or the two pistols strapped to her waist.
>
> Of good family, she had children cared for in New Orleans school. Often visited them. Loved dancing. Yet during the war, did extremely hazardous "man's work." (1964)

Women who used guns indiscriminately were, of course, a minority among frontier ladies. Most women wanted only to protect themselves. The proficiency of ranch women in the use of firearms, however, caused those who were taking a closer look at what was going on west of the Mississippi to describe what they saw. They could not be blamed if they noticed the accoutrements of those who would be fashioned into folk heroines on the cattle frontier.

4

Into Their Own Hands

Over cactus and rock the Rurales pursued a female rider across the border into Texas. Only minutes before, the woman had galloped into Rancho Conejo in Coahuila, Mexico, where some fifty men, under the command of a Captain Rivera, were camped. She entered a building, took a rifle, and dashed away. The astonished Rurales went after her and probably would have caught her, except that she chanced upon a fresh mount. The fresh horse belonged to Ed Lindsay, who just happened to be leading a wagon train across the path of the pursued and the pursuing. The woman asked Lindsay for his horse, and, since she was holding a gun on him, Ed didn't mind in the least. The woman left the Mexicans eating her dust.[1]

The rider was Alice Stillwell Henderson, who did her riding and shooting in the rough and lonely expanses of the Big Bend country along the Rio Grande of Texas. Those who knew Alice were glad to give her all the room she needed. Mrs. Henderson's incident with the Rurales was part of larger trouble among Texas cattlemen, border bandits, and law enforcement. The trouble extended into other parts of the West where other women took up arms or whatever was handy in order to protect their herds and property whether in full-fledged cattle wars, fence-cutting wars or in border skirmishes because the law would not or could not protect them. Their stories prove that the myth of helpless women had little place on the range and that women, when given sufficient cause, were quite capable of taking the law into their own hands.

The same day that Alice took the rifle from Rancho Conejo, her husband was forced to leave the area because of some difficulty of his own with the Mexican police. During the trouble, whatever it was, Henderson's cattle and Winchester rifle were confiscated. Mr. Henderson asked Alice to recover the rifle and cattle for him and the wife wasted no time. Alice got the rifle back almost immediately. It took her longer to recover her husband's cattle from across the Rio Grande, but in time she managed to do it. Mrs. Henderson had four brothers, and with their help she was able to get two thousand of the livestock back over the next two years. She bought a ranch in the Davis Mountains some one hundred thirty miles from the border and drove the cattle back in small bunches. The Mexicans did not approve, but they were able to do nothing about the fearless Alice and her helpful brothers.

Alice Stillwell Henderson's family had helped to settle Brewster County in the Big Bend. In 1890, after her marriage, she and her husband established a ranch on Maravillas Creek. Her home was a typical cow camp—no house; just a tent for shelter. Her nearest neighbor, Jim Wilson, was thirty miles away.

Although Mexican bandits were accustomed to raiding the Texas ranches across the Rio Grande, they bit off more than they could chew when they tangled with the Hendersons. On one occasion, bandits raided the herd, taking food, saddles, and other equipment as well. Mr. Henderson headed for the river in hot pursuit after he had instructed Alice to ride to the Wilson camp for help.

Canyons, rocky trails, Spanish dagger, and the blackness of night barred the way, but Alice finally reached Jim Wilson's camp after riding all night.

Jim and his two hands, along with Alice, made the long ride back. They left Alice at her camp to rest after her long night's ordeal while they went on to help Henderson recover his cattle. Mrs. Henderson had no more than settled in when five bandits rode into her camp. She was not unprepared, however, and, by her own methods, persuaded them to get rid of their weapons.

She entertained them at gunpoint all that long day until the men returned with the stolen herd.

Little is known about Mrs. Henderson's physical appearance. One historian declares that her face was not beautiful, and yet her photograph attests to the fact that neither was she plain. Most remember her character, which they describe as "enduring and splendid."[2] It was said that "every man and woman who knew her, though women were mighty scarce over her range, respected her."[3]

A relative of Alice's, Hallie Stillwell, who was a Justice of the Peace in Alpine, remembered that Alice rode astride, wearing men's trousers and a man's hat. When she rode to town, however, she marked the occasion by slipping a divided skirt over the trousers, which she pushed down into her boot tops. She was reputed to be a lady at all times, and even riding, as she did most of the time with her brothers and other men, she was respected and deferred to. Says Miss Stillwell: "Alice made many trips alone from Mexico leading a pack horse, and had no fear of making camp alone." Alice also found time from her ranch duties to teach in the first school established in Marathon, Texas.[4]

On another occasion when Alice and her kin were driving a bunch of cattle across the Rio, they were intercepted by about thirty Mexicans who tried to prevent their crossing. Alice got the drop on them, threatened to kill the first one to move, and held them at gunpoint for two or three hours until the herd was crossed.[5]

This intrepid lady was very fond of a large sombrero which she always wore. Returning from a cattle-retrieving expedition into Mexico, Alice and her brothers had a large bunch of cattle pointed toward Texas when darkness prevented them from proceeding. They made camp and started a fire, leaving no guard with the cattle since they were certain they had not been followed. It was one of the few mistakes Alice ever made, but she paid dearly for it. During the night a bunch of bandits attacked, taking everything they had, and the group was forced to run for cover. While they were making their getaway, a bullet clipped the chin strap on Alice's sombrero. She might have lost everything else, but Alice was not about to lose her beloved hat, too. She stopped in a hail of lead to retrieve it.

Alice Stillwell Henderson faced her life's obligations in a man's way, yet those who knew say that even "when called upon to face loneliness, danger, cold steel and blood, she remained a womanly woman."[6] Her life was as grand and dramatic as the Big Bend that was her home.

Alice was interested in that other frontier woman whose exploits were well-known in the Bend, Sally Skull, horse trader from Refugio County. Alice wrote a book on Sally's life, but the manuscript was lost before it was ever printed.[7] One wonders what Alice saw in Sally's life that was any more remarkable than her own.

While Alice Henderson's quarrel was with officials of another country, Ann Bassett Willis of Brown's Park, Colorado, had problems with local cattle barons. She, too, was prepared to lead men to help fight for what was hers. Ann was also prepared to stand up alone in the defense of her beloved park. Her controversial and stormy existence, lived in the tradition of the cattleman's code, puts to shame any of the wild tales by dime novelists in which violence, gun play, Indians, outlaws, cattle stampedes, righteous cowboys and damsels in distress were the stock in trade.

Ann's life began in 1878 in the proper dramatic setting. The Ute chief Marcisco and his tribe were encamped some two hundred yards from the cabin where Ann was born. Unable to nurse her baby, Mrs. Bassett had to find a substitute quickly. Among the women at the Ute camp was See-a-baka, the mother of a newborn son. After much consultation, See-a-baka agreed to be Ann's wet nurse, and the white baby was carried through a snow storm to the lodge of the Indian mother.[8]

Brown's Hole, or Brown's Park as Ann's mother called it, lay in the northwest corner of Colorado and the northeast edge of Utah. It was a place of abundant game and verdant grasses, of steep mountain passes through which swept the mighty Green River. And for Ann, it was a place of enchantment, a place to stand and fight when the time came for fighting.

The people of Brown's Hole were a convivial, hardworking group and they lived according to the range code which dictated that strangers were welcome, that a person's real name was his own business and so was his past. As a result of living by this code, Brown's Hole suffered a bad reputation among some outsiders as a place where outlaws could find refuge from the law.[9] Ann's family, for instance, counted among their friends Elza Lay, one of Butch Cassidy's gang. But as Ann pointed out, no stranger was asked to submit his genealogy. In Brown's Park friendships were based on today's deeds, not on yesterday's mistakes.

Ann had a western-story-book childhood. She rode the expanses of Brown's Hole at will and unchaperoned. She was both the pet and the pest of the ranch hands. Her nature was wild, and she often got herself into dangerous situations. On one occasion she roped a bear cub and barely missed death when the mama bear made a swipe at Ann and broke her horse's neck instead.[10]

Ann was the center of an early episode involving the cattle barons of the Middlesex Cattle Company and the small operators of the Hole. The outcome was peaceable enough, but the incident cast a shadow toward things to come.

The Middlesex Cattle Company made an effort to run herds into Brown's Hole, which was largely public domain. The company was stopped not by bullets and bloodshed but by sheep deliberately pastured there by those who believed that cows would not cross territory grazed by sheep.[11] From 1877 to 1888 Middlesex cowboys gathered their herds near Brown's Hole and moved them to the mountains in the summer and on to the lower ranges during the winter. There were always strays in the Hole during such roundups. In the spring of 1883, Ann found a stray Longhorn calf, and, although it had been branded and ear-marked, she claimed it for her own rather than let it starve. In the months to come Ann became so attached to the animal that she went to see the general manager of the Middlesex company and offered one of her daddy's purebred Durhams in exchange for her pet Longhorn. The manager would not accept such a generous trade and insisted that Ann keep the calf for her own. During the year, the management of the Middlesex changed hands, and when a new puncher saw the cow wearing the Middlesex brand among the Bassett herd, he cut the animal out and put it with other Middlesex cows.

When eight-year-old Ann found her pet missing, she guessed what had happened and went to take back what was rightfully hers. The ramrod did not see it Ann's way and refused to give up the animal. Ann took a quirt to the man. It was not long before other cowboys took sides in the matter and a fist fight broke out between the foreman and another cowboy who thought Ann should be allowed to take her calf home. Ann's champion won and the child drove her pet home where in secret she took drastic steps to insure that the Middlesex boys would never bother her again. She altered the brand.

When Roark, the foreman, next saw the Longhorn and the blotted brand, he sent for the sheriff who in turn issued warrants for the arrest of nearly everybody in Brown's Hole including a visiting Englishman who was just passing through. The issuing of warrants was the first time Ann's parents knew what their eight-year-old daughter had been up to. Everyone who had been issued warrants dutifully filed into court, but the case was dismissed for lack of evidence.[12]

It might be supposed that Ann learned her lesson from that day in court, but she did not. In 1899, when Ann was a teenager, she and some friends found a small herd of cattle which did not belong in the Hole. The group forced the herd to cross Green River, and some of the cattle were probably drowned. The incident did not enhance her reputation.[13]

The threat of big operators overrunning the range and the murder of some of Ann's friends led her to take a more determined stand. In 1910, Ann, then married to H. H. Bernard, informed the stockmen that her watering hole, long enjoyed by all cattlemen, was off limits to them. After this action a range detective gathered evidence which caused Ann and her foreman, Tom Yarberry, to be charged with stealing and butchering a heifer on March 13, 1911.[14] It looked bad for Ann, but she was not only schooled in the western traditions of handling range problems, she also knew how to be a lady in grand style. The combination of talents was hard to beat.

Ann had learned to act the part of a lady when, as a teenager, her family sent her away to Salt Lake City where the sisters at the Catholic convent undertook to gentle and tame the coltish girl. Instead of feeling shut away from her freedom, Ann imagined that school was all a great play put on for her benefit.[15] Her education, blended with her western ways, made her a formidable opponent in court when she met Ora Haley, owner of the Two Bar, whose heifer she was accused of stealing and butchering. Ann blamed Haley for the murder of one of her best friends, and more than cows must have been on Ann's mind when she entered the courtroom.

The room was crowded and tension high as the actress, Queen Ann—beautifully dressed, daintily fragile, and seemingly defenseless—made her way into the courtroom. Newspapers of the day were anxious that nothing of the procedures be left out. They tell for instance that Cliff Rowe took stenographer Spruil's place so that Spruil could attend the Knight Templar's Conclave at Denver.[16]

It was not really Ann who was on trial, as it turned out, but cattle baron, Ora Haley. Attorney Saunders spent time asking a lot of seemingly pointless questions and then "without altering the monotonous tempo of his questions or his tone of voice" he asked Haley how many cattle he had. With pride, Haley replied that he had close to ten thousand head. Attorney Saunders then lowered the boom by asking Haley why only four months ago he told the county assessor that he had only five or six thousand? Not waiting for Haley to answer, Saunders turned his back to the witness, looked at the jury and answered for Haley—"Mr. Haley lied." The trial was as good as over. John Rolfe Burroughs, who knew the history of Brown's Hole, concluded:

> That Ann Bassett was guilty as sin was beside the point. In her writings, Ann says. 'I did everything they ever accused me of, and a whole lot more.' Everybody knew it, and very few people in North-

> western Colorado cared two hoots in a hollow. She was a heroine. She looked—and acted—the part. A lone woman, a smallish woman, a woman still young and exceedingly attractive had fought the mighty Haley to a standstill. Holding him up to public obloquy, Ann Bassett had whipped the daylights out of him.[17]

In 1920, Ann took a second husband, Frank Willis. They moved to California and then to Arizona, where they ranched. Ann enrolled as a forestry student and applied for a position as a forest ranger. In spite of her proven ability to back down Colorado's mightiest, she was not accepted into the Forestry Service because she was a woman. In her later years Ann lived quietly compared to the lively years of her youth. She died in Leeds, Utah, at the age of 78 among friends who probably never knew the tales she might have told them.[18]

The actions of a colonel in the United States Army and the death of her husband at the hands of neighbors caused Susan McSween of New Mexico to take, or try to take, matters into her hands in the Lincoln County War of 1878.

It is recorded that Nero fiddled while Rome burned, and, while New Mexico is a long way from Rome, it has also passed into the lore of the Lincoln County War that Susan McSween played the piano while men burned the house out from under her.[19]

The Lincoln County War was not entirely a cattle war, although rustling and range rights eventually entered into it. The struggle began as a mercantile war over government contracts for beef to supply army posts and Indian reservations. In the 1870s, Gustav Murphy, and later James J. Dolan, acting for a group known as the Santa Fe Ring, monopolized government beef contracts. John Chisum wanted a piece of the pie, and, along with such men as Alexander McSween and John Tunstall, made a successful bid to supply beef to the army. That's when the shooting started.

It is not necessary to offer opinions as to which side was right or wrong in order to judge Mrs. Susan McSween's part in it. Susan did not really get warmed up until the last day of the war, July 19, 1878, when her husband was killed. The lady's wrath centered as much on Colonel Dudley of the United States Army as it did on the Murphy-Dolan gang.

When Susan decided to appeal for help to the Army on the day the Murphy-Dolan gang was shooting it out with her husband's men at her front door, she crawled out of the house on her hands and knees because bullets were flying and no one seemed disposed to stop shooting. Colonel Dudley, who did not like McSween and his men anyway, was not touched at the sight of Susan crawling. He was even less impressed when Susan arrived before him and in haughty tones demanded to know why he had a howitzer aimed at her house. The colonel was forced to explain that Mrs. McSween could not tell the front end from the rear end of a cannon and that actually the cannon was facing away from her home. She probably dismissed that as a petty detail. The important thing was that pompous Dudley had that cannon, and since he would not use it for her, then he must be against her.

Beginning with the failure of Mrs. McSween's plea for help in stopping the Murphy-Dolan gang, things went from bad to worse. Remembering the episode later, she said, "Bullets were flying all around me that day. I feared nothing." When Dudley refused to help, Susan laid it on the line about how things were going to be: "Some day these deeds will recoil on your head! If I live, I will do all in my power to bring that about."[20] Susan returned to the house, played the piano for awhile, and did not leave until fire had burned all but the last room. As the group left, Mr. McSween was shot.

Susan decided to stay on in Lincoln if for no other reason than to tell all she knew about who murdered her husband. The woman was threatened openly by the Murphy-Dolan element and when Andy Boyle and John Kinney threatened to kill her on the spot, she invited them to have at it. They, however, declined and decided instead to prove that while sticks and stones may break your bones, words will very nearly ruin you. Among other things, her enemies circulated the story that she and Mr. McSween were not legally married. Dudley accused her of intimacy with several men. Some even said later that she and John Chisum were carrying on.[21]

In retaliation Susan forwarded affidavits to Washington naming the ones who had killed her husband. During a hearing in court over the matter, Susan and Dudley got into it again and spent most of the time hurling accusations at each other.

When the situation had cooled off, Mrs. McSween was able to salvage some of her husband's estate, marry lawyer George Barber in 1884, and establish a ranch of her own in the Three Rivers area of New Mexico.

Nothing in Susan's background had prepared her for the rough life in New Mexico in general or for ranching in particular. She was living in Atchison, Kansas, where her social life probably revolved around the Presbyterian church, when she met and married Alexander McSween. He had been educated for the Presbyterian ministry but chose law instead. The couple came over the trail to Santa Fe and perhaps planned to settle near Las Vegas. During a chance meeting, Miguel Otero advised them to go to Lincoln where they settled down and later became involved in the troubles of the county. Otero had lived in the area for some years and was a citizen of importance.[22]

Susan's ranch, called Tres Ritos, may have been stocked with about forty head of cattle given to her by John Chisum because of his regard for her late husband.[23] That Chisum and Susan were intimate was probably malicious gossip and not in keeping with Chisum's reputation as a woman-avoider.[24] It seemed to be a local pastime to accuse her of intimacy with anyone from well-known Lincoln County personalities to passers-by. Susan in a letter to Maurice Garland Fulton mentioned that John Chisum "never put up at any other place than ours."[25] Alexander, Susan and John once made a business trip together, but there is no real evidence that they were more than friends and business partners.

The Old Abe Eagle of September 1, 1892, ran an article telling about Susan's fabulous ranch house and thousands of cattle,[26] but Tobe Tipton, a pioneer Tularosa merchant, said that the story was a "pipe dream."[27] It is difficult to know just how many cattle Susan ran on the ranch, but acquaintances such as

Clara Snow and Roy Harman of Carrizozo, New Mexico, did remember that Susan, who was by then Mrs. Barber, was a good manager and kept close contact with ranch affairs. She wanted the stock well-cared for and used a surrey and team to check the range. Mrs. Snow never remembered seeing Mrs. Barber on horseback and concluded that her foreman probably supervised her cowboys.[28] Another acquaintance, Reverend Lacy Simms of Alamogordo, New Mexico, recalled that a Mexican called Pompey was her foreman.[29]

It must have been a lonely existence at Three Rivers for a woman accustomed to being in the center of things. There was not even a church in the area. Lacy Simms recalls that "social life for all the families there then was almost a minus quantity." Mrs. Barber relieved the monotony on at least one occasion by giving a "baile" or dance for all six families who lived in the area. It was an all-night affair and even Lacy and the other children attended.[30] Others remember that Susan was an excellent dancer and made "quite a figure on the dance floor as she was slim and very active."[31]

Susan divorced George Barber for nonsupport in 1891. Barber apparently never had much to do with the ranch but spent most of his time at his law office.[32]

Susan's declining years, after the sale of her ranch to A. B. Fall, were spent in White Oaks, New Mexico. Still proud and courageous, she tried to make her life as meaningful as possible. She kept up her appearance as an elegant, stylish woman. Mrs. Snow, a resident of White Oaks, remembered that she wore diamonds, stylish hats and veils, and that "her clothes were the expensive kind and made her outstanding in any crowd." Although she dressed elegantly she was "extremely gracious to everyone, rich or poor."[33]

Susan visited her neighbors, took part in Ladies Aid Society meetings and drove frequently to Carrizozo in one of the few cars in the area. According to Eve Ball, prominent New Mexico historian:

> She was always fastidious in grooming and dress, and bought one of the first cars in this area. John Littell,

> who when a very young man, drove her car for her, told of how very careful she was to prevent tanning and how she kept up appearances.[34]

Roy Harmon and his brother Lloyd went to Mrs. Barber's house in White Oaks as children and remember that she gave them cookies. After refreshments Lloyd was sometimes allowed to learn, with Susan's help, the notes on her prized piano. In addition to the piano, Susan had a ouija board and she used it frequently to "talk" with Alexander, her first husband.[35]

Although Susan's later life was often lonely, she kept active. She spent much time corresponding and talking with Maurice Fulton about his book on the Lincoln County War. She chided him for not coming to see her more often and for not staying long enough when he did come. She expressed concern over such matters as the fact that she was "living very humble and crude,"[36] that she thought her niece was stealing her papers about the Lincoln County War,[37] and that her health was bad. Her memories of the Lincoln episode only served to bolster her belief that her husband had been a saint. She reinforced her claims by quoting her minister. On hearing that McSween was dead, she remembered the minister saying: "Oh, merciful God[,] if they killed such a man as McSween they would kill Jesus Christ if he were to come down here as every act and deed . . . proved him to be a merciful good Christian."[38]

Susan's one hope for financial gain came not from cattle but from oil. In her letters she continually reminded Maurice Fulton that he had said he would try to put her in touch with some oil company about drilling on her land.[39]

While other women on the Mexican border, in Colorado and in New Mexico were busy punching cattle, throwing lead and words and keeping their spirits up, Mrs. Mabel Doss Day of Coleman County, Texas, got caught with her fences down. It was called the Fence Cutting War of 1883 and the principal areas of destruction were Jack, Wise, Clay, Coleman and Frio counties.[40] The cutters were not, at first, mad at Mabel personally. They were mad at the barbed wire which was enclosing the open range.

Long before becoming embroiled in a fence-cutting war in Coleman, Mabel Doss had been the belle of society in Sherman, Texas, where she taught music. The highlight of the Sherman social season was the Fourth of July celebration called Natal Day. In 1878, Mabel was the candidate most likely to be crowned queen of the event. The whole town was considerably surprised when another candidate was chosen. An investigation into the matter showed that the winner's father had appeared in town the day before with a bag of Mexican silver pesos which were deposited, evidently, in the right hands.

Mabel's friends and supporters rallied around her, held their own celebration and presented Mabel with a chain and gold watch on the back of which was an inscription attesting their love and loyalty. The group attended the Natal ball to which Mabel wore an elegant princess-style dress embellished with a rose sash draped in flowers. Taking in all the festivities was William H. Day, a prominent cattleman.[41]

Mabel and William Day were married in 1879, and Mabel began her life as a ranch wife in Coleman County. William gave his bride a pony and saddle and she, in a blue riding habit, accompanied her husband on the range. Day's primary concern was fencing his land—some forty thousand acres of it.[42] In addition to her own horse, William bought Mabel a "traveling she-bang," as she called it, which was a vehicle with three seats. It was ordered from St. Louis and cost $973. The contraption had seats that could be let down for a bed or used on a rainy day for dining.[43]

In 1880, Willie Mabel was born to the couple and life looked stable, but in 1881, the horn of a saddle severely injured Colonel Day and he died from gangrene. Before his death he told Mabel about his business and instructed her to take over. The operation was $117,000 in debt.[44]

The widow was determined to refinance and carry on the ranch operations on land that was already bought and not part of public domain, but instead of using local capital, she went outside the state for backing. When the news got around that Mrs. Day had formed a two hundred thousand dollar corporation known as The Day Cattle Ranch Company with Kentucky backers, the fence cutters declared war on her. When the cutters were not hanging out with Madge Barker and her girls at the Blue Front Saloon, they were getting rid of Mabel's fences as group therapy. Just in case Mabel was not getting the message, they posted a notice on the streets of Coleman complaining not only of Mabel but of a few more grievances which were beside the point:

> Down with monopolies. They can't exist in Texas and especially in Coleman County. Away with your foreign capitalists. The range and soil of Texas belongs to the heroes of the South. No monopolies, and don't tax us to school the nigger. Give us homes as God intended and not gates to churches and towns and schools. Above all give us water for our stock.[45]

Mabel was not much on guns—yet. She wrote a calm, friendly reply in the paper telling the offenders of Coleman that 1) She owned her own land; that she was not fencing public land; 2) It was not the place of anyone but civil authorities to remove her fences; 3) There were plenty of gates which anyone might use when they wished to pass through her land; 4) If certain people did not leave her fences alone, she just might not live in Coleman County any more; 5) Wasn't there some way law-abiding men could put a stop to the lawlessness. In reply, the fence cutters ripped out some more fence.

Mabel tried other methods to stop the destruction of her fences. She persuaded a friend in a high place to get the Texas Rangers to come to Coleman. When the Rangers came, they mixed and mingled with the population to see which way the wind was blowing and decided that, according to a General King who helped arbitrate:

> There was no real foundation for apprehending any organized outbreak or contest with arms between pasture men and fence cutters, and that personally the most friendly feeling existed between many of the owners of pastures and those who openly opposed large pastures, and who thus gave encouragement to

> those who were lawlessly and secretly cutting down and destroying these pastures.[46]

Apparently General King's men forgot to ask Mabel what she thought.

The Rangers were no help. The local sheriff refused to help. He was too busy with rustlers who were, no doubt, finding lots of wandering cattle on the ranges. When the head of the local law-and-order league asked Sheriff Jones to investigate the wire cutting, he replied, "I love to live too well to do that."[47]

Mrs. Day even went outside the law by promising help to a man accused of murder in exchange for his services as a fence rider with his Winchester for a companion. The fence cutters took the man's Winchester, pointed it at him, and made him help them cut six more miles of fence.

The legislature finally considered the problem of fence cutting and made several suggestions. One lawmaker thought the offenders ought to be shot on sight. Another thought fences ought to be built around Coleman and all the fence cutters armed with nippers put inside it:

> As the fence cutters preferred to do their work at night, the plan was to propose stretching a great awning over the county, paint it black to represent night, and cut holes in it to represent stars. They would then be able to cut all the time and would all die of sheer exhaustion from the lack of sleep.[48]

Finally a sensible law was passed under which fence cutters were assessed from one to five years imprisonment. When they realized that they would have to face more than a few angry cattlemen, the fence cutters studied war no more.

In 1889, Mabel married Captain Joseph C. Lea and moved to New Mexico. She continued as an influence for good in her new life and among other things founded New Mexico Military Academy in her home in Roswell.[48]

Not all ranch women were entirely successful in their attempts to solve their problems inside or outside the law, but with words, guns, and other interesting and questionable weapons they managed to trample a good many wrong men who got in their way. And they proved that life could be dangerous when a woman took matters into her own hands.

5

The Lady Rustlers

Anne Richey of Lincoln County, Wyoming, was "thirty, purty, and full of life."[1] She was the daughter of a well-known ranching family. Educated, married to a school teacher, she had some claim to culture, though she knew how to ride, rope and brand. Maybe it was the "thirty, purty and full of life" part that caused her to do what she did—and what she did was rustle cattle.

While Westerners put up with a good deal of nonsense from women (even murder) they got tough now and then with rustlers. Rustling was generally a man's game. There were not many lady rustlers, but what they lacked in numbers, they made up for in ingenuity. Sometimes leading the men, sometimes taking orders from them, the women rustlers learned that the penalty for getting caught was terminal and soon.

In November of 1919, Anne Richey had the distinction of being the only woman ever convicted of cattle rustling in Wyoming. Anne probably had accomplices. Her neighbor, Charles King, may have been one of them. But Anne, in the true spirit of honor among thieves, never named any names not even when, as she was on her way to her preliminary hearing, a masked rider shot at her and shattered her arm. The rider was never identified.[2]

Wyoming's Supreme Court upheld Anne's conviction two years after her sentence was appealed,[3] but the court allowed her time to make her ranch ready against the Wyoming winter. Before the time set for Anne to begin serving her sentence, she was mysteriously poisoned.[4]

Anne Richey insisted that she worked alone, but Mrs. Grace Newton of the La Plata Valley of New Mexico made rustling a family affair.

Grace Newton was described as a "big strong woman of the out-doors with a firm jaw."[5] She was also a mother who believed in togetherness by instructing her son, Orlando, on how to do things by doing things with him. Mostly Grace showed Sonny how to steal and butcher other people's cattle in the La Plata Valley. Orlando and two other men were sentenced to state prison terms, but when Grace got caught, the loyal mother claimed she did not know anything about what Orlando had been up to. To top it all off, Grace screamed some four-letter words in the courtroom, and the judge ordered her out until she could behave.[6] The judge gave her three years.

Sons are not the only good helpers. Husbands, too, make good rustling accomplices, and Mrs. Gatlin of Menard, Texas, was just as loyal as Grace Newton when the chips were down.

"Oh Lord, for what we are about to receive, make us truly thankful"—or something close to that must have been on Sister Gatlin's mind as she and her husband went about doing good. Mrs. Gatlin was a traveling lady evangelist and with the aid of her husband, she helped people relieve themselves of their burdens of sin. After services Mrs. Gatlin changed her white evangelist's robes for men's overalls and relieved her congregation of their cattle. The sheriff around Menard and Rochelle, Texas, got suspicious and found some stolen animals with the Gatlins. Mr. Gatlin was convicted, but his evangelist wife pleaded insanity. They locked her up in the insane asylum in San Antonio where she, no doubt, gave the Word to a captive audience.[7]

Another couple who practiced togetherness by rustling cattle in the 1880s were Mr. and Mrs. F. M. Baker of Oklahoma. The couple was arrested by Marshal Evett Nix and his deputy near the Bill Halsell ranch and taken to Guthrie, Oklahoma. During the trip the group stopped for the night and bedded down on the prairie. Sometime in the night Mr. Baker escaped across Bird Creek. While Mrs. Baker was being held in Guthrie, she sent word that she wanted to see Marshal Nix. Nix complied and was greeted with a tirade from Mrs. Baker against Nix's deputy. She claimed he had stolen her husband's coat and tie, killed him while he was swimming Bird Creek and had not tried to find his body. Mrs. Baker punctuated her ranting with curse words. Nix assured the woman he would investigate but she sent a letter to Washington, just in case. When the Department of Justice wrote back to the marshal and asked for a full report, Nix sent out the deputy to bring the escaped husband in. When Baker was at last reunited with his wife behind bars, Nix reported:

> From the reception he received at her hands, I have often wondered if he wouldn't have preferred to have been shot at Bird Creek. I have heard tongue lashings before, but hers eclipsed them all. Where had he been? What had he been doing? Why had he been doing it? Who had he been with?[8]

Occasionally a lone woman got all the blame for rustling. *The Texas Livestock Journal* reported in 1883 that Mrs. Helen Loveless was found guilty of killing cattle belonging to stock raisers in Paradise Valley, Texas. Mrs. Loveless owned her own ranch but apparently fed her hired hands from beef on the range—anybody's beef. The reporter added that although Mrs. Loveless was probably forty-five years old, she married a youth of nineteen who later hightailed it with some of her horses. The conviction of a woman for rustling was unusual, and the reporter concluded that perhaps the jury might not have found her guilty if she had "been young and loveable instead of Loveless."[9]

Some female rustlers just could not help themselves. The devil, or some no-account man, made them do it. Seventeen-year-old Annie McDoulet and sixteen-year-old Jennie Stevens, known as Cattle Annie and Little Britches, were delinquent teenagers who rode with the Doolin gang in 1894, in the Oklahoma Territory. It is reported that they stole cattle and horses.[10] They found other business enterprises as well—peddling whiskey to the Osage for instance.

The girls were daughters of two poor neighboring farm families. After taking up a life of crime, they went about heavily armed and no one doubted that they were good shots.[11] James Horan thinks the girls provided comic relief—and other services—for the Doolin gang. They seemed to spend most of their time keeping the road hot, riding up and down country lanes and listening for secret information. Of course, every one in Ingalls, Oklahoma, a town where the Doolin gang was well-known and relatively safe, knew who they were, but they must have felt important dashing, heavily armed, up and down the roads.

After the Doolin gang was brought to justice, Marshals Bill Tilghman and Steve Burke were ordered to bring in Cattle Annie and Little Britches from their hiding place at Pawnee. Little Britches saw the men coming, leaped out a window to a horse, and galloped off. Marshal Tilghman, not wanting to shoot a woman in spite of the fact that she had no compunction about emptying her gun on him, shot her horse instead. The horse fell on the girl, no doubt saving the marshal a foot race to capture her. She fought like a wild cat until Tilghman spanked her.

Meanwhile, Marshal Burke captured Cattle Annie when she leaned out a window to shoot at him. They, too, had a free-for-all but Burke managed to subdue his captive with a bear hug. The girls were taken to Perry, Oklahoma, cleaned up, and sentenced to short jail terms. Cattle Annie later married and settled down near Pawnee, Oklahoma. Little Britches went to New York and died of consumption.

The Doolin gang was blessed with the presence of another young cattle rustler—Rose of Cimarron. Her real name was Rose Dunn and she came to Oklahoma when her parents made the run in 1889. Rose enjoyed a good home and received an education in a convent in Wichita, Kansas. She probably met the Doolin gang through her brothers who were cattle thieves. An excellent rider and an expert with gun and rope, Rose was known to have crossed the border of Pawnee County on more than one occasion to help her brothers rustle cattle for a drive to Guthrie where a certain butcher waited to receive the goods.[12]

One of the members of Doolin's gang was Bitter Creek Newcomb who was described as "handsome as a movie star."[13] Rose fell for Bitter Creek and shared her affections with no one else. When she joined the gang, she became "nurse, scout, spy, courier, and horse holder for the gang."[14] But in case anyone had the idea that Rose was a loose woman, Bill Doolin himself vouched for her conduct: "The entire gang worshipped her. If anybody had ever dared to intimate that she was not all a good woman should be, any one of the crowd would have killed her accuser instantly."[15]

During one encounter between the law and the Doolin gang, Rose proved herself a true daughter of the range. The gang was holed up in Ingalls when the posse found them. The women, including Rose, had taken refuge in the Pierce Hotel. The hotel was really a kind of boarding house run by Mary Pierce who provided beds, meals, and certain other comforts for the boys. The building was a crude place with no stairs leading to the second floor. A ladder provided entrance to the top floor. When Rose looked through the window and saw Bitter Creek fall wounded by the livery stable, she buckled two belts of cartridges around her waist, grabbed a Winchester and bailed out the window holding on to sheets tied together to make a rope. Running into the line of fire, Rose gave Newcomb the revolvers while she manned the Winchester.[16]

After the gang got away, Rose nursed Bitter Creek back to health only to have him meet his day of reckoning not long after. According to Nix, Rose was later arrested, brought to court and placed for a short time in a federal prison.[17] James Horan insists that Nix is wrong, that Rose was never arrested, arraigned, or spent time in jail.[18] Both agree that she married into a substantial Oklahoma family and lived a long and respectable life.

Another woman who let a man lead her down rustler's road was Ella Watson, known as Cattle Kate. On a summer day in 1889 in Wyoming, A. J. Bothwell, Tom Sun, John Durbin, R. M. Galbraith, Bob Conner and E. McClain knocked on Kate Watson's door and told her to go get in the wagon which they had thoughtfully provided for her. Kate was surprised by the invitation and she wanted, as any woman would, to change her dress first. The men insisted that what she had on was fine. With Kate seated in the wagon, the group went over to the home of Kate's friend, Jim Averill, and invited him to go, too. Averill did not much want to go either, but since his neighbors insisted, he decided he would. After a four-mile drive to Spring Canyon the group walked to a tree and hung the honorees, Kate and Jim. The pine tree was a short one, and since the victims did not have far to fall, they strangled to death slowly.[19] Kate's moccasins came off when her neck jerked the rope. According to Mari Sandoz, Kate's skirts were "blowing and ballooning in the updraft and the slow dying."[20]

If Kate could have been content with the drudgery of Kansas farm life, she never would have got mixed up with Wyoming cows, but Kate did not like scrubbing, and milking, and working in the fields. She hit the trail and exchanged hard living in Nebraska for easy pickings in Wyoming in saloons and bawdy houses. One story is that when a soldier told her he did not like her name, Ella, she changed it to Kate.[21]

There are two versions of Kate's life in the Wyoming cattle business. One version says that Kate was a hardnosed business-woman. She could ride as well as any man and she could swing a loop with the best of them. It was reported that Kate "could throw a steer and hold him while the men put on the brand."[22] More important, Kate was hailed as Wyoming's Cattle Queen and was admired by cattlemen who declared that she lived by the best of the cowboy's code. One story made her the heroine of a raid in which she stormed a gambling house and at gunpoint recovered a sum of money which she claimed had been stolen from her hands in a crooked card game.[23] She was known as "The Duchess of Winchester" because of her skill with a rifle.[24] Some who did not think of Kate as a heroine described her as an Amazon—160 pounds of muscle.[25] Another added long brown hair and an easy smile to the muscle.[26]

The portrayal of Kate as an honest woman is not necessarily a true one, even if such a picture is pleasant to believe. The truth is that Kate probably was a frowzy, dumpy, hard-drinking tart who got herself mixed up in cattle rustling because she did what Jim Averill told her to do.

Jim Averill was considered something of a gentleman on the rough frontier. He ran a combination saloon-store-post office in the Sweetwater Valley of Wyoming between Casper and Rawlins. Kate was his partner in the saloon, and in their side business of filling their corrals with cattle—either theirs or somebody else's.[27]

Just how much rustling Kate and Jim were actually doing is a matter of conjecture. Some say Kate took stolen cattle from cowboys in return for her favors.[28] Others say Kate knew nothing of the rustling, that Averill was the thief.[29] The fact is, there was a lot of rustling going on in Wyoming in the late 1880s, but perhaps Kate and Jim would hardly have been noticed except for Jim's one bad habit. He wrote letters to the leading newspapers condemning the large cattle owners who were squeezing the small operators off the open range. In particular, he incurred the wrath of A. J. and J. R. Bothwell, who were trying to buy out all the small owners in the valley. Averill called so much attention to Bothwell's land grabbing during a time when feelings were running high that Bothwell and his vigilante committee decided to close Averill's mouth for good. After the lynching, Bothwell's crowd was brought to trial but never to justice, and the people of Sweetwater Valley continued to war some more.

There were many other female outlaws but they favored stage robbing, not cattle stealing. Of course, no roster of female desperadoes is complete without mentioning Belle Starr and Calamity Jane. Although neither fits into a study of cattlewomen, they do qualify as probably the best known and most notorious western women. There remains little to say about either Belle or Calamity. Both fit the category of "girl sports" popularized in dime novels. Calamity was herself the subject of several novels. Calamity was also her own best publicity agent, and she mixed and mingled in whatever enterprises her imagination thought of. Belle was too refined to steal cows. Fine-blooded horses suited her better. From time to time tales about Belle continue to surface. One story told at the Texas Trail Drivers

Association meeting some years back, and passed on to me by the late Mody C. Boatright, has it that a puncher by the name of Pete rode into San Antonio one evening:

> The hotels were overflowing, but the proprietor of one small place agreed to house him in a room with another guest, provided the consent of the first guest could be secured. This was easily done and the two shared a double bed. Pete and the roommate talked of many things, among them Belle Starr and her escapades. During the conversation Pete entertained a keen desire to meet this famous western woman.

The story goes on:

> The next morning Pete found that the other guest had arisen before him. When he went down to the veranda, a fine horse stood saddled at the rack. His late roommate came out and mounted.
> "Did you say you would like to see Belle Starr?" he asked.
> "Yes."
> "Well," said the other, turning to gallop away. "You slept with her last night."[30]

Guns used expertly either for right or wrong, herding cattle up the trail, ranch work which included roping, branding, and penning combined with household chores and mothering, specialized clothing (costume, if you will) adapted to horseback riding, expertise with horses—all in the world of women on the cattle frontier—reveal that the elements were in place for the creation of a western heroine who would be known as the cowgirl. But the label, cowgirl, never had general approval during the time when the term really fit. By the time "cowgirl" caught on nationally, cowgirls had already hybridized. Still, it is interesting to scan the dim horizons of the western past, point to a rider on the rim and declare "Look, there she is —maybe; well, it looks kind of, sorta' like one, a cowgirl?"

Wallace Stegner in an introduction to A. B. Guthrie's *The Big Sky* makes the point that "Like any other part of a human tradition, history is an artifact." History isn't history until someone not only remembers it but writes it down. The problem is, however, that not everybody writes it down the same way and often the slant on history depends on the one doing the remembering or the writing down. In many cases, information about cowboys and cowgirls, too, was interpreted in purple prose and not undertaken just by those who had copying down dry facts in mind. Writing of women and men on the cattle frontier early served the purpose of information, but it served as entertainment, too. It might appear that to discern between fact and embellished fact is easy. Truth to tell, in the West, it isn't always easy. It may be that reporters, writers, rememberers sensed that women on the range were viewed through a glass darkly, that their images were distorted, hazy, and that with words they might become focused, sharp, clear, and defined. Obviously, a new Western type was being born.

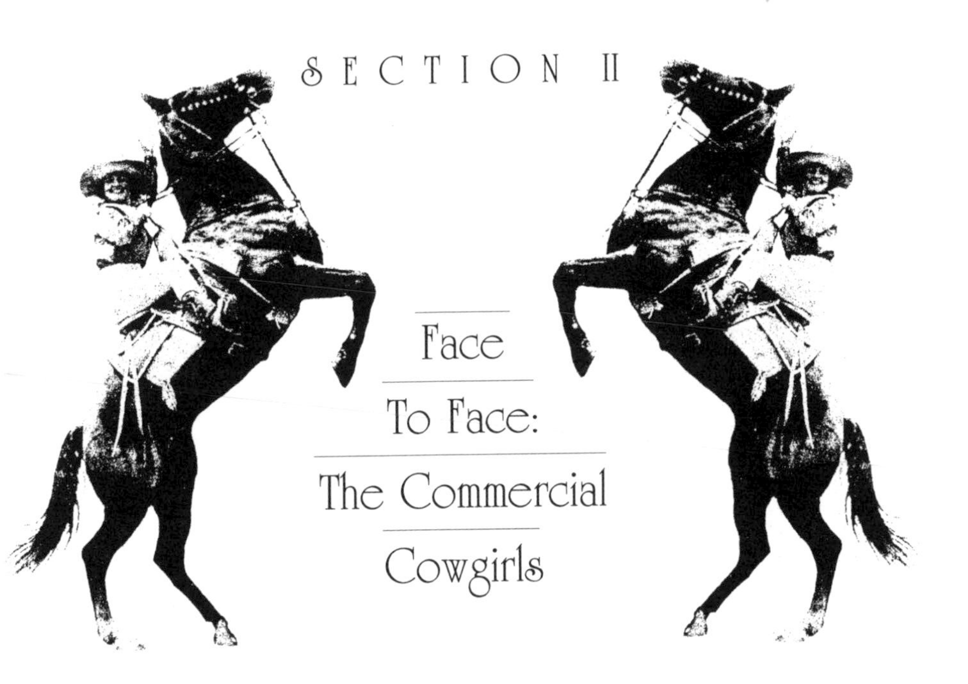

SECTION II

Face To Face: The Commercial Cowgirls

Cowgirls might never have become folk heroines if they had all been stay-at-homes. If the public had not been offered a look at ranch women and to see what they could do, what they wore and how they behaved, cowgirls might have been forever doomed to anonymity. One of the first glimpses the public had of the cowgirl was as she came out of the chutes in Wild West shows and rodeos.

Some women in the audiences liked what they saw enough to take up the rodeo cowgirl life themselves, either through marriage to a cowboy or on their own. In the early 1890s, the word cowgirl was first used nationally and realistically, or so it seemed to an eager public both in the United States and abroad. During this era when the public was getting its first glimpse of ranch life, the majority of women connected with Wild West shows and rodeos had never been on a ranch. The image of a cowgirl, then, was already in place and all that was necessary was to imitate it. The reflection was a composite—a western portrait of a western woman, not a farmer's wife, not a "squaw," not a "señorita," not a schoolmarm, not a dance-hall queen, not a prostitute, but an All American Western Amazon, that girl of the Golden West, THE COWGIRL!

Out of the chutes during the early years of the century came such a woman riding not just a horse but a bucking bronc. A paraphrase of an old cowboy song tells it best:

The first time I seen her was early in spring,
Ridin' a bronco, a hard headed thing.
She tipped me a wink as she gaily did go,
For she wished me to look at her buckin' bronco.

The rider leaves the impression that she wanted the cowboy to look at more than just her horse. She wanted him to see her and what she was doing. Ever since the early days of Wild West shows and rodeos, crowds have been doing just that—appreciatively watching a woman on horseback.

6

Out of the Chutes: the Early Years

The twin spectacles of rodeo and Wild West show brought the frontier to the doorstep of civilization so that it could be inspected at close range. Other heroes needed the woods, the mountains, or the ocean, but cowboys and cowgirls were portable, needing only an enclosure, a horse and a rope. Even more important, real cowgirls and cowboys could be imitated, as thousands of youngsters know, and the actors could learn their parts, not from firsthand experience in cattle country, but from those who were already authentic participants in the rodeos and shows. And when the masses did inspect closely, they could not tell the old hands from the newly initiated. Perhaps they need not have cared anyway since, real or fabricated, the heroines and heroes satisfied both Americans and Europeans, as Mody C. Boatright called them, "the taste makers of the era."[1]

Trying to determine which came first, the Wild West show or rodeo, is not an easy task. In some instances it is hard to tell when rodeo leaves off and the Wild West part begins, and in other cases a Wild West show looks mighty like a rodeo. The truth of the matter is that the two are inextricably woven together.

The cowgirl heroine first made national headlines in Wild West shows. The unlikely figure on which attention first centered as the ideal woman of the western frontier was none other than that sweet young thing who observed sadly, in the Rodgers and Hammerstein version, that "you cain't shoot a male in the tail like a quail"—Annie Oakley. As is often the case with heroines, Annie nearly stole the show from the hero, Buffalo Bill.

In 1882, the ranchmen of North Platte, Nebraska, had asked William F. Cody to arrange some kind of celebration in honor of the Fourth of July. The entertainment for the Old Glory Blowout, as it was called, consisted of cowboys in riding and roping events and of Indians in a mock attack on the Deadwood stagecoach. This celebration developed into Buffalo Bill's Wild West Show in 1883.[2] In the same year that Cody was getting up a celebration for North Platte, one of the first rodeos in which prizes were awarded was produced in Pecos, Texas.[3] Neither the Texas nor the Nebraska contests of 1882 featured any cowgirls, but by 1885 Annie Oakley was on the scene as a member of Buffalo Bill's Wild West Show.

Phoebe Ann Moses, who changed her name to Annie Oakley for no special reason, who had never been west of Cincinnati before getting into show business with a shooting act, and who knew nothing of horses, cattle, or cowboys, seems at first glance a poor choice as a western heroine, but Annie managed to hold the fort until the genuine thing could get there. Mostly she, and the other ladies like her, held the Wild West fort with guns. The story of how Annie helped to feed her family by trapping and shooting quail and squirrels, and, consequently, of how she met, had a shooting match with, and married Frank Butler has been most attractively told in the musical comedy *Annie Get Your Gun*. Equally well known are her exploits with a gun in behalf of Buffalo Bill's Wild West Show, but Annie's abilities were not restricted to firearms. She combined her shooting skills with a sense of drama and a winning personality. Biographer Dexter Fellows explains Annie's impact on America:

> Even before her name was on the lips of every man, woman, and child in America, the sight of this frail girl among the rough plainsmen seldom failed to inspire enthusiastic plaudits. Her entrance was always a very pretty one. She never walked. She tripped in,

> bowing, waving, and wafting kisses. Her first few shots brought forth a few screams of fright from the women but they were soon lost in round after round of applause. It was she who set the audience at ease and prepared it for the continuous crack of firearms which followed.[4]

Little Sure Shot also combined primness with a dash of individuality which endeared her to crowds. Between shows, Annie often worked fine embroidery while the other performers were out on the town. When she was introduced to the Prince of Wales, Annie ignored protocol and the prince by greeting the princess first with a handshake. Her behavior caused the prince to remark that it was too bad there weren't "more women in the world like her." Wild West historian, Don Russell, concludes that besides Buffalo Bill himself, Annie Oakley is "the only . . . universally recognized personality who was entirely a product of the Wild West shows. . . ."[5]

Although Annie at first did no more than perform with her gun, no doubt the audience was able to imagine that she could shoot Indians like a real frontier woman if she had to. It was, after all, an Indian, Sitting Bull, who gave her the title "Little Sure Shot." They probably felt, too, that she could have ridden a horse, and it was not her fault that in her childhood she lacked horse and saddle. In 1887, Annie made up for that deficiency by riding a horse in a race against Lillian Smith, who had joined the show in 1886. Lillian was fifteen years old at the time, and, in addition to being a crack rifle shot, was already an expert horsewoman.

By 1887 there were a dozen women in Buffalo Bill's show. One woman was featured in an attack on a settler's cabin, and a Mrs. Whitaker was in charge of costuming. Mrs. Georgie Duffy, "rough rider of Wyoming," and a Colorado equestrienne, Miss Dell Ferrel, were also featured. Using these and other ladies, a square dance on horseback was performed in which Emma Lake Hickok and her trick horse were the main attraction.

By 1893 Buffalo Bill had enjoyed a successful European tour with such acts as Annie's guns, other shooting performances including his own, demonstrations of foreign styles of horsemanship, races, "cowboy fun" in which roping, riding, and buck-jumping were demonstrated, a pony express ride, a buffalo hunt, an attack on the stagecoach, and the depiction of Indian customs. Women appeared in the square dance, in the cast of acted-out scenes, in the working crew, and in an event listed as "Races Between Prairie, Spanish, and Indian Girls." Although the format was merely an expanded version of his 1893 show, Cody now billed his offering as Buffalo Bill's Wild West and Congress of Rough Riders of the World.[6]

Buffalo Bill's show enjoyed too much success not to be imitated. Pawnee Bill's Historical Wild West featured May Lillie in a shooting act. May, a Smith College graduate from a Quaker community in Pennsylvania, married Gordon W. Lillie, known as Pawnee Bill, hastily took her degree in subjects western, and became a goldmedal winner in rifle shooting in 1887 in Philadelphia and in 1889 in Atlanta, Georgia. With May appeared Bright Star, an Indian Princess, Señorita Rosalia from south of the border—or south of somewhere.[7] By 1893 Pawnee's group numbered three hundred men and women, the latter billed as "beauteous, dashing, daring and laughing Western girls who ride better than any other women in the world."[8] Among the authentic cowgirls participating in his show was Bertha Blancett. Bertha was raised on a Colorado ranch and joined Pawnee Bill in 1906.[9]

There were more imitators (at least 116 according to Don Russell) and probably they all made use of women in the program. Generally they followed a routine similar to Buffalo Bill's.

Meantime, back at the ranch, rodeo was developing and it is necessary to return to the Great Plains in order to see what had been going on while Buffalo Bill and his imitators were applying quirt and spur to the imagination of the American public, assisted by a corps of cowgirls.

It is generally agreed that the Pecos, Texas, contest of 1882 was one of the earliest recorded rodeos. There were rodeo-like affairs, however, as early as 1847. In June of that year Captain Mayne Reid described a "roundup" held in Santa Fe:

> This round-up is a great time for the cowhands, a Donneybrook fair it is, indeed. They contest with each other for the best roping and throwing, and there are horse races and whiskey and wines. At night in the clear moonlight there is much dancing on the streets.[10]

The early rodeos were called Stampedes, Round-Ups, Frontier Celebrations, and Pioneer Days, and they were often part of a Fourth of July celebration. An exposition in Denver offered prizes in 1887.[11] The oldest continuous rodeo, called Frontier Days Celebration, has been staged yearly in Prescott, Arizona, since 1888. The first commercial rodeo was advertised in 1893 in Lander, Wyoming. Montana joined in 1896 and Cheyenne Frontier Days was organized in 1897.[12] Features of all these early-day celebrations were relay races, stagecoach holdups, and pageantry depicting pioneer days with, of course, rodeo contests. In other words rodeos were local versions of Wild West shows with heavier emphasis on cowboy contests.

Women came into the rodeo picture before the turn of the century. Milt Hinkle, who participated in early rodeo, recalled seeing Annie Shaffer of Arkansas ride a bucking horse in 1896 at the Fort Smith rodeo.[13] Warren Richardson, the first chairman of Cheyenne's Frontier Days, named a Miss Bertha Kaepernick as riding broncs and entering a wild horse race at the first celebration in 1897. On the day of the rodeo a torrential downpour ruined the arena and nobody wanted to ride. Richardson's brother persuaded Bertha to do an exhibition ride in front of the grandstand so the people would not leave and ask for their money back. The cowboys decided that if a woman could ride in such conditions, they had better do it, too.[14]

Prairie Rose Henderson challenged the judges and rode a bronc at Cheyenne in 1901. Prairie Rose was the daughter of a local rancher, and when she tried to enter the contest the judges told her that no women were allowed. Prairie Rose demanded to see the rules, pointed out that no mention was made of women, and got her ride.[15] Her campaign smacked of a publicity stunt since at least one woman was riding in 1897, but, reports Clifford P. Westermeier, Prairie Rose "created such a sensation that many of the rodeos soon included as a feature event a cowgirls' bronc riding contest."[16] Rose eventually married a Wyoming rancher, and she died as dramatically as she had lived. She rode off one night into a blizzard and her body was not recovered for some nine years. Her championship belt buckle identified her.[17]

Women were riding in races as early as 1903 at Cheyenne, and in 1904 the *Denver Post* offered a silver loving cup to the champion lady rider of the show, who turned out to be Mrs. Bill Irwin. In 1905, Bertha Kaepernick came back to Cheyenne, riding one hundred miles horseback to get there, and then when she did get there, her horse threw her.[18] Bertha Blancett rode broncs in 1904 and 1905 at Cheyenne, and in 1911 at Pendleton, where she competed with men and almost won the championship.[19]

Women may have been competing in rodeos large and small just prior to and just after 1900, but they were not known as cowgirls until President Theodore Roosevelt applied the phrase to a performer from Oklahoma. Although the term was in use before Teddy bestowed it on Lucille Mulhall, few would argue that she was the first to give the word national meaning.[20] Roosevelt played no small part in calling attention to the West. In extolling such women as Lucille, he also helped to mold people's thinking about cowgirl heroines.

Lucille's father, Zack Mulhall, made the Oklahoma run in 1889 and established a ranch in Logan County. In spite of her mother's attempts to civilize her by sending her to a convent in St. Louis, Lucille was more interested in her daddy's world, and he allowed her to remain in the city only one year. She made a hand by the age of ten—roping, branding, herding and breaking horses. She was further instructed in the ways of western showmanship by her brother Charley and her sisters Bossie and Georgia. Legend has it that when Zack told Lucille she could have her own herd when she was big enough to brand her own cattle, she went out and managed to brand all the unmarked cattle she could find using the cinch buckle on her saddle.

In 1899, when Lucille was thirteen, Colonel Mulhall organized his own Wild West show. It was headquartered at his ranch and from it the family entered various carnivals and fairs. The ranch did not sponsor a traveling show. A shy young fellow named Will Rogers was among Colonel Zack's cowboys, and he and Lucille were close friends. In 1900, the Mulhalls performed in a Cowboy Tournament at the Rough Rider's reunion in Oklahoma City, and Roosevelt, then a candidate for vice president, saw Lucille. An estimated twenty-five thousand watched the Mulhalls perform. Lucille was allowed to participate in the show by riding her horse in a mock Indian massacre, and she briefly displayed her roping skill. Roosevelt is reported to have invited her and her sisters to dinner and the Mulhalls in turn invited him to visit the ranch. In a few days Roosevelt, accompanied by some of his Rough Riders, came to call and he asked Lucille to ride and rope for him. When she had roped some calves and ridden a bucking horse, Teddy told her if she could rope a wolf, he would invite her to the inaugural parade if he was elected vice president. In a manner in keeping with the standards of modest folk heroines, Lucille went about the task immediately and privately. Three hours later, so the story goes, she rode up, dragging a dead wolf behind her. She supposedly scared up a wolf with the help of her pet dogs and accomplished the rest of her grisly task with the end of her stirrup iron.

It did not take long for Colonel Mulhall to decide to build a show around Lucille. In 1900, the Oklahoma group appeared in St. Louis and again Lucille stole the show with an impromptu exhibition. Included in the group was a Mexican lady steer rider who promptly fell off. Dispatching the hero of the show, Ellison Carroll, to minister to the limp señorita, Lucille approached the loose steer, but instead of roping him, she jumped upon his back and rode him until her brother and father relieved her. What became of the señorita is unrecorded, but it was obvious that Lucille was fast entering the gates of legend and lore.

In 1901, the Mulhalls participated in a horse show in Des Moines, Iowa, where Lucille's roping was a sensation. She roped five horses simultaneously. Later she was to rope eight, but five seemed adequate for a fifteen-year-old.

When Lucille was sixteen, the family was invited to participate in the McKinley and Roosevelt inaugural parade, just as Teddy had promised. After the Washington trip the Mulhalls headed for El Paso, where Colonel Zack allowed Lucille to compete in steer roping for the first time. It took two throws to land her steer and tie him, but, at that, she beat all the men with whom she was competing.

Heroes and heroines never win all the time, if only to show what good sports they are, and neither did Lucille always emerge victorious. The public, however, usually remembers the winning. In 1903, she won one thousand dollars for the best time tying three steers. Next she appeared at Denison, Texas, and was first among thirty ropers. Harry Stephens, an old time drover, remembered seeing her there. He recalled:

> They had a big steer tying show, Zack Mulhall and his bunch at our fairgrounds, and his daughter, Lucille. She looked about eighteen and wore a divided skirt. First woman I'd ever seen that wasn't on a side saddle. . . . And she was a fine steer tier. She could rope those steers, drag 'em down and tie 'em just like a man.[21]

In 1904, in Wichita, Kansas, Lucille won again, this time having to chase her steer over a five-foot fence. In the same year she appeared at the St. Louis World's Fair.

Legend has it that Will Rogers came to fame because of a steer that Lucille missed in 1905 in Madison Square Garden. While the characters vary according to who is doing the remembering, one version is that when Lucille missed her steer, Tom Mix threw a loop and came up empty. By this time the steer felt safer with members of the audience and, in great haste, proceeded to join them. Only the trusty loop of Will Rogers could bring the steer back to the arena again.[22]

Lucille's popularity as a cowgirl was not entirely due to her skill, although her skill was awesome, the result of perfect timing with her rope and unusual balance on her horse. Like

Annie Oakley, Lucille was small, weighing only ninety pounds, and she had about her a little girl's shyness and daintiness. One of the most appealing pictures of Lucille shows her wearing a long skirt and a rather feminine hat, and she is standing inside a loop swung by her friend Will Rogers. Lucille was pretty enough to become a silent-movie star, and it was rumored that in her lifetime she made and lost a fortune but died a pauper. She was married twice—ten years to a musician and briefly to Tom Burnett, son of Texas rancher Burk Burnett, whose cattle carried the famous 6666 brand.[23]

Later cowgirls such as Ruth Roach and Mildred Douglas attested to Lucille's kindness and helpfulness to fellow contestants. Mildred said that Lucille, "riding her big White Man horse, snubbed many bucking horses for me . . . and never turned one loose until I told her I was ready."[24] Ruth remembers that Lucille never got involved in petty jealousies but offered help to all even when they were competing against her.[25]

In 1905, the same year that Lucille and her family were romping and stomping in Madison Square Garden, still another ranch group, the Miller Brothers' 101 Ranch (also of Oklahoma) was gathering cowboy and cowgirl talent for the purpose of presenting a Wild West show. When the Mulhalls and the Millers came together, two of the most authentic groups of cowboys and cowgirls were joined and many heroines worthy to apply for Lucille's title of Queen of Cowgirls were present. The women were, by now, well out of the chutes and from about 1910 to 1930 the heroines would spur from shoulder to flank as they became established in the minds of the onlookers from New York to California. The women who appeared in the arena in this era have rarely been equaled and left behind a lasting impression of what a western heroine ought to be.

The Miller Brothers' 101 Ranch, founded in 1892, was busy with many enterprises before wild westing came along. In 1903, the brothers, Joseph, Zack, and George, began running the ranch as a family business, and in time they could boast of more than prime cattle, a slaughter house, a tannery, and a packing plant. In addition, the brothers operated a dairy, a saddle shop, fruit orchards, and a cannery. When they struck oil, they set up a refinery and a filling station. Since so many employees were required for the various enterprises, they had to install housing, a laundry and a company store. The Millers always enjoyed good relations with their Ponca Indian neighbors, and they established a trading post for them.

In June of 1905, the National Editorial Association came for a rodeo at the 101 Ranch. Lucille Mulhall was on hand doing what she did best. Geronimo, brought from Ft. Sill where he was a prisoner, was there doing what people thought he ought to do best—hunting down a buffalo for the evening barbeque. Geronimo thought so much of Lucille's performance that he gave her a beaded vest.

The Miller Brothers' cowboys and cowgirls appeared in 1907 in Jamestown for the Tercentenary Exposition and in Richmond, Atlanta, and Louisville. In 1908, the 101 Ranch Wild West show took to the rails, and, for the next ten years or so, was one of the better traveling shows in the nation.[26]

If you can believe the Miller's own ballyhoo, the talent for the 101 show was provided by friends and neighbors right off the Oklahoma prairie. Mrs. Alma Miller England, co-author of *The 101 Ranch*, states: "The cowgirls riding 'buckers' and twisting the lariat in the show arena were, like the cowboys, recruited from the 101 and adjoining ranches." She further reveals that these Oklahoma prairie girls "rode astride" and performed various ranch chores such as carrying mail, buying supplies, and helping with roundup.[27] No doubt the girls did perform ranch tasks, but it is not likely that women showed up at the 101 for the job of doing a little neighborly totin' and fetchin'. As Don Russell points out, "there was a suspiciously large lot of top talent waiting at the 101 for all this lightning to strike."[28] One suspects that the excitement of show business and travel lured some to the 101. Cleo Tom Terry, co-author of a book about an early day cowgirl, Florence Reynolds, confirms the suspicion by saying that she believes some girls "went to the 101 to get into show business, just as girls go to Hollywood to get into the movies."[29] Still another authority adds that "a rodeo championship was the easiest road to a career in the silent films."[30] One of the ones who made it into silent films when the

101 was not in session was Bertha Blancett, the early Cheyenne contestant, who rode broncs as the men did with no hobbles tied under the stirrups. Bertha worked for the Bison Moving Picture Company and did stunts such as tripping her horse while he was in a dead run.[31]

In 1914, the Miller Brothers took their show to Europe with a program that looked much like any other Wild West show. There was something of the usual circus atmosphere with Prince Lucca and his Wild Riding Cossacks, a shooting act, and the mock massacre, this time taking place on the Old Chisholm Wagon Trail. But there were also top cowboys and cowgirls such as Bill Pickett of bulldogging fame, and Bertha Thompson, a featured rider.[32] And there were more:

> Lucille Mann was the leading bronc rider. Florence LaDue of Bliss, Oklahoma, roped a steer from the back of a running horse. Alice Lee of Dallas, Texas, made a specialty of falling off her horse, catching one foot in the stirrup, and doing a frog-hop along the ground. Lottie Alridge of Greeley, Colorado, lay flat on her horse's back and fired a Winchester at hordes of imaginary Indians. Babe Willetts of Chickasha, Oklahoma, rode a horse and cut out a steer from a bunch of cattle. Other girl champions present were: Mabel Klein of Pecos, Texas, Dot Vernon of Phoenix, Arizona, Ruth Roach of Ponca City, Oklahoma, and Jane Fuller of Eagle, [Engle] New Mexico.[33]

In 1916, Buffalo Bill and the 101 Ranch Show combined for a week and became the Chicago Shan-Kive and Round-Up. Says Don Russell, "Here a Wild West show became an instant rodeo, providing the missing link between these two forms of entertainment."[34] What made this contest different was that there was a list of events with rules given and some world championship titles awarded. The contests were "trick and fancy roping, steer roping, trick riding, bucking steer riding, bucking mule riding, steer bulldogging, and wild horse race."[35] Lucille Mulhall and Prairie Lillie Allen appeared in addition to the other women of the 101.

The outbreak of World War I brought to a close many of the major Wild West shows, but the same era brought prosperity for rodeo and a continuation of heroines on horseback.

In the same year that Buffalo Bill and the 101 appeared together, another contest of importance was being staged. It was a rodeo, but it was called the New York Stampede. The show was produced by Guy Weadick at Sheepshead Bay. Clifford P. Westermeier suggests that it "was one of the first occasions when name contestants of the West were introduced to the East."[36] It appears likely, however, that audiences had probably seen some of the top names already in Wild West shows. Among the women appearing were Dorothy Morrell, Prairie Lillie Allen, and Fannie Steele. Fannie rode "slick broncs," that is, without hobbles.[37] Prairie Lillie was at her peak as a bronc rider and won the contest at Sheepshead. Those looking into her background would be disappointed to discover that she was from Columbia, Tennessee, but her various jobs as bronc rider, stock supplier for western movies, and operator of a riding school made up for her error in being raised east of West. It is true that she joined circuses as a featured performer and that she retired not to a little home on the range but, of all places, to New York City, and the truth must be borne.[38]

Another contestant making her appearance around 1916 was Fox Hastings. Whether or not she appeared at Sheepshead Bay is unknown, but by 1917 she was a heroine of the first order, and her career, which was filled with injury and spectacular performance, may be considered typical.

Fox, a small but shapely and muscular type, began her career as a trick and bronc rider, and she was known for her unusual daring and grit in a sport already filled with people who were long on those two commodities. At the Kansas City Roundup, Fox mounted her bronc and lasted only four jumps. The horse fell, and, worse still, it fell on Fox. Two times the animal tried to get up and two times fell again on the rider, who was apparently tangled in the rigging. It was the kind of scene that sends a crowd into hysterics, a bunch of cowboy rescuers to horse, and thinking people for a stretcher. Those near at hand could see that Fox's neck was twisted so that it looked broken.

All was silence as Fox was transported from the arena, and, as the crowd probably thought, to the great bucking chute in the clouds.

In about fifteen minutes, however, just as the people were beginning to recover, who should appear riding in "an open car with the top down," and waving to the people? T'was Fox who ceremoniously stepped to the judges' stand and asked for a reride. Naturally, she was not denied and she rode splendidly, even managing to dismount at the end of her performance.

But the story was not ended. Foghorn Clancy, who remembered Fox, says:

> The crowd never knew that Fox Hastings collapsed just a few minutes later and that she was in agony for days afterward before the results of that fall eventually wore off. They did not know that they had seen an incredible display of sheer nerve, of courage that would have stacked up well against the courage of the pioneer women who trekked west with their husbands and who fought Indians and loneliness and disease and starvation while they raised children and built homes.[39]

Fox's ride and recovery and Foghorn's speech wrap it up in terms of who and what cowgirl heroines are and what their portrayal represents. It might be well to remember that while Fox Hastings' performance looked like something out of a western melodrama, it probably happened just that way, and while Foghorn's speech smacks of the sentimental, it nevertheless expresses exactly how a good many people felt about Fox and others like her.

In 1924, Fox traded the bone-jarring, body-trampling broncs for the pointed horns of a running steer, and became one of the few women bulldoggers. Again she sustained injuries, but again she performed. Fox was often teased about her figure. Although she was small in stature, she was full-hipped, and she made jokes about her size which she felt aided her in bulldogging. Often her final remarks before leaving the chute were, "If

I can just get my fanny out of the saddle and my feet planted, there's no steer that can last against me."[40]

Considering the daredevil courage and stamina Fox displayed in the arena and tallying the serious injuries she sustained, it is a wonder that she was not killed in rodeo. Her death came, however, not in the glare of arena lights but in the privacy of a hotel room in Phoenix, Arizona, and at her own hand.[41]

The Calgary Stampede, begun in 1912, was another major rodeo where women figured prominently. Among the participants were Mrs. H. McKenzie, Fanny Sperry, Bertha Blancett, Florence LaDue, and Lucille Mulhall.[42] Mary Dumont was a participant at Calgary in 1919 but she achieved no great distinction on her early bronc rides. After bucking off on her first ride, and popping like a rag doll on her second try, she approached Foghorn Clancy and asked him what he thought. The best Foghorn could offer was that she had nerve. Apparently she kept her nerve, learned what was needed to go with it, changed her name to "Ma" Gibson, and rodeoed some fifteen years as a champion before being killed in the arena.[43]

In 1918, Fort Worth launched its original indoor rodeo and declared it to be not an exhibition but a contest in which the contestants paid entry fees and took home money only if they won.[44] These arrangements are worth noting, because until the time of the Fort Worth show and even later, contestants sometimes performed on a contract basis. While the entrants did vie with each other for prizes and awards, they were not necessarily dependent on just the money they might win, since they were paid a salary and sometimes a percentage of the gate to compete in some rodeos.[45]

One competitor in the early Fort Worth show was the enthusiastic, vivacious Mildred Douglas Chrisman. She remembers that in 1917 the prize money was small. Leonard Stroud, a champion bronc rider, Mildred and others had just come from the El Paso show. The El Paso group decided that if they refused to ride for the small purses, there wouldn't be so many contestants and Fort Worth would increase the rewards. The outcome was that Mildred and her friends were not permitted to ride. They sat in seats and watched the show and, according to Mildred, it was good—without them.

Mildred was born in Philadelphia, Pennsylvania. Her father was a professor of mechanical engineering at the University of Pennsylvania. She was educated in a Connecticut boarding school where horseback riding was part of the curriculum, and she acquired a greater love for horses than for books.

During school vacations Mildred visited in the homes of friends. She particularly enjoyed being in the home of Ray and Minnie Thompson, renowned High School horse trainers in Bridgeport, Connecticut. In their large indoor riding arena they held horse shows and trained their own horses. There Mildred learned to ride and jump, both English and sidesaddle. With such training it was not long before she found her way to Barnum and Bailey's circus and then to rodeo. Bronc and steer riding were her specialties. She had no intention of getting into trick riding but she ended up doing it anyway. In 1916, the Royal American Stock Show in Kansas City, Missouri, advertised trick riding but since only two entered—Mayme Stroud and Babe Willetts—the contest was cancelled unless a third rider turned up. Lucille Mulhall offered Mildred her dependable White Man horse and told her that she would help by telling Mildred what to do each time she came around the ring. Mayme won first and Mildred placed second.

In 1917, Mildred rode relay horses for the first and last time at Cheyenne. Mr. C. B. Irwin had two relay strings entered but he did not want his daughters to ride them because his son Floyd had just been killed roping a steer. Irwin asked Mildred if she would ride one of his strings. Mildred agreed and spent some anxious moments trying to make the changes from one horse to another during the race. When it was all over Irwin told her it was also the first trip out on the track for the horses.

In 1931, Mildred married Pat Chrisman and they both worked with Tom Mix. Pat was business manager for Mix for nineteen years and the original owner and trainer of Tony, Tom's famous horse.[46]

The Fort Worth rodeo had offered exhibition bronc riding as early as 1917. In 1920, a cowgirl entered the event in competition who, although she remembers placing only second, was destined to win first place in a variety of events in the years to come. Her name was Mabel Strickland, a quiet beauty from Walla Walla, Washington. Mabel's father was not a stockman, but he rendered the ranchmen of the area a valuable service as a bootmaker. He provided the same service for his daughter, and she never forgot the boots which were literally handmade and handstitched. Mabel owned a saddle horse too, and she found it hard to stay away from a Frontier Days Celebration where she saw for the first time Bill Donovan doing trick riding. The high school youngster decided she could do tricks and with the help of Mr. Donovan she vaulted herself into the saddle and a career in rodeo.

Mabel won the trick riding in Walla Walla in 1913, 1914, and 1915. She started relay racing in 1916 and for two years won first place in Washington, Oregon, Montana, and Idaho. In 1918, Mabel became Mrs. Hugh Strickland. The couple settled down on some land near Mountain Home, Idaho, and tried farming. They soon found themselves in debt. Hearing about a roundup in Twin Falls, Idaho, they both decided to enter, hoping to win enough prize money to pay off their debts. As Mabel recalled: "We were very lucky. Strick got a job running the arena. He also won the bronc riding." Although the Strickland's baby daughter was only two months old, Mabel entered steer riding but found that she did not have the strength to hold on. She continued:

> On the way home we had to cross the Snake River on a ferry boat. The young fellow running the boat asked us if we had been to the Twin Falls Round Up. Of course, he did not know any of us. He said he sure would like to own the saddle that was a prize for the bronc riding. So Strick asked him how much he would pay for it. The boy said $250.00 he had saved. Strick got the saddle out and did his eyes shine. He dashed up to his house and paid for it.[47]

Hugh's winnings in addition to the money from the sale of the championship saddle provided the couple with enough to pay off all they owed. Deciding that rodeoing paid more than farming, Hugh and Mabel began to travel the circuit. In 1920, Mabel tried bronc riding and a skill learned from her husband, steer tying.

Mabel was an honorary member of the Western Heritage Society and in 1971 she was honored as the first woman in the Pendleton Round-Up Hall of Fame.[48]

There were scores of other large and small rodeos which made their appearance in the early part of the twentieth century and there were, as well, countless women who helped provide the entertainment expected from cowgirl heroines. While it is not possible to elaborate on the careers of all the women in rodeo, their names do at least merit being called. Some of those participating were Alice Sisty, Lula Bell Parr, Goldie Griffin, Belle Lynch, Montana Belle, Dixie Devere, Mabel Hackney, Sara Glasser, Dorothy M. Robbins, Rene Shelton, Pauline Nesbitt, Grace Runyan, Vaughn Kreig, Bonnie McCarroll, Bonnie Gray, Bea Kiman, Rose Smith, Donna Cohan, Mabel Baker, Hazel King, Alice and Margie Greenough, Mary Parks, Lola Hunt, Fay Blackstone, Mae Lambert, Tillie Bowman, Mabel Cline, Alice Adams, Pearl Brion, Opal Wood, Lucylle Richards, Mabel Tompkins, Louise Hardwick, Marie Gibson, Mrs. Ed Wright, Rose Davis, Maxine McClusky, Ruth Benson, Lorena Trickey, and a score of others.

7

Out of the Chutes: the Later Years

The year 1924 was special for a group of rodeo cowgirls. In that year John "Tex" Austin, who began producing rodeos prior to 1924, took a group to Europe which included most of the top female as well as male hands of rodeo.[1] Using a ship called the *Menominee* to accommodate performers, mounts, and stock, Tex set sail in May for a tour which still remains vivid in the minds of those who participated. They were all much admired and the cowboys were besieged by ladies wherever they went. The English gentlemen, however, stood somewhat in awe of the cowgirls. Charlie Smith, who still had a twinkle in his eye when he remembered pretty cowgirls, recalled that the Englishmen seemed to think that women who could dog steers, ride broncs, and rope the wind were too much women for them.

The cowboys were in competition against men from other countries, and, even though the humane society protested, the show was a smashing success. Not only did the performers shine in the arena but they were welcomed into British high society. From dances to high teas to receptions at which they were requested to appear in "full cowboy kit," the cowboys and cowgirls were at their charming western best. At dances white ties and tails mixed with chaps and satin shirts, and boots and patent leather stepped to the same music. At one dance, to which a Rumanian prince had been invited, the cowboys, tired of sedate waltzing with composed British gentility, decided enough was enough.

One by one the musicians were relieved of their instruments until there was a large enough group of cowboys to render "Alexander's Ragtime Band," the tune most popular at the time, with a little extra feeling. After the English guests had begun to get the hang of the beat, a young cowgirl with a dazzling smile and a charming manner gently guided her bald-headed partner to the center of the floor and called for a square. The band took up "Turkey in the Straw;" the heroes and heroines went into their native routine, and, literally and figuratively, swept the English off their feet.[2] The smile and the charm of the one who brought it all off belonged to Ruth Roach.[3]

The 1924 tour was not the first time Ruth had been to Europe. In fact, she really began her career there in 1914 with the Miller's 101 Show. Ruth spent her childhood in Excelsior Springs, Missouri. Like other girls who later became cowgirls, she did not let town living interfere with finding horses to ride. There were donkeys and Shetland ponies near at hand, and her uncle's farm provided her with more mounts. After her 1914 tour, Ruth joined the Hagenback-Wallace circus. She did only trick riding in 1914 but by 1917 she was ready to try bucking horses, and she was the first woman to ride them at the Fort Worth rodeo. Lucille Mulhall's group was appearing there in exhibition. Some of her female performers refused to ride, and Lucille needed somebody to try the broncs. She approached Ruth. Still a beginner and knowing she ought to think it over, Ruth asked to see how it was done. Lucille had a man ride "Memphis Blues" for her, and what Ruth saw was a demonstration of how quick and hard a man could get thrown. Ruth did not let the demonstration stop her. She rode the mare and a news story said:

> The audience was treated to the sight of this small girl coming out of the chute on a bucking bronc, pigtails flying, spurring and screeching like a wild Indian.[4]

Bronc riding remained Ruth's favorite event although she performed and won championship titles in other areas. During her career she won the titles of World's Champion All Around Cowgirl, World's Champion Trick Rider, and World's Champion Girl Bronc Rider. Ruth rode at Madison Square Garden from 1916 until 1934.

Some of Ruth's fondest memories are of the 1924 trip to Europe. After the tour was completed, Tommy Kirnan formed a group which continued to perform in London and also in Paris. They appeared at the London Palladium on a stage and were booked along with a puppet show and other acts.[5] Pictures made at the time indicate that there must have been nearly as many people outside watching the horsed performers exit and enter as there were inside watching the show.

During the same season Ruth and other Wild Westers gave a command performance for the royal family in which they were not allowed to make their usual commotion with their guns. In the noise of yelling Indians, Cossacks, cowboys and cowgirls the guns were probably not missed. During their stay in London, the group also was given special permission to ride on the royal bridle path, sometimes in the company of the King. It must have been a sight—posting and galloping, derbys and Stetsons, jodphurs and angora chaps, royalty and roughness.

Ruth was not only a top rider but she was also a great beauty and to her often fell the job of posting the colors at grand entries and publicizing the rodeo when it came to town. In 1922, in the Texas Hotel in Fort Worth, officials had the lobby floored with a special straw mat so that Ruth could trick ride up and down to call attention to the rodeo.

The eastern press probably did as much to publicize western heroines as anyone, and, while the articles emphasized the spectacular, they contained enough truth to make their releases realistic. The problem was that people remembered the spectacular features better than they remembered the facts, and the women came to be larger-than-life images of themselves when what they really were was quite impressive enough. Following is an example from the *Boston Sunday Post* dated October 30, 1932, by George Brinton Beal. Beal mislabels the pickup man as a hazer:

> The shrill cry of a woman's voice, the roar of the crowd, the thundering of flying hooves in the hard

> packed dirt, Ruth Roach, her red silk shirt flaming through the dust . . . like a freshly lighted match came heaving out of chute number one aboard a bronc seemingly composed of equal parts of TNT and dynamite loosely bound together in a tight fitting suit of piebald horsehide. In that first wild leap into the comparative freedom of the Garden area, Ruth parted company with her broad brimmed black hat and her short curly hair was making a desperate effort to follow it from her tossing head. Sunfishing along, that bronc started due West for the land of his fathers . . . .
>
> When the whistle blew Ruth was dragged unceremoniously from her still pitching and weaving mount, her arms clasped with ardent firmness about the waist of the hazer as he rode in to get her. Tucking her shirt which had left its natural mooring place and breathing a little heavily, Ruth retrieved her black hat and retired to the comparative privacy of a squat seat in the dirt just to the right of the mounting chutes. "Gee kid, but you've had a ride," was the admiring comment from Dogtown Slim spread out along the fence where he hung apparently suspended by his elbows. And that was the end of the day's work for Miss Roach who has been riding her way to fame and fortune through the rodeo world for nearly ten years now . . . .

The steady and dependable Vera McGinnis was another among Tex Austin's group in London in 1924. She won the trick riding trophy and also the relay cup—two championships in one show. Vera was also in Tommy Kirnan's group of cowboys and cowgirls when they toured the continent after the London engagement.

Vera joined the Hugo Brothers in 1926. Theatrical promoters who had been staging shows of various kinds in the Orient for several years, the Hugo Brothers decided to take a rodeo to Japan, China, Indochina, Vietnam, Siam, the Malay

States, Java, Penang, and Singapore. Some thirty people including Vera, Opal Wood and Princess Red Bird made the trip.

Vera married another top hand, Homer Farra, in 1931. Consistently among the winners on the circuit, they went on the road together and, as Vera recalls, "it was so much easier than bucking the game alone." In 1934, a racehorse fell with Vera, breaking her back in five places, her neck, her right hip and some ribs. After the doctors decided she was going to live, they told her she would never walk again. It is hard, sometimes impossible, to keep a good cowgirl down, however, and Vera did walk again.[6]

Always a daring racer, Vera was almost unbeatable on her Thoroughbred, Cassandra. One of her friends, Mildred Douglas Chrisman, remembers the time in Phoenix, Arizona, when Cassandra and Vera were in a race:

> There was a company of Army artillery on exhibit in the centerfield of the race track and when the race started, the artillery pieces started out of the centerfield and across the race track. If I remember right, one horse crashed into the cannon and Vera's horse tried to jump over it. It was quite an accident, one I'm certain Vera will never forget.[7]

Another of the cowgirls who crossed the ocean with Ruth Roach and Vera McGinnis and the rest of Tex Austin's group experienced a most unheroine-like but, nevertheless, real problem. Florence Randolph spent the entire voyage in her cabin, seasick. Florence's career began when she was fourteen years old, and she proved that cowgirls are where you find them, even in the circus.[8] Born in Augusta, Georgia, where her father was superintendent of an iron works, Florence's first experience on a horse was riding with her grandfather on his cotton plantation. When she was fourteen she persuaded her parents to apprentice her to a family traveling with the Ringling Circus. Eventually the circus disbanded and Florence formed her own group known as "Princess Mohawk's Wild West Hippodrome." When the Hippodrome went out of business because of an accident in Kentucky, the grandstand collapsed, Florence joined the Barnum and Bailey Circus, where she learned resin-back riding.

In 1919, Florence entered the Roman races at the Calgary Stampede, and her experience as a resin-back rider served her well. She won against fourteen men and received the Prince of Wales trophy, a fifteen-hundred-dollar saddle, which she promptly sold to a movie star. From Calgary the cowgirl went on to perform in rodeos all along the circuit which at that time began in March at Fort Worth and ended up at Boston in November.

After a rodeo in Phoenix, Arizona, Florence decided to visit friends in Hollywood and consequently got into movies for a time. Although she was for a brief period one of Mack Sennett's bathing beauties, most of her work in Hollywood consisted of doubling for movie star Shirley Mason and doing such things as riding horses over cliffs. The Hollywood pay was good but Florence had rodeo fever and she returned to the circuit.

Injuries and broken bones were Florence's constant companions and, as she said, "I have been carried out for dead several times." In 1923 a horse called School Girl somersaulted over on Florence and she was pronounced dead in the arena. On another occasion in Washington D. C., a bucking horse fell on her and the verdict at the hospital was that if she lived she would never walk again. Reviving just in time to hear the last part, Florence jumped off the table wearing only a sheet, rushed past the doctors and Ruth Roach, who had accompanied her to the hospital, and out into the cold night air.

In 1925, after returning from England, Florence married Floyd Randolph. Between housekeeping duties, Florence continued to perform. She won her first all-around championship trophy along with six thousand dollars at Philadelphia in 1926. Florence added the George W. Nixon Trophy in 1926 at Chicago as World Champion Girl Bronc Rider, the Juergens Anderson Trophy in 1927, and World Champion Trick Rider title in 1928. In 1930 she won the Champion All Around Cowgirl trophy in Philadelphia and she was twice awarded the ten thousand dollar Metro-Goldwyn-Mayer trophy. Her crowning achievement came much later when she was chosen as one of the women honored by the Cowboy Hall of Fame in Oklahoma City, Oklahoma.

Another honoree in the Cowboy Hall of Fame, Tad Lucas, was among those on the 1924 trip to England.[9] Tad had become Mrs. Lucas shortly before the tour and the trip must have been like a honeymoon on Noah's Ark. The year 1924 was not only the beginning of Tad's married life, it was also the beginning of an international reputation which would equal, if not surpass, Lucille Mulhall's. It seems fitting that Lucille's successor should come from the plains and that she should know ranch life firsthand.

Barbara "Tad" Barnes was born in the northwest section of Nebraska near Cody, and she got into rodeo the way the public would like to believe all true cowgirls get there—by first growing up on a ranch with a real frontier family. Lorenzo Barnes came west after the Civil War to make a fresh start like so many others. He was the first white settler in the Cody area, and, in addition to establishing a store for which he hauled supplies some two hundred miles by ox team, he also homesteaded a ranch.

Tad, the twenty-fourth Barnes child and the baby of the family, had plenty of brothers and sisters with whom to play games that often centered on horses and cattle. Tad was expected to do the work of any ranch hand from roundup to branding, and she learned to ride on the family spread as all little ranch children learn—by riding often and riding bareback.

Naturally, there were Indians in Tad's early life and it would be in keeping with romantic notions about cowgirl heroines to tell that Tad learned to ride and race with the noble Sioux on their ancestral hunting grounds, but such a story would not be entirely the truth. The days of the Sioux's glory as horse Indians had passed when Tad was learning to ride, and their ancestral haunts were but reservations. She remembers that her horsemanship was superior to that of the Sioux women against whom she rode in squaw races at local fairs and rodeos. In fact, Tad probably never had an occasion to be impressed by Sioux horsemanship. She did witness the degrading government check day when the Indians were given their allotments. She recalls hiding with her brother behind some sand dunes to watch the Indians returning from town in their wagons. Drunk and wild, they ran their wagons crazily, turning them over, strewing family and possessions about the countryside. It was a far cry from the horsed and feathered noble savages she would see portrayed in the Wild West shows and rodeos in her adult years.

Tad began her public life as a cowgirl amid the familiar surroundings of a ranching community. When she was about thirteen, along with other children, she rode wild cows and other outlaw stock brought to town by local ranchers each Saturday. They eared down the stock in the middle of the main street, and, if the youngsters performed well, the crowd passed the hat. Later, Tad exercised horses for a neighbor, and, when he took her as his jockey to the fair in Cody in 1918, she was attracted by the twenty-five dollar prize money offered in cowgirl steer riding. She won the money.

In 1920, Tad's family moved to Texas, and in 1923 she joined Colonel Frank Hafley's show, which toured Mexico. In the same year the budding cowgirl rode exhibition rides on Brahman steers in Madison Square Garden and tried saddle-bronc riding for the first time.

One would like to imagine that Tad spent her leisure time at the ranch playing dangerous games and learning tricks as she sped across the plains and that when she first did trick riding in 1924 she burst full speed into the arena, dazzling the crowd with the spectacular antics learned in solitary prairie practice. Such scenes are entirely imaginary. Tad knew nothing of trick riding before 1923, when a friend began to teach her. What her prairie riding had already taught her, however, was fine timing, balance and coordination. In 1924 Tad was ready to do exhibition trick riding at Wimberly Stadium in London with Tex Austin's group.

Tad and Buck, her husband, returned from England and rode for a time with the 101 in 1925. They bought their home in Fort Worth the same year and headquartered there between seasons.

In 1925, Tad, always exuberant and daring, won the trick riding championship at Cheyenne and she continued to win for the next six years. In 1925, she also won the All Around Championship in Chicago. She was All Around Champion and Trick Riding Champion at Madison Square Garden for eight years straight, the only one ever to complete such a record. By winning for three consecutive years—1928, 1929, 1930—she was awarded permanent possession of the ten thousand dollar Metro-Goldwyn-Mayer trophy. She also won the Selfridge Trophy for All Around Champion Cowgirl in 1929 and the Australian Trophy for best bronc rider at Sidney in 1940.

It was again a Boston newspaper, *The Boston Evening American* of Saturday, November 9, 1946, which reported Tad's abilities and revealed how western girls came to be doing what they were doing. While there is truth in the report by Austin Lake, it is not exactly unvarnished:

> Nor according to Mrs. Lucas are these chuck wagon beauties a special breed of hairbreadth hellions blessed with reinforced frames, rubber-sheathed nerves and a passion for sensations of train wreck. They are, says she, normal girls who fell victim of their environment—rugged daughters of a rugged frontier. In fact, she thinks, any eastern "perty" lass of the lipstick and fluffy female type might have taken to bronc-busting if born in the leathery surroundings of a daddy-owned stock-ranch, cradled in the saddle, teethed on a cinch buckle, and nourished on cooked cow.

People who remember Tad are always quick to mention her generosity, her honesty in competition, and her helpfulness to newcomers. She refrained from gossip and never seemed to take herself too seriously. In addition to those virtues, which make a heroine in any walk of life, she was the rider supreme—daring and skilled. Because Tad came from a genuine ranch background, because of the unusual skill, timing and style which marked her performances, and because of the personality she projected in and out of the arena, she was the ideal western heroine. She was a cowgirl's cowgirl and a cowboy's too, and her induction into the Cowboy Hall of Fame honored her for her contribution to rodeo. As indication of further esteem she was elected president of the Rodeo Historical Society in 1970.

After 1924 and into the thirties, the lives of most of the cowboys and cowgirls were spent in the routine of following the circuit. Times were good and money plentiful. A good many of the cowgirls had come to rodeo from Wild West shows which by the 1920s had about played out. According to Mrs. Bob Crosby, who followed the circuit with her husband, cowgirls were "making more in a week than they had formerly made in a season." In addition to good pay, the girls were staying only at expensive places and wearing only custom-made clothes. Gone were the days of sleeping in third-rate hotels and eating in the performers' tent as they had done in Wild West shows.[10]

Not everyone who joined the rodeo circuit felt that it was a step up. Juanita Gray McCracken remembers that when she married and joined rodeo performing with her husband in his roping act, she made only ten dollars a week compared with the sixty-five dollars she had been earning as a dancer.[11] Still, generally speaking, money was adequate for most of those competing, on contract or in exhibitions.

Velda Tindall Smith remembered the happy times and good years.[12] Velda did not find rodeo through any of the usual routes of circus, Wild West show, marriage to a rodeo cowboy or life on a ranch. Rather she came along at a time when the cowgirl legend was well-established, and her first glimpses of the glorious life on horseback were as a little girl watching westerns at the Saturday afternoon movies in Longview, Texas. It was easy for Velda to see that while you could dress up like a cowgirl, walk and talk like a cowgirl, you could not really be one unless you had a horse. As it turned out, a doctor's advice helped her into a saddle. Velda was a sickly child and there were many things she could not do. The family doctor suggested to Velda's parents that if they got her an old, gentle horse to play around on, it would give her something to do. If the budding cowgirl's parents had only known how she was going to play around on the old, gentle horse, she might never have been allowed to have one. The movies turned into reality when, in 1923, Velda went to Dallas to see Ruth Roach and Florence Hughes Randolph ride in a rodeo there. After that, Velda did not waste any time in finding a man named Curley Griffith to teach her riding. In 1924 she was ready to perform, and she was so scared that she fell off in the course of two out of three tricks she performed.

Between 1925 and 1927 Velda worked as a featured trick rider with Miller's 101. She later added steer riding, relay races and broncs to her repertoire and followed the circuit. In the early seventies she was still riding in barrel races in local rodeos.

For many years Velda and her family lived next door to Tad and Buck Lucas and their daughters. The public does not think of cowgirls as wives and mothers, but most of them were. Usually when the women were busy during rodeo season the children stayed at home in the care of grandmothers or trusted friends. By the time Velda and Tad's daughters were four and five years old, they were skilled enough to join their mothers in some rodeo performances. Mabel Strickland's daughter accompanied her parents on the circuit until she reached school age. When school prevented the children's regular participation in rodeo, they went with their parents during summers and holidays.

During the off-season most cowboys and cowgirls had some place they called home. Velda and Tad called Fort Worth home and so did a good many other performers. Fort Worth was a major railhead and stockshipping center with holding pens. It was a good place from which to ship rodeo stock. Trucking and the roads to truck on were not satisfactory and railroads were the mainstay of rodeo transportation just as they had been the mainstay of the cattle industry. When the season opened, a special train was often put together at some point west where other cowboys and cowgirls were located, and it chugged its way east, picking up stock and rodeoers along the way. There was much visiting to be done aboard the trains, and there were other diversions. Poker games kept the cowboys holed up, and the stakes were often high. The cowgirls played a milder form of penny-ante. There were costumes to be repaired or made, and they often took sewing machines along and set them up in their rooms during the rodeo. One activity, quilt making, was certainly in keeping with the cowgirl's image as frontierswomen. One year Velda Smith cut up white squares of muslin and had all the top hands sign their names on a piece of the material. For several seasons she embroidered the autographs until she had enough to make a spread. Florence Hughes Randolph remembered tearing up old costumes to make satin quilts until she had many more than she needed.[13]

Places like New York, Boston, Chicago, Philadelphia, and other large cities provided cowgirls with unusual places to shop. Usually they stayed at hotels near where they were performing. The women took care of getting located and unpacked while the men unloaded and quartered the stock. Other places were remembered for special reasons. The Indians were a special treat at Pendleton. Usually Indians were featured at the rodeo, and the cowboys and cowgirls were quite as captivated by them as were the crowds. Cheyenne was probably the favorite place on the circuit because of the scenery. Often the performers came prepared to camp out. Velda Smith recalls that many of the contestants cooked their meals over a campfire and slept out. At night after the rodeo she and her friends would square dance until the wee hours and then arise at five o'clock to work out the relay horses. No doubt the camping at Cheyenne helped to enhance the legend of the sons and daughters of the western soil.

When the season was over, the cowboys and cowgirls returned to home ground, where they learned new tricks and routines, tried out and practiced for events which they hoped to enter, and settled down to what was for them a normal routine. Many cowboys and cowgirls bought ranches and by living there in off-season helped at least part of the western myth come true.

The 1920s were golden years for rodeo. Cowboys and cowgirls were a part of the national landscape. Money was good, popularity was high and life was sweet. While few realized it, the whole shebang was about to come to a jarring halt as the heroes and heroines bucked their way into the year 1929 when an outlaw horse called Depression would ride the circuit, bringing to an end some of the make-believe of rodeo.

In 1934, another tour of Europe was undertaken but the cowboys and cowgirls had lost some of their charm. They were not so cordially received and the humane society used a heavier hand.[14] Perhaps the Depression, which had toppled more than one idol, caused a loss of interest in rodeo abroad and at home. Perhaps it was time now for the nation to take its eyes away from the reflection of itself growing and strutting, an image of which rodeo was only one facet. Whatever the reason, the glories of the western frontier as expressed in rodeo were stripped away, and rodeo came to be as much a business as a show. Whatever it became, the important thing is that it survived. As Mody C. Boatright suggests:

> It would survive by becoming a ritual in which, on the obvious level, the last frontiersman, the cowboy, or, more accurately, a man in ceremonial garb representing him, re-enacts the conquest of the West, and on a deeper level symbolizes man's conquest of nature.[15]

Sally Skull was one of the most memorable gun women of the West. She was never without a rifle, and pistols hung from a cartridge belt around her waist. She feared neither Indians nor Mexican bandits and frequently taunted both on rides to Mexico for horse trading.

Cora Viola Slaughter (top photo) was the wife of famous rancher and law officer John Slaughter of Arizona. Viola often rode with John to bring herds of cattle from Mexico to their ranch in Arizona. Famed for her kindness, Viola gave a home to Apache Mae (bottom photo), after the child was found abandoned in a tepee following a raid on her tribe by Arizona ranchers.

Sharlot Hall of Arizona is best remembered as a writer and historian. Daughter of a buffalo hunter, she once took over management of the family ranch plus her own 160 acres when her father's health failed. A serious spinal injury from a riding accident turned her to writing. She became the territorial historian for Arizona, and a collection of her poems was published after her death.

Cattle roundups in the West were often rowdy and downright dangerous. Many cowgirls took part at their husband's side or alone. Two unidentified women and a young girl posed for this photograph (top) during a roundup in the early 1890s. The Becker sisters of Alamosa, Colorado, (bottom) didn't let their long dresses get in the way when there were calves to be branded. This photo was taken in 1884.

Life on the frontier held many hardships and little leisure time for the cowgirls. They might have looked with envy or possibly scorn on this full-dress parade outside Flagstaff, Arizona, on July 4, 1907. Many women might have been shocked at these riders sitting astride in their long skirts and hats. Alice Stillwell Henderson (right) had little time for parades. She was chasing Mexican cattle rustlers along the Rio Grande of Texas. These bandits finally learned to leave the Henderson ranch alone.

Susan Haughian (far right) came to Montana from Ireland. She was widowed and left with 10 children to raise during a crisis in the livestock market. Undaunted, she continued driving her herds in search of grazing land, buying pastures where she could until she amassed a considerable empire.

Ella Watson was better known to the people of Wyoming as "Cattle Kate." She was alternately called Wyoming's "Cattle Queen," for her way with cows, and "The Duchess of Winchester," for her skill with a rifle. She met an untimely end at the hands of large landowners in the Sweetwater Valley.

The most famous of the early day ranch women who found careers in rodeo was Lucille Mulhall of Oklahoma. Her father began a Wild West show in the 1880s which attracted national attention—including that of President Theodore Roosevelt. Lucille was one of the first women to compete against men and win.

Copyrighted 1909
by J.V. Dedrick.
View by Dedrick

Dorothy Morrell was a contestant at the New York Stampede in 1916, one of the first occasions where rodeo stars of the West were introduced to the East. Note her long "corkscrew" curls hanging down under her hat.

Tad Lucas of Fort Worth, Texas is one of the best loved and most remembered of all early day rodeo queens. She and Florence Hughes are the only women honored by the Cowboy Hall of Fame. This photo was taken in 1923.

Tad Lucas was the all-around champion and trick-riding champion at Madison Square Garden for eight straight years—an unparalleled record. Her "suicide drag," shown above, thrilled thousands of rodeo spectators for many years, as did her steer and bronc riding (right and top photo following page). The saddle and trophies she poses with (bottom photo, next page) are representative of many honors in her long and colorful career.

Tad Lucas
World's Champion Steer Rider
Copyright by C. D. Ostrom

One of the prettiest cowgirls was Mabel Strickland (above). Mabel was a trick rider before her marriage to Hugh Strickland in 1918. The young couple tried farming for a while but found rodeoing paid more and began riding the rodeo circuit. Mabel eventually tried bronc riding and steer tying, a skill learned from her husband.

A glance at the cars in the background of the photo at the top of the facing page will give you an idea when Tad Lucas and her horse Sunshine posed for this portrait. Notice her jodhpurs. At left, Tad shows off her angora chaps which were practical and protective and added another embellishment to her already spectacular attire.

Ruth Roach began her rodeo career in 1914 with the Miller Brothers' 101 Show. She began competing in trick riding and was later one of the first women to try bucking broncos.

Ruth Roach was not only a top rider but a great beauty who was often called upon to post the colors at Grand Entries and to publicize the rodeo when it came to town.

MABLE STRICKLAND-TAD LUCAS

Ruth Roach, on the bucking bronco at the top of the facing page, was often seen in satin bloomers and heart-embossed boots. The photo above shows her dressed in bloomers, which begame popular after 1918. Mabel Strickland and Tad Lucas (at left) model another popular fashion—jodhpurs. Notice the silk sash around Mabel's waist. In this era you could also see sleeve holders made of elastic and decorated with satin streamers.

The pretty smiles in the top photo belong to Mabel Strickland and Tad Lucas. They posed in 1926 in Kansas City. Posing above in riding regalia are from left to right: Bea Kirnan, Tad Lucas, Florence Hughes, Ruth Roach, and Curley Seale.

Mabel Strickland, Fox Hastings, and Bea Kirnan pose at a rodeo in San Antonio. Note Bea's fur coat.

The *Rough Rider Weekly* was one of the early adventure series designed to capture the excitement and romance of the cowgirls. The issue above appeared in 1906 and sold for a nickel.

The photos on the facing page capture many of the rodeo queens in the period following World War I. In the top photo, from left to right are: Kitty Canutt, Ruth Roach, Mabel Strickland, an unknown cowboy, Florence Hughes, Bea Kirnan and Prairie Rose Henderson shown in 1918. The middle photo shows the rodeo girls of 1920: Rene Hafley, Fox Hastings, Rose Smith, Ruth Roach, Mabel Strickland, Prairie Rose Henderson, and Dorothy Morrell. The bottom photo taken in 1932, pictures Reva Gray, Grace Runyon, Fox Hastings, Betty Meyers, Tad Lucas, Ruth Roach, and Ruth Benson.

Artist Ace Reid continues to poke fun at ranch women and their hardships in cartoons such as this. (Used by permission of Ace Reid Enterprises, 1977).

The author and publisher are indebted to Tad Lucas and Ruth Roach for their kind cooperation in allowing the reproduction of many of their personal photographs in this pictorial tribute to the cowgirls.

8

With Quirt and Spur

The events of rodeo developed from the cowboy's life of work and play on the range. Women's rodeo events reflected range activities too, but only when they were the same jobs as the men performed. It was a real novelty to watch cowgirls doing cowboying. That is, for a time, exactly the purpose women served — novelty.

Novelty or not, the kinds of events women entered did much to promote their image as heroines. The cowgirl was the frontierswoman riding by her man's side, spurring as he spurred, laughing at danger, roping and tying, and playing his games on bulls and broncs. The cattle needed tending, and the cowgirls mounted up with the rest of the outfit. Wild West shows and rodeos declared that it was so.

Nothing seemed to prove the cowgirl's worth more than the bronc-riding event because it was as dangerous as anything in rodeo, and it was breathtaking to watch.[1] Prior to 1925, and maybe even after that year in some places, broncs were snubbed right in the arena where the audience could see what was going on. Later, when the animals were confined to chutes, it was easier to give a score on the performance of horse and rider, but it took away some of the excitement of watching as the cowboys subdued the animal so the rider could mount. Women were allowed hobbles on their broncs: that is, a piece of leather tied under the horse's belly from one stirrup to another. This prevented the women from spurring, but it helped them stay in the saddle. As in the men's event, the horse was given a score for how well he bucked, and the rider was given a score for how well she stayed on. The souvenir program of 1927 from the Fort Worth rodeo indicates that the women were allowed two reins and hobbles. If the women rode without hobbles, they were awarded twenty-five extra points on their score, provided, of course, that they stayed on until the end of the ten-second ride. The purse that year was for ten thousand dollars, a good sum of money.

Fannie Steele and Bertha Blancett both rode without their stirrups tied down, and, while it looked more dangerous, there may have been good reasons. The hobbles served the purpose of tying the rider to the horse, and, when it was time to get off, the rider had to wait until the pickup man caught her rope and dallied the horn. Only then could she work her feet out of the stirrups and be transferred behind the pickup man on his saddle. Velda Smith remembers watching Bonnie McCarroll receive fatal injuries at Pendleton because she could not free herself from her hobbles. Bonnie drew a rank horse, and she was tied too tightly in the stirrups. During the violent ride, she lost her hold on the ropes. Unable to grasp mane or horn, the rider was whipped and snapped over and over again. Finally her feet came loose and Bonnie was flung violently to the ground. She died eight days later from her injuries.[2] The sight was enough to keep Velda from trying broncs for a while.

While tragedy sometimes occurred during the bronc riding event, there were moments of fun as well. Friends of Tad Lucas remember a time in Monte Vista, Colorado, when the cowgirl drew a bad one. Buck, her husband, was worried enough about Tad to make it a point to be close by in the arena when she came out of the chute. Buck's fears were justified because after a few wild jumps, Tad came flying through the air. Buck, who was standing at the right place at exactly the right time, managed to catch her just before she hit the dirt.[3]

In spite of the fact that bronc riding was labeled a contest, it was often a contracted act which only appeared to be a contest to those watching. Other times when three or four purses were being offered and there were not enough entrants to make a contest, the contestants already entered would rustle up other riders to enter whether the extras knew how to ride or not so that the contest could go on and the money be paid. This was practiced in some of the other events of rodeo as well. Foghorn Clancy tells how he solved the problem of too few riders at San Antonio in the early days. Because the women were all trying to get to another rodeo in another town, he was left with only Ruth Benson entering bronc riding. Since it took two to make a contest, Ruth rode twice, once as herself and once as someone else. After she rode the first time she changed her clothes, boots, and hat and rode again. The crowd appeared to like the second rider better than the first, but, after all, the second woman had had more practice, even if the crowd did not know it.[4] Still another way to fill the contest in some events was to let the women contest with the men.

> Women riding broncs were usually not given the same horses as the men, and the contractors had to provide two strings of bucking stock. The cowgirls were given animals that "bucked high and showed pretty" as the saying went, but generally they were not twisters or outlaws. Such names as "Pinto Pete," "Triangle Paint," "I-b-damned," and "Recitation" showed up among women's stock in the 1920s.

Pickup men, those dependable life lines which mean the difference between injury and safety, found their jobs in the women's events particularly enjoyable. In the men's events, cowboys grabbed on to the pickup man's saddle or waist and jumped to the ground. A woman, because of the hobbles, required a pickup man's arm about her waist to steady her and assist her to safety. Needless to say, all the cowboys seemed available for the ladies' events and the cowgirls could pick and choose from among the best. The close contact provided some bawdy stories and moments of hilarity in the midst of real danger, as this story illustrates: One contestant had reason to want off her horse in a hurry. She had drawn a rough bucker and the animal's violent landings caused her to hang her blouse on the saddle horn. On the next trip skyward, the cowgirl's blouse and underclothing were ripped open. Her ample upper anatomy, now unfettered, received a severe lashing along with the rest of her body. Everytime her head went down, her bosom heaved upward. It was a few minutes before the pickup man could get to her, but thinking of her embarrassment, he hurried. When the man finally got there, her words were not about her embarrassing predicament, but rather, "For gosh sakes, somebody get me off this horse before I black both my eyes."[5]

Women's steer riding was probably not as spectacular as bronc riding, unless you happened to be the one doing the hanging on, but it was still a good event to watch. The cowgirls were again allowed special stock. In addition to riding steers, they also rode stags, which were old bulls that had been castrated. The women rode without hobbles, holding with both hands to a surcingle.

In later years, after Tad Lucas and Velda Smith had started rodeoing, women began to ride Brahman bulls, pronounced Braymers in the West. Cheyenne was one of the first rodeos to offer the event, and, since all the other women were trying it, Tad and Velda thought they would too. Both were entered in the relay races, for which they wore different shoes. They put their boots in a handy place so that they could hurry and change and get entered in time to ride. After the relays they scurried behind a fence, changed into their boots and dashed over to the chutes only to discover that they were too late to enter. Velda and Tad had reason to be glad of their lateness. As they watched between the boards of the enclosure, one bull after another exploded from the chutes, turning neck, shoulder and hind quarter in that twist peculiar to one-ton Braymers. And as the bulls jarred and tore up the ground, and as the women, all top cowgirls, sailed through the air one by one, the watchers could see that the reason the bull twisted and turned was that the animal not only wanted to dislodge the rider—he also wanted to trample her after she was unseated. Velda and Tad looked at each other in relief. Someone came up later and asked why they had not ridden the bulls. "Oh, we were sure going to, but we were too late to enter, and they have rules about things like that, you know," was their reply.

Steer tying was an event in which women excelled, and that they excelled seems an unlikely thing because the steers were large and the women small. Steer tying, not to be confused with calf roping, pitted a mounted roper against a steer. The rider would approach the running steer, throw the loop and "gather the horns," roping just the horns of the steer. Casting slack to the right side of the saddle horn the roper would ride to the left at a forty-five degree angle. The steer, upon hitting the end of the rope, would be jerked off its feet. While the horse kept the slack out of the rope by dragging the steer, the roper would dismount and tie him with the usual three wraps and a hooey, a half-hitch to secure the wrap.

Lucille Mulhall was the first and undisputedly the best woman steer roper rodeo ever witnessed. She competed in all the early contests against men and often beat them. Because women were given no special stock or favors, and because the event was also a part of real ranch work, it was one of the favorite events of both cowboys and cowgirls.

While skill with a rope and the help of a smart, strong horse enabled women to compete on equal terms with the men in steer tying, the ladies sometimes required help in bulldogging. It was not unheard of for some of the cowboys to practice throwing the steers several times before the ladies dogged them, and, with their necks already sore from twisting, the steers succumbed to the cowgirls' touch. Claire Thompson, Vivian White and Fox Hastings excelled in the event.

Trick riding was the one event above all others which lent itself to a woman's touch, and it brought forth thunderous, stomping approval from crowds. The rules from Tex Austin's Chicago program of 1925, from Fort Worth's program of 1927 and from Madison Square Garden's program of 1928 indicate that trick riding was a contest to be taken seriously. Each rider had to submit a list of her ten best tricks and be prepared to perform twice daily any tricks called by the arena director. The rider was judged on ease, gracefulness, skill, number of straps (the more straps, the lower the score), speed of horse, and the degree of difficulty of the tricks.

The tricks fell generally into three categories: top work, which indicated various stands on the top of a saddle equipped with a longer, slimmer horn for easier grasping; vaults, executed by hitting the ground with the feet and vaulting back into the saddle; and drags, or strap work, accomplished by grasping specially designed holds on the saddle and hanging near the ground on the side or back of the horse. The three easiest tricks were considered to be the Roman stand, the shoulder stand and the Cossack drag. Among the most difficult was the back drag, devised by Tad Lucas, during which the rider hooked her feet into straps on the horse's rump and hung head down over the flying horse's hooves. Going under the belly or under the horse's neck was expected as a grand finale, and the women, because of their smaller size, were generally better at these final tricks than the men.

It goes without saying that an absolute requirement was a horse with control of his nerves and a smooth gait. It also helped if the animal was not overly fond of what was going on in the grandstands. Tad Lucas' Candy Lamb was such a horse. He was widely admired and nearly priceless to her. Smooth trick horses, along with the skill and grace of the rider, caused the event to look easy when, in fact, it was anything but that. Women trick riders sustained many injuries from being dragged and stepped on, and a rider could end up just as dead from trick riding as she could from a bronc tromping. None of the riders who saw Juanita Parry killed while trick riding in Madison Square Garden ever took the event for granted.

The Northwest, specifically Cheyenne and Pendleton, was the scene of another dazzling women's event—the relay race. The races required a race track, which none of the other regions had, and three horses. The women would walk their horses to the starting line, and, at the signal, ride the distance of the track, where they would change to another horse and continue the distance of the track once more. Then the cowgirls would change to the third mount and race for the finish. The changing of horses was as astonishing to watch as the race itself. Depending on the rules, the riders would either stop their horses with their heads resting on the rumps of the waiting mounts and change over the tops of the saddles, known as pony expressing, or they would dismount completely, grab the horn of the saddle of their next mount and vault into the seat with the horse already in a dead run. A short neck rein, left lying loose, was grasped by the rider once she got herself safely situated in the saddle. The waiting mounts, race horses every one, were very nearly impossible to keep still without twitches on their noses. When a cowgirl made the change, the twitches were released and the animals bounded away. Tad Lucas, who was especially good at vaulting into the saddle, once got such an extra push from the bound of her horse that she flew up and over, not into the saddle, but to the ground on the other side. Finding herself in a dangerous predicament with other riders and horses on every side, she did what any heroine would have done—she vaulted back in reverse and finally found leather.

The Roman races in which the rider stood with one foot on each horse around the track was another sensational event, and often men and women competed against each other. Florence Hughes Randolph was the only woman ever to win the Roman race against men, at Calgary in 1919.[6]

There were other events in rodeo in which women participated such as trick roping, flat races, stake races and something called steer undecorating in which a ribbon tied around the steer's flank had to be removed.

Rarely did cowgirls specialize in one event, although some were naturally better at some things than others. Usually the women entered all the events because of a system in which the championship was based on points accumulated in events rather than on money won. In order to win, the cowgirls had to enter nearly everything.[7]

While all the contests had rules of one kind or another, some ladies' events lent themselves more to exhibition than to real competition, and, while some may protest that all the events were competitive and legal, there is no question that in some events the rules were badly bent if not altogether broken. It apparently made little difference to the crowds who came to see the cowgirls and cowboys. Within the heroic circle, however, there arose a need for rules and order. Many of the performers were trying to make a living at rodeoing, and the awarding of World Championships needed to be on a more uniform basis. As Vera McGinnis Farra tells it:

> It used to be that most good shows, with what was then considered large prizes hung up, called themselves championship shows. We'd win one this week and go to another one maybe next week and contest the same people and lose and yet both were [called] championship rodeos.[8]

Around the time of the founding of the Rodeo Association of America in 1929, cowboys and cowgirls had become lax in appearance, low in morale, and unsure of the fairness of promoters, contractors, and fellow contestants. In 1936, the Cowboy's Turtle Association, which later became the Rodeo Cowboy's Association, came into being. The RCA helped to insure more consistent rules and more uniform conditions under which to perform.

Another benefit of organizing seems entirely out of place in cowboying circles, and that was the strike.[9] Although threatened several times, strikes rarely happened, and only one time did the cowgirls play a part. In 1939 the women thought about a strike against the Fort Worth show because the rodeo did not include a cowgirl's bucking event. Their plans failed because the girls remembered how fairly they had always been treated at Fort Worth and decided not to carry through the strike.[10]

About the same time that the cowboys were organizing—a step which should have benefited the women too, although they had no voting rights in the group—forces were at work which would eventually destroy women's events and relegate cowgirl participation to a minor place in rodeo. The 1930s brought to an end many of the spectacular contests in which women competed, and the Depression played a part in it. Roman races required two horses, relay races required three, and it became increasingly difficult to maintain and transport so many mounts, especially when the prize money was small and the contestants few. The percentage of women competing in rodeo had always been small compared with the number of cowboy contestants. Contractors also had to provide special bucking stock for women. More important, the heroines proved to be their own worst enemies. Bronc and steer riding had always been touchy events because of the scoring system. If a rider drew an animal which was a poor bucker, she got a lower score. If she claimed she had not received a fair animal to ride, then husbands and sweethearts got involved with judges and sometimes the fur flew. The other events became merely contracted exhibition features.[11] Without the incentive of competition for money and world-championship titles, the cowgirl events soon died on the once vigorous vine.

Women's events experienced some revival during the forties when all-girl rodeos came into vogue. This kind of rodeo was probably created to fill the gap when the men were engaged in World War II. Included in the events were bareback bronc riding, bull riding, ribbon roping, breakaway roping in which the calf is roped but not tied, steer undecorating, and barrel racing.

On February 29, 1949, the Girl's Rodeo Association was formed at San Angelo, Texas. Like the RCA, the GRA uses a point system in choosing the all-around champion and the champions in each event. A point is given for every dollar earned and the all-around titles go to the high point winner in two or more events. Some of the purposes of the organization are to promote better performing conditions, to protect members against unfair management, and to publish information regarding dates, prize money and contestants entered in various rodeos.[12]

One of the cowgirls instrumental in forming the association was Jackie Worthington, sister of Ada Worthington Womack. Jackie served as the association's president and was active on the rodeo circuit from the early 1940s through the late fifties. The Jack County cowgirl was World Champion for six years running and held some seventeen individual world class titles. Jackie was a worthy successor to those cowgirls from ranch backgrounds who gained their skills on the range, and who spent time in rodeo competition while continuing to help run their family's ranches. She was the third inductee into the Cowgirl Hall of Fame in Hereford, Texas. Through her work with the Girl's Rodeo Association in promoting fair competitions and insisting on high standards and because of her own life's example in the rodeo arena and on the cattle range, Jackie Worthington made the term cowgirl a better word.[13]

Cowgirl participation in rodeo today is largely confined to grand entries, occasional participation in cutting horse events, and barrel racing. In the latter, the women run their horses around barrels in a cloverleaf pattern. It is exciting, but not as exciting as the early-day events when women pitted themselves against the men or against each other in men's events. Still, glad to participate wherever they can, the women have formed an association which promises to keep the cowgirls in the saddle. In 1955, a group of women under the guidance of Velda Smith, Fay Oglesby and NaRay Ratliff formed the Texas Barrel Racers Association. Soon there were other state groups aiming to promote women in rodeo through barrel racing competitions. One important aspect of their promotion was to insist that women dress as real cowgirls, at a time when tennis shoes and ragged jeans were becoming the order of the day.[14]

9

I See By Your Outfit

There is a modern paraphrase of "The Streets of Laredo" which says:

I see by your outfit that you are a cowboy.
I see by your outfit that you're a cowboy, too.
I see by our outfits that we are both cowboys.
You get you an outfit, and you can be a cowboy too.

While it took much more than clothes to make a rodeo hand in the early days of the sport, it is nevertheless true that the clothes worn by cowboys and cowgirls did much to enhance their image as heroes and heroines, made them readily identifiable to the public and popularized some romantic notions about them. For instance: cowboys and cowgirls are always ready to leap into the saddle. Where else would they go dressed like that?

What began as merely working clothes took on the trappings of a costume when cowgirls began to appear in public. The ladies began performing on ranches, in rodeos, and Wild West shows in what they were wearing at that period in history—long skirts which had been stitched up the middle much like the culottes of today.

Lucille Mulhall was one of the first women to make the transition from ranch life to performing cowgirl. Various pictures indicate that Lucille at times wore a woman's frilly hat and at other times donned a high-crowned Stetson. Boots, spurs, and a long-sleeved blouse completed the outfit.[1] Will Rogers remembered Lucille most often wearing a long, gray divided skirt of whipcord or broadcloth, patent leather boots, a white shirtwaist of silk, and a small hat.[2]

There was, of course, an element of danger in wearing long skirts. In 1905, Lucille appeared with her family in Madison Square Garden. While she was exhibiting her skill on a horse called Governor, she leaned from the saddle to pick up a handkerchief from the ground and her long skirt became tangled in the stirrup. Lucille was dragged for a distance but managed to free herself.[3]

During the era of long skirts there were some who preferred not to stitch a seam up the middle and did not ride astride. It is reported that a Mrs. Riordan thrilled audiences by riding broncs sidesaddle.[4]

A picture of an early day performance of Cheyenne's Frontier Days shows women riding astride in races wearing long skirts which do not appear to be seamed up the middle. Their blouses seem to be of a feminine type with long sleeves and high collars. Their hats vary from jockey caps to cowboy hats, and the winner is headed for the home stretch in an ordinary lady's hat.[5]

In the early 1900s, when some women were performing in long skirts, others had already shortened their dresses. Annie Oakley is shown in an 1887 picture in a shortened but undivided skirt.[6] Cowgirls' skirts were usually made of leather, often fringed on the bottom. High-topped boots covered the legs so that no "bare limbs" would shock the Victorians. Fringed leather vests, blouses with flared sleeves, cowboy hats, hair ribbons, neck scarves and leather gauntlets added decoration to the riding costume. One doubts, however, that any of the embellishments made riding or roping any easier.

A mixture of long and short skirts continued into the 1920s and later when "flappers" and cowgirls, too, donned bloomers and bared their knees for all the world to see. While the costume may have seemed daring, it at least provided the first real freedom for women performing on horseback.

The most reliable source of information on cowgirls' clothing was Tad Lucas.[7] Tad remembered the first bloomers she ever saw. They were worn by Prairie Rose Henderson in 1918 in Gordon, Nebraska. Rose wore an ostrich plume skirt over the bloomers. Later other cowgirls wore bloomers made of corduroy or satin and fastened with elastic under the knee. Bright-colored stockings made of silk showed between the boots and the bloomers. The shirts were loose blouses with low necklines. Large triangular scarves, which hung to a point in the back and tied in a knot in the front, were worn with the blouses. Enormous bows perched on the back of long curls were complemented by wide-brimmed western hats. Cowgirls were also bedecked with bright silk sashes worn around the waist. Often, during the same period of the 1920s and 1930s, women wore sleeve holders made of elastic and decorated with satin streamers.

The leather-fringed skirts and high-topped boots continued to supplement the bloomers in the arena until the mid and late 1920s and into the 1930s when jodhpurs became popular. The jodhpurs bloused at the hip and buttoned tight at the calf. Colored silk hose and matching scarves continued in use as did sashes around the waist. During this time the rodeos and Wild West shows were still making trips abroad, and the jodhpurs may have reflected English influence. The pants may also have been an adaptation of the doughboys' trousers.[8] From this period on it may be observed that the ladies were copying men's styles instead of adapting ladies' clothes as they had done with skirts and bloomers.

For relay races jodhpurs were combined with rubber-soled shoes and leather leggings which laced from ankle to knee.

Both men and women often competed in chaps. Tad's chaps, made of angora, were practical and protective but they also added still another embellishment to her already spectacular attire.

During the 1920s ladies began to bob their hair. While the haircuts may have had nothing to do with it, it was reported that cowboys often wove strands of their favorite cowgirl's hair into their ropes.[9] Such gestures no doubt pleased the crowds and added a touch of romance to the heroines who competed with, if not against, the men.

Boots and hats posed no particular problem for women during the early period because there was a limited supply to choose from and because they were considered men's articles. The girls had to take what they could find. They, like the cowboys, sometimes ordered Stetson hats from Philadelphia. The hats came only in brown, black or cream. Boots were produced primarily in neutral colors and were often handmade for the performers.

Tad Lucas remembered that one of the first girls to wear long pants was Vera McGinnis. She appeared at the 1927 Fort Worth Fat Stock Show and Rodeo in a pair of men's white trousers which she had altered by removing the front fly, fastening them on the left side. The same year Tad, and later Fox Hastings, wore the first Mexican-style suits featuring a bolero and pants made of velvet or satin which belled at the bottom. Inserts of a complementary color were sometimes sewn into the bells. The style was influenced by a rodeo tour of Mexico with California Frank's show where the girls observed the flared legs of the flamenco dancer's costumes. The dancer's costumes were in turn copied from clothes the Mexican charros and rancheros wore, but it was the dancer's outfits which impressed the cowgirls.[10]

Tad and other cowgirls made, or had seamstresses make, their costumes because no commercial firms manufactured them. By 1927, rhinestones and sequins were being used, and a wider variety of cloth such as gabardine was being processed. From the earliest days cowgirls and cowboys made use of beaded Indian belts, gloves, vests, and jackets to glamorize their clothing. Other early-day accessories included fur coats and jackets made from plaid blankets.

Some women added extra-special personal touches to their costumes. Bernice Taylor, known in the East as the Gardenia Lady, always wore the white flower in her hair during her performances.[11] As an added touch Kitty Canutt combined the unusual with the practical by having a diamond set in her front tooth. Periodically Kitty had the diamond removed and pawned it when she needed entry money.[12]

The 1940s could be called the beginning of the modern era in western and cowgirl clothing. Yokes in shirts and pants came into style along with fitted rather than blousey sleeves in shirts.

Lamé for decoration and men's denim pants for practicality came into vogue for women. Hair styles ranged from short cropped hair to long pigtails and every length in between. It is interesting to note, however, that from the earliest days until the present, cowgirls have generally favored long hair. The consensus is that it is more feminine, looks better under a western hat, and adds an element of the dramatic when blowing in the wind.

While clothing became primarily a matter of costuming for rodeo cowgirls, there were others out on the range who had to make some clothing changes too. When women began leaping into the saddle, hurling ropes, tailing up cows, chasing steers through the brush and drawing guns from the hip, they probably went around mumbling that well-known female phrase, "I haven't got a thing to wear." Just getting to the frontier was difficult work and some women adopted knickerbockers which were covered with knee-length skirts. Dee Brown in *The Gentle Tamers* noted: "Any woman starting west in a silk dress was immediately suspected of being a prostitute; a respectable woman was supposed to wear working clothes, at least until she completed the journey."[13]

Isabella Bird, the Englishwoman who toured the Rocky Mountain region in 1873, was considered a dude and not a genuine frontierswoman. Nevertheless, she stayed long enough to make a hand on a ranch owned by two Scottish families, the Evans and Edwards, and she did not let English propriety prevent her from finding a comfortable way to ride cowponies, which she greatly admired, or keep her from going after the cattle. She wore "a half-fitting jacket, a skirt reaching to the ankles, and full Turkish trousers gathered into frills falling over the boots. . . ."[14] Eventually the skirt became bothersome and when she took it off, not without some embarrassment, the guide insisted that no one thought less of her for trying to be comfortable.

Eventually most women on ranches wore pants of some kind. Alice Stillwell Henderson wore pants, the bottoms of which she stuffed into her boot tops. When she went into Alpine, Texas, from her Big Bend ranch, she wore a long skirt over her outfit.[15] Sally Skull is reported to have worn everything from rawhide bloomers and men's pants to long dresses.[16]

Thelma Crosby continued to wear a divided skirt while working on the ranch because her husband did not approve of her wearing men's pants.[17]

Agnes Morley Cleaveland's *No Life For a Lady* gave one of the better descriptions of what she and, no doubt, others wore. She says:

> First, I discarded, or rather refused to adopt, the sunbonnet, conventional headgear of my female neighbors. When I went unashamedly about under a five-gallon (not ten-gallon) Stetson, many an eyebrow was raised; then followed a doublebreasted blue flannel shirt, with white pearl buttons, frankly unfeminine. In time came blue denim knickers worn under a short blue denim skirt. Slow evolution (or was it decadence?) toward a costume suited for immediate needs. Decadence having set in, the descent from the existing standards of female modesty to purely human comfort and convenience was swift. A man's saddle and a divided skirt (awful monstrosity that was) was inevitable.[18]

The cowgirls of Miller Brother's 101 Show made hands at the ranch between rodeos. Their first glimpses of fashion came as they performed in large cities:

> Some of the ranch belles had never seen a parasol and could not understand why one should not welcome the tan which accompanied buoyant health. Lorgnettes, vanity bags, dresses *en train*, and turban bobs were beyond their puzzled comprehensions. The plaits, coils, and tresses of fashionable coiffure evoked their curious interest but no desire for emulation.[19]

Apparently some cowgirls were interested in fashion, however, as evidenced in the adoption of such styles as bloomers and bobbed hair.

C. L. Sonnichsen suggests in his book *Cowboys and Cattle Kings* that the reason cowboy clothes are noticed in such places as New York is not because they are "outlandish," but because people know what the clothes stand for.[20] The same is true about the cowgirl's clothes. To see the ranch and rodeo cowgirl today dressed in her best proves that the heroine is still glamorous, but she is also durable, just as she has always been.

Because of traveling Wild West shows and rodeos along with reports in newspapers about performances and competitions, it did not take long for audiences to believe in the mythical West. Neither was the myth centuries old and separated by time from the facts that spawned it. The western myth was fresh, based on truth, verified by enthusiastic live characters wearing costumes and subduing wild animals with strange and splendid equipment. The West became transportable truth, accessible to view even as it was being born. Rodeo and the life it imitated seemed to be an entirely American epic composition, and it gained acceptance beyond the continent of its creation. By wagon, train, truck, and boat, rodeo and the Wild West show and notions about cowboys and, yes, indeed, cowgirls, entered the gates of embellished fact and emerged through the chutes of legend.

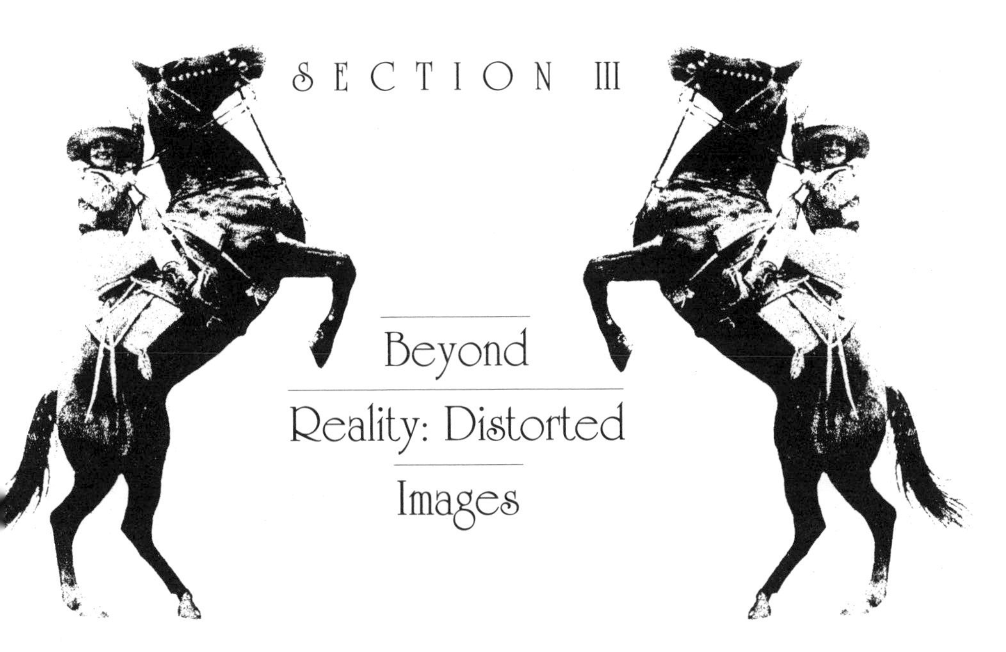

SECTION III

Beyond Reality: Distorted Images

By the turn of the century, the United States with only a bit more than a century of experience to write about, wrote about it a lot. Teddy Roosevelt, who did much to point out the fabled West, gave the subject importance and impetus. The West along with other slices of Americana began to show up in inexpensive, pulp publications known as dime novels. Long on plot, exaggerated truth and moral applications, the little books became the American version of the fairy tale. Using a real person or someone who represented him, the pulps surrounded characters with problems to solve in dramatic settings. The characters responses were also dramatic with positive, victorious, morally uplifting conclusions. Fiction took up the formula and method. Some, however, began to move into excellence and revealed unvarnished truth. Beyond the printed word was the development which would catapult the West right into the laps of those who wanted to sit down and see for themselves—the movies.

From the very beginnings of all three—dime novels, fiction and movies—the West was equal to other American subject matter. Those entering the gates of legend and lore, cowgirls included, found themselves enshrined, and, for better or worse, immortalized.

10

Wild, Wild Women

The desperadoes are gaining fast.

"Leave me, Ted, " she cried. "They will kill you if they get you, and you can escape on Sultan, which can outrun any of their horses."

Ted looked at her and laughed.

"I guess not," he called back. "Keep it up, we'll win yet."[1]

Naturally Ted does not leave her, and the couple get out of their predicament. This happy conclusion, however, is brought about by Stella, the "girl pard" of Ted Strong, not by the bumbling hero. Stella knows a solution when she sees one and Ted is sitting on it—Sultan, the stallion. When Ted is shot out of the saddle and left hanging thereon by the skin of his chaps, Stella approaches the "superb Sultan" who has never worked up a head of steam, catches him by the bridle and suggests to him that he ought to whoa. Sultan, like most dime novel stallions, understands Stella's every word, and allows the heroine to leap from her own mount after which, "as Ted reeled and was about to fall, she sprang into his saddle, caught him, and dashed away to safety." This 1906 adventure from *Rough Rider Weekly* entitled "King of the Wild West's Nerve; or, Stella in the Saddle" is a typical portrayal of what frontier heroines had become since 1860 when Beadle and Adams started issuing their versions of adventure in the form of dime novels.

There were other inexpensive weeklies before the firm of Beadle and Adams began to produce and there were cheap novels about people in all walks of life. As historians Joe Frantz and Julian Ernest Choate point out, "the cowboy, like America waiting on Isabella, needed only a sponsor to make his presence felt throughout the nation."[2] One of the sponsors turned out to be dime novels.

Before 1880, heroines seemed to exist solely to give the hero something to rescue. The women were not necessarily cowgirls but they were western types and often the reader made no distinction between the two. Certainly the cowgirl owed something to the behavior of her frontier sisters and predecessors, and the situations frontierswomen got into involved the same perils any cowgirl might face. In the early novels, the ladies manage to get themselves into one compromising situation after another and one wonders how that can be, considering that their study day and night was to protect their purity. Indian attack, for example, was one menace the ladies wished to avoid at all costs. Every reader knew, perhaps hoped, that a "fate worse than death" awaited the heroine at the hands of Indians, but with the authors, it was only a threat. The Indians of most dime novels were in great awe of maidenhood. They might dangle the victim over the coals, tie her to a stake, or devise other interesting tortures, but, as Edmund Pearson points out, "their honor was as safe as if they were in a convent. Indians were, all of them, gentlemen."[3]

Other dangers such as desperadoes, famine, flood, prairie fire, and disease were shared by all western heroines, but most of the ladies were of the helpless, fainting, fragile variety found in the tales of Cooper. Henry Nash Smith in *Virgin Land* sets 1880 as a general date when the western heroines began to change from genteel creatures placed around the scenery for rescuing, into active, vigorous women who, with pistol, whip, battleax and anything else they could lay hand to, were able not only to defend their own purity but also to snatch the hero out of sticky situations.

The transformation of heroines from passive objects to active ones began with the introduction into the action of Indian girls who could ride and shoot. Next followed the ancient device of disguising heroines in men's clothes. The disguised heroines often committed acts of violence, usually for revenge. Finally the heroine assumed all the skills and functions of a western hero. By 1878, with the appearance of Edward L. Wheeler's Hurricane Nell in *Bob Woolf, the Border Ruffian; or, The Girl Dead-Shot*, the heroine began to act like something out of a Wild West show. Nell can ride, shoot, rope, and yell like a man. She ropes a wild mustang, then rescues the hero (a Philadelphia lawyer) from the Indians by grabbing him around the waist and assisting him atop the back of the wild horse she has roped for him. She kills three of the enemy with as many shots from her rifle.[4] Nell is a girl among girls, and she is joined in similar exploits by Wild Edna, Calamity Jane and others.[5] Henry Nash Smith concludes that the heroine, when "freed from the trammels of gentility, developed at last into an Amazon who was distinguished from the hero solely by the physical fact of her sex."[6]

Douglas Branch believes that the "greatest writers of Dime Novels have not been pale young men from Connecticut, but men who had known the frontier."[7] Some writers who did not know the frontier, however, still wrote good novels. Perhaps it is safe to say that the authors knew *about* the frontier, if not from personal experience, at least from newspapers, travel journals, or, beginning very close to 1880, from Wild West shows and rodeo. Except for Calamity Jane, characters usually were not based on real people, but some were at least reminiscent of real people. Smith chalks up the outrageous behavior of heroines to an increase in and love for sensationalism.[8] While that is, no doubt, partly true, there are some heroines who bear enough resemblance to real people to cause one to wonder. A few examples will suffice: Rowdy Kate of *Apollo Bill, The Trail Tornado, or, Rowdy Kate From Right Bower*, written in 1882, announces in a typical southwestern boast, "I'm a regular old double distilled typhoon, you bet." There was actually a Rowdy Kate in the 1870s. She was a dance hall girl, among other things, and she probably was thought of as a double-distilled typhoon.[9] Katrina Hartstein of *The Jaguar Queen; or, The Outlaws of the Sierra Madre*, written in 1872, goes about with seven pet jaguars on a leash and is the leader of a gang.[10] Annie Sokalski, who around the mid 1860s, accompanied her soldier-husband to his duty posts, was herself accompanied by thirteen trained hunting dogs which she kept on leash. She had the personality to control not only the dogs but a good many other people with whom she came in contact. Annie's riding habit, made of wolfskin and trimmed with wolf tails was topped off with a fur hat. She spent a good many hours at target practice, was a deadly shot, and could ride better than some of the cavalry.[11] Such a personality could have inspired a Jaguar Queen, and Frederick Whittaker, who created her, had been in the army.[12] The previously mentioned Hurricane Nell shows up in the Pike's Peak area dressed like a man.[13] Mountain Charley, who was actually Mrs. E. J. Guerin, joined miners at Pike's Peak dressed like, and passing for, a man in 1859. She published her autobiography in 1861—in plenty of time for a dime novel writer to have heard of her.[14] Iola of *A Hard Crowd, or Gentleman Sam's Sister* was "capable of shooting down instantly a man who accosted her in the street."[15] Any number of women previously described, such as Sally Skull, or the South Texas woman who blew a man's head off when he got fresh, could pass for Iola. C. P. Westermeier, in *Trailing the Cowboy*, quotes from six newspapers dating from 1877 to 1885 about cowgirls and cattlewomen, any of whom could have passed for a dime novel heroine.[16]

Many of the sensational women of dime novels fit the classification of "girl sports." Sports are usually beautiful women who dress in mannish fashion. They can perform all the manly feats with gun, whip and knife. They take their liquor straight and often swear expertly. Sports almost never get the hero's romantic attention, although they save the hero in time for him to fall into the arms of some other woman.

There were real-life Sports, among them Calamity Jane, who could have served as models. Mary E. Sawyer, known in Arizona as Mollie Monroe, had all the qualifications of a Sport. In the 1890s Mollie was known, according to the *Phoenix Herald*, as "the girl cowboy who in her day, would ride anything with four feet, chew more tobacco and swear harder than any man in Arizona."[17] *The San Francisco Mail* of May 27, 1877, reported that:

> It was customary with Mollie to accompany all the leading scouts against the common foe, the Apache. Dressed in the uniform of the country of that day—buckskin pants, the usual appendages of beads and fringes, broad-brimmed hat, armed with a Henry rifle, two six-shooters, and a bowie knife, she was ready for the fray. And when it came down to a good square Indian fight, Mollie was there, as many a one of the Apaches found to his cost.

Mollie always had her purse open for those down on their luck, and she attended the sick like a "visiting angel." Supposedly unrequited love drove Mollie from her home to the wilds of Arizona.

Mollie was declared insane in 1877 and committed to the Clark and Langdon Sanitorium at Stockton, California. When a reporter visited her there, Mollie told him that "she was the meanest thing on earth, and intended to be so until she was turned out and allowed to do as she pleased."[18]

In *The Barranca Wolf, or, The Beautiful Decoy, A Romance of the Texas Border* by Joseph E. Badger, Jr., Lola is the Sport. She is dressed in white doeskin with leggings to match. She wears a cap of fur adorned with eagle feathers "such as the Kiowa wear." The dark–eyed brunette is pretty to look at as she sits her piebald mustang "savage style." Her rifle is balanced across her Mexican saddle and "other weapons gleamed from the belt that encircled her round, compact waist."[19]

Although Lola's father has taught her to hate men and to lure them into the Barranca for the purpose of foul play, she falls for Ned, the hero. Ned is promised and Lola dies defending him, but not before she asks Ned to marry her. Sports lack a certain tact when it comes to getting what they want, and they hardly ever get it, even when they are dying.

In *The Detective Queen; or, The Denver Doll's Devices* by E. L. Wheeler, the heroine is a Sport and a humdinger. She wears a "plumed slouch hat of snowy white" over her brown curls. Her figure of "symmetry and grace" is clothed in "an elegant suit of gray" with which she wears patent leather top-boots, a diamond studded "biled" shirt, and a sash about her waist—a costume "at once dashing and characteristic of the wild roving existence she led." Wheeler insisted that the Doll was a respectable woman sworn to break up a roadagent gang with the assistance of her helpers—a Negro, a Dutchman and a Chinese man.

The Doll is a formidable card player and one game features a duel with guns loaded with salt and pepper. Typical of Sports she declares, "I take but precious little stock in men,"[20] but the reader must take into account that the phrase is uttered before a suitable male wanders into the story.

Another of Wheeler's tales, *The Girl Sport; or Jumbo Joe's Disguise* features Leadville Lil. Lil takes her whiskey straight and smokes cigarettes while wearing a suit of "flawless fitting white duck," patent leather slippers, a diamond pin and a gold watch. Upon entering a bar armed with revolver and rifle, Lil puts up a kiss as her entry fee in a poker game.

There is another sporty type in the same story. Her name is Sadie. Sadie gets the hero, Joe, in her clutches and declares that she will have him tortured if he doesn't marry her. That rips it with Joe and he responds:

> Were death to stare me in the face in a hundred horrible shapes, I would welcome it rather than ally myself to a woman who takes the burden of match-making upon her own shoulders.[21]

Joe can afford to make smart remarks because Lil is waiting in the wings to rescue him. In the end Lil and Sadie fight and Sadie gets hers, not from Lil, but from Joe who shoots her. In an unexpected twist Lil turns out to be an heiress, a fact which does much to excuse her sporting ways, and she gets to marry the hero.

E. L. Wheeler's most famous Sport, Calamity Jane, is given detailed treatment in *Deadwood Dick on Deck; or, Calamity Jane, The Heroine of Whoop-Up*. When someone asks if Jane is a hard case, someone else explains that she is merely a daredevil. Some say a man deserted her and she took up a roving life to hunt him down. Others tell that she married a brute and ran away from him. Jane has a pretty but hard face. She wears buckskin pants "met at the knee by fancifully beaded leggins," dainty slippers, a velvet vest, and a boiled shirt. Her jacket is of velvet and her Spanish broad-brimmed hat is "slouched upon one side of a regally beautiful head."

Jane wears one revolver around her waist and carries a rifle strapped to her back. She rides a black pony richly equipped in Mexican style. When asked why she dresses like a man, Jane replies,

> I don't allow ye ken beat men's togs much fer handy locomotion an' so forth, an' then, ye see, I'm as big a gun among the men as any of 'em.[22]

In *Deadwood Dick in Leadville; or, A Strange Stroke for Liberty*, Jane saves a man's life in a crooked card game. When she draws her gun, everyone knows she means business. No one even dares look at Jane too long for fear it may anger her. She boasts that she enjoys a good fight and never shoots at the same target twice. Jane refers to ammunition as "condensed death."[23]

George Waldo Browne's *The Tiger of Taos; or, Wild Kate, Dandy Rock's Angel* features the exploits of a Sport who feels that she is shunned by society because of her father's reputation as a horse thief. It apparently has not occurred to her that the shunning may be because she totes a rifle and a pair of revolvers and lives up to the name of Wild Kate.

Kate is not beautiful, but she has other things to recommend her. She is "attired in a fancifully trimmed and frilled suit of border gray, encircled at the waist by a belt of buckskin, which was nearly reached by dark chestnut waves of silken hair falling down over her shoulders." Riding a "strangely-spotted mustang" Kate saves the heroine, Alice, and the hero more than once.[24]

Most dime novel heroines fall into the general category of frontier women. They are not necessarily cowgirls. Their lives may be involved in any number of western activities—shooting, swearing, popping a whip, wielding a battleax, fist fighting, pounding leather, and dressing up like men—and their activities influenced what people believed about pioneer females. There were two heroines, however, who rode the dime novel range from 1900 until the 1920s and who were genuine cowgirls.

Arietta Murdock, created by Cornelius Shea, first appeared in 1902 in the *Wild West Weekly.* She is rescued from the Sioux by Young Wild West and his stallion, Spitfire. West is a doer of good out on the prairies—that is, he tries to be the doer, but with Arietta around he sometimes becomes the doee.

Arietta is described as a golden-haired blonde, and that should be a clue that she is going to have all the fun. Her father, Sam Murdock, is the postmaster of Weston in the Black Hills. She is a native of Wyoming and she shoots, not like the best cowboy shot, but "with the skill of the average cowboy or man of the border," and she rides vicious broncs too, provided they have been ridden at least once before. She is, then, for a woman, a cut above the average man, but just a shade under the hero. In "Rawhide Ralph; or, The Worst Cowboy in Texas" (the title refers to the villain, not the hero) of the August 14, 1908, issue of *Wild West Weekly,* Arietta shows what she is made of. While Wild and company are off somewhere, Arietta and two other lady friends decide to take a ride to see the neighbors. One of the other women is Eloise Gardner, the sweetheart of one of West's bunch. Reminiscent of some Wild West cowgirls, Eloise was once a circus performer. Although her occupation may appear a strange one for a western heroine, it indicates that Shea knew what was going on in the arena. Florence Hughes Randolph, for example, got into Wild West shows after being in the circus.

Once out on the prairie the girls discover a burned-out ranch, and guess, with astonishing accuracy, that "Rawhide Ralph" has done it. At that moment Rawhide himself rides up. Arietta knows from the condition of the villain's face that it has been in contact with young Wild West's fists. Rawhide is not feeling kindly toward West, and, seeing Arietta, he plots revenge. The girls try to ride away, but, unfortunately, only the heroes get to ride stallions, and, being poorly mounted, they are caught. Rawhide has sense enough to take the girls' weapons. They are, after all, western girls and the rifles hanging beside their saddles aren't just for decoration.

Fiendishly, Rawhide proposes marriage to Arietta, and he prepares for a mock ceremony. The other two women are allowed to go, and as the gang's attention is drawn to the doorway, Arietta pulls a revolver which was hidden in her buckskin jacket. In keeping with the code of other real-life heroines before her, Arietta, without hesitation, points her gun at Johnny Cole, one of the gang, and does not merely wing him, but blows him to kingdom come. In a second she is mounted and joins the other girls as young Wild West, just a shade late, rides to the rescue. J. Edward Leithead, writing for *Dime Novel Round-Up*, points out that Arietta's killing of Cole marks her as different from most western heroines:

> No hesitation, no girlish squeamishness about shooting to kill when she had to, no conscience-stricken aftermath, which marked Arietta as so different from pallid heroines of Western fiction who, even though fighting for their lives or in a good cause, seldom more than wounded a human target if they hit him at all or didn't down his horse instead. In Arietta Murdock, Cornelius Shea presented the type of girl who helped to win the West.[25]

Arietta is displayed on about eighty percent of the covers of *Wild West Weekly* and her name appears often in subtitles. She rescues the hero with regularity by such feats as hurling dynamite, leaping chasms, shooting her revolver, riding for the posse, producing Indian amulets and charms, and stealing guns or horses from the outlaws.

Another series featuring a cowgirl heroine was the *Rough Rider Weekly*. Many of the stories were written by Ned Taylor, the pen name of St. George Rathbone. The series about the range and range life was probably launched to compete with *Wild West Weekly*, and in spite of what was considered better writing than appeared in the *Weekly*, lasted only 175 issues.[26]

Ted Strong, owner of a ranch in the Black Hills of Dakota, spends his time doing cowboy things with his group, the Rough Riders of Black Mountain Ranch. Ted was once a sergeant with Teddy Roosevelt's group; hence the name, Rough Riders.

There is realism in such stories as "Ted Strong's Wild West Show; or The Making of an Indian Chief" which features a rodeo contest between the boys of Black Mountain and the waddies of Sunset Ranch, in which incidentally, the hero loses. Ted saves the girl spectators by shooting a steer which charges the stands in an act reminiscent of Will Rogers' roping feat at a rodeo which brought him to prominence. Many of the performers of the 101 Ranch are even mentioned by name.[27] On a similar theme the *Wild West Weekly* referred to West's group as being caught in World War I.[28] The 101 group actually did get caught at the beginning of the war and their stock was impounded.[29] It would appear from such allusions that both series were well-acquainted with what went on in rodeo and Wild West shows and borrowed freely from both.

In *King of the Wild West's Haunt; or Stella's Escape From Sacrifice*, the heroine is introduced into the series. Stella is known in Texas as "Queen of the Range." She has been raised on her father's Sierra Blanca Ranch near El Paso, and when she is orphaned, the Rough Riders adopt her as their girl "pard," short for partner.[30] A Mrs. Graham accompanies Stella everywhere as her chaperone except when Stella rides out hell-bent for danger. Shooting and riding, Stella has no time for hanky-panky, anyway.

Stella is also a blonde. Her costume of white Stetson, bolero jacket, white leggings and red skirt embellished with a gun strapped on her hip, is reminiscent of costumes featured on Wild West posters.

In *King of the Wild West's Nerve; or, Stella in the Saddle* which introduced this chapter, are all the elements of a typical Rough Rider story. The tale begins in the San Simon meadows, where Captain Henry Foraker and Don Luis Fernando are in contention for land and cows. The meadow actually was a place frequented by Mexican and American outlaws, indicating that Ned Taylor was up on his history of the region.[31] Don Luis not only has his eye on Foraker's cattle but also on Foraker's beautiful and bountifully endowed daughter, Bonito. Bonito is a combination of her Spanish mama and her Puritan, Nordic papa—fire and ice. She has learned the social graces from convent schooling and the skills of riding, hunting and shooting from life with father on the range. The señorita is daddy's girl, and from him she inherits her love of the land. Bonito is large for her age, whatever age that is, "tall for a woman of the Southwest," and muscular from all that riding. In other words, another Amazon. Don Luis wishes to gain Bonito's hand in marriage along with her daddy's cattle. When the Forakers decline, Don Luis gets nasty, and his villainous behavior prompts the Forakers to summon Ted Strong. Wherever Ted goes, Stella is never far behind.

Bonito and Stella become instant, bosom friends. They must form an instant friendship because the book is not long enough to allow things to progress at normal speed. While Ted is out looking for trouble, the girls decide to take a ride to look at the cattle which remind Stella of the good old days on Daddy's ranch in Texas. That the ladies mount up and take an innocent ride is a giveaway that, while the hero is hunting trouble, the girls will not only find it first but get in it with both feet. Don Luis captures them (oh, if only those heroines could get hold of a stallion to ride!) but not before Stella has a chance to cut Don Luis down verbally by calling him a "dirty greaser." Such language may not have been unkind or in bad taste in 1906, but it was dangerous. Eventually Ted appears on his horse, Sultan, and the sound the animal makes is "pitty, pitty." When Ted cannot locate the girls at home, something wonderful happens:

> Something told Ted that the girls were in danger. It was that wonderful intuition of which he was possessed. It had never failed him yet, and he relied upon it as much as he did his senses of sight hearing and smell.[32]

The reader can only conclude that Ted certainly needs all the help he can get. The girls are treated to an unnecessary rescue. They could have managed it themselves, but Ted arrived prematurely.

Girl "pards" in literature, if dime novels count as literature, are not necessarily a new type, but they are an interesting variation on an Amazonian theme which predates Shakespeare's Hippolyta of *A Midsummer Night's Dream*. "Pards" are not like gun molls, who hang around to decorate the scenery or offer physical consolation to the boss. They are not like women such as Belle Starr who acted as a kind of gang boss. Although "pards" are definitely masculine in their abilities and sometimes even in their manner, they have a healthy interest in the opposite sex. While "pards" often wear men's clothes, they do not fall into the category of women who try to pass as men, and they are not to be confused with the rougher girl "sports." They are rather, as their name implies, partners of the cowboy, able to do almost everything he does, sharing equally the danger and the daring, and needing only occasional concessions to their femininity. It does not appear likely that the dime novelists were following any literary traditions, but rather based the female characters on actions, or what they thought were the actions, of real western women.

Girl "pards," although their roles become highly refined and they bear little resemblance to dime novel predecessors, show up in later literature. Several early writers of western stories mention partner-types. Wilson M. Hudson, in his study of Andy Adams, tells about a novel entitled *Tom*, after the heroine's nickname, which Adams never published. The story concerns a woman who can ride, shoot, herd cattle, and wrangle horses like a man. She marries the hero, Bob, in the end.[33] *The Virginian's* Molly, who does not at first understand the code of the West, shows signs of developing into a partner near the end of Owen Wister's novel. Emerson Hough's *North of 36* contains a genuine pard, although she seems a bungling one. Taisie Lockhart, possessing all the qualities which make a lovable and helpful pard, cannot seem to stay in the saddle once out on the trail. She keeps losing a trunk filled with valuable land scrip, falls in the river, and, it seems to me, cramps the cowboy's style in language and behavior. She is a pard who somehow gets off on the wrong foot, but apparently that is the way Hough wished it. Mattie Ross of *True Grit* is certainly one of the best pards and Charles Portis writes so convincingly of her that readers forget that the author's work is a parody of western dime novel. There was even an old dime novel series called the *True Grit* series.[34] The heroine of *Cat Ballou*, born during a thunderstorm and aided in her cause by all sorts of frontier types, is another "pard" of the dime novel variety.

The portrayal of western women and cowgirls in dime novels as Amazons is far from the truth. Dime novel authors generally stress that their heroines are large women, or the ladies' actions suggest that they must be bigger than average. Nearly all of the heroines surveyed by Henry Nash Smith are described in Amazonian terms and most are above average height, although no one ever specifies what the average is. Lola of *The Barranca Wolf* is "tall for a woman, several inches above the medium height. . . ."[35] The Denver Doll and Wild Kate are above medium height. Calamity Jane is only medium height but she performs as if she were *much* taller! Arietta and Stella are likewise quite capable of tall feats.

For whatever reason the actions of the heroines are depicted on a grand scale—sensationalism or an awareness of real western women's behavior—it is probably easy to imagine that only a large woman could accomplish such manly acts. However, a survey of women in Wild West shows, for instance, shows that most of them were not even average height. Annie Oakley and Lucille Mulhall were barely five feet in height. Of Mabel Strickland, Tad Lucas, Fox Hastings and Ruth Roach—all top names—none was over five feet three inches. Florence Hughes Randolph was only four feet six inches.

There were probably some larger women but one would be inclined to think that the horse was the great image builder and that seeing women on horseback performing ranch feats added to their stature. Observing women participating as pickup men and hazers—chores which Lucille Mulhall, particularly, often performed—must have caused writers to think of them as giants who like Stella Fosdick could hold the hero on her saddle.

Still another reason for portraying women as Amazons may have been that the actions in dime novels, according to Charles M. Harvey, "were physical, and they were told in language that made pictures in the mind."[36] Perhaps it took large women to create big mental impressions.

Dime novels perhaps even more than Wild West shows and rodeo helped to popularize notions about western cowgirls, and while it is difficult to approach the study of dime literature with anything but levity, the novels are a valuable tool for historians. William A. Settle, Jr., indicates that because of the glorifying and idealizing of the frontier, the West "entered for the first time into the consciousness of a large number of Americans."[37] Merle Curti writing for *Yale Review* found that the dime novels reflected "a much wider range of attitudes and ideas than the ballad or folk song," and were "the nearest thing we have had in this country to . . . a literature written for the great masses of people and actually read by them."[38]

The novels gave not only a picture of the Wild West, but, in the actions of the heroes and heroines, encouraged self reliance. Says Harvey: "Manliness and womanliness among the readers were cultivated by these little books, not by homilies, but by example." If we can believe Harvey, even the "taste and tone of the life of the generation which grew up with these tales were improved by them."[39]

11

A Book By Its Cover

The woman on the cover of the book is pretty. Her hair is long, her lips red and inviting. That she is a woman of the cattle range is evident in her buckskin shirt laced loosely in the front, her leathery looking skirt which the wind whips against her legs, the cartridge belt hanging upon shapely hips, and the spurs buckled on dainty boots. The heroine is a far cry from the sunbonneted statues which stand weatherbeaten and trail-worn, children at their large and weary feet, testifying on courthouse lawns that coming west was mighty hard on the women. Some readers looking at the voluptuous ladies on the covers of the pulps hope they can tell a book by its cover and buy—and buy and buy. Often the readers are not disappointed and get what the cover depicts—a sexy woman involved with western heroes in a variety of action-spiced situations out on the range. The covers as well as the contents of some western books have helped to shape public opinion that women on ranches had a lot more to offer than hot biscuits.

Western women have even managed to capture some publications all their very own among a field which runs the gamut from *True Confessions* to *Ladies Home Journal.* The publications known as *Ranch Romances* are much tamer than the confession variety. They go in for such titles as "A Bullet for Brenda," "Winchester Wedding," "Too Young, Too Far Away," and "Flower of the Mescalero." Unlike confession magazines in which sex is all, the romances on the range are only slightly earthy. Action is always more important. The heroine very often saves herself or the hero—a dime novel type who has found the modern joys of romance.

According to W. H. Hutchinson, ranch-romance stories came into vogue in the mid 1920s to "provide self-identification for women readers with the story line and plot."[1] Alan Bosworth refers to the ranch romance format as "Sally's Sweater" in which a good deal of wordage is "devoted to the inevitable movement of her second-skin sateen blouse. The story, setting, and characters are quickly introduced, and then back to Sally's Sweater."[2]

If the ranch-romance stories are tamer than short stories and novels which came later, there are other compensations in the magazines. There is, for example, a section devoted to letters in which the readers express not only pleasure in the publication but also request that other readers correspond with them. The letters are often from lonely widows who give their age, color of their eyes and hair, who tell that they are interested in country ways, the out-of-doors, gardening, collecting rocks, making quilts, reading about the West, country and western music, crocheting, and who would like to correspond with others of similar rustic mind. The letter page is reminiscent of early day newspaper and magazine ads by which some cowboys found mail-order brides.

Western paperback novels are sometimes judged by the women on their covers. The main ingredient is still action, but romance runs from flirtation to raw sex. Instead of loathing all that lonesome, hateful western space and monotonous landscape, the cowboys and cowgirls discover interesting diversions by the creek, over the next rise, up the draw, 'neath the stars, in the gully, beyond the ravine, beside the arroyo, at the bottom of the hill, in the shade or noon-day sun, over the divide, under the mesquite, behind the ocotilla and amongst the grama grass.

Some insist that paperbacks featuring sexy, western women and gory scenes are merely trash and give distorted views about anything western. Not all the books, however, are intended to distort. While it is true that some authors know little of the West, others try to be faithful to essentials. Louis L'Amour and Max Brand represent the two extremes. Brand, it is said, was once persuaded to visit El Paso, but he did not like what he saw and locked himself in a hotel room and read Sophocles instead. Louis L'Amour, on the other hand, is said to have researched carefully and could boast of a pioneer background in which his great-grandfather was scalped by Sioux Indians.[3] Although considered for some years as only one of the better pulp merchants, the late L'Amour now has a following of doctoral students studying his many novels. The various attitudes of western writers of paperback novels only prove that you cannot always judge a book by its cover and that the authors may be telling more of the truth than we at first suppose. Consider the fact, too, that many hardback books eventually get into paperback complete with the kinds of covers that help sell them.

Western hardback books which do not have anything provocative on the dust jacket or covers often do have something to say about ranch women. And if magazine authors and paperback writers found western women all sexily alike, the writers of what is thought of as serious literature of the range found a rich variety of personalities and attitudes among the women of the cattle country. A few examples from early literature to the present will illustrate.

The fiction of the West clearly divides ranch women into two camps—those who love the range and adjust to the hardships and those who hate and fear ranch life and never quite come to terms with the environment. For those who like tales of physical deeds and adventure there are stories in which ranch women who love the West, or who were to the saddle born, figure prominently. Such literature is vigorous and action packed and not always particularly introspective.

One of the early pieces of adventure literature dealing with a ranch heroine is a story written in verse in 1908, *Nancy MacIntyre, A Tale of the Prairies* by Lester Shepard Parker. The melodramatic tale deals with a cowboy, Billy, who is trying to prove up his eighty acres in Kansas. He loves Nancy who lives on a neighboring ranch. Bill worries considerably about his abilities in the courting department:

If this making love to women
Went like breaking in a horse,
I might stand some show of winning,
Cause I've learned that game, of course.

Nancy is a girl among girls. She is pictured wearing a long skirt, blouse, gun and cartridge belt. Billy describes her:

Now, those women that you read of
In these story picture books,
They can't ride in roping distance
Of that girl in style and looks.
They have waists more like an insect,
Corset shaped and double cinched,
Feet just right to make a watch charm,
Small, of course, because they're pinched.
This here Nancy's like God made her
She don't wear no saddle girth,
But she's supple as a willow
And the purtiest thing on earth.
Hair as black as fire-burnt prairie,
Eyes that dance and flash and flirt;
Every time she smiled she showed you
Teeth as white's my Sunday shirt.

Nancy is not only a "natural" girl, she is resourceful and brave. When the couple gets caught in a storm and their wagon ends up on the top of a dug-out with the settler shooting at them, Nancy saves the day. Billy is shot through the hand, and Nancy calms the frightened horses, then lashes them all the way back. She dresses Billy's wound and sees him safely home. Later she reveals that she, too, was wounded, but, not wanting to cause her sweetheart any more anguish, she goes home and has her father cut out the bullets.

Later in the story Nancy shows her spunk again. The heroine's family must flee Kansas because Nancy's father steals a horse. When the law catches up, Nancy stands off a posse so her family can escape.

Nancy MacIntyre is not a story for sophisticated, demanding readers. It falls into that body of material published early in the century which lends itself to public recitation. While *Nancy MacIntyre* may be considered by some no more than a cleverly rhymed, lengthy bit of trivia, it is nevertheless valuable for its memorable scenes of western landscape, of the harsh life of the prairies and of the unforgettable Nancy.

Another early writer who used cowgirls in his stories was O. Henry (William Sydney Porter). He lived for two years on a ranch managed by Texas Ranger Lee Hall in La Salle County, Texas. In 1884, he worked in a bank in Austin, Texas, and later for a newspaper in Houston. O. Henry wrote a series of stories about the West published in 1907 in a volume entitled *Heart of the West*. "Hearts and Crosses" presents a cattle queen who, after inheriting a ranch from her father, manages the ranch so well that her husband feels that he is little more than a hired hand. The husband leaves his wife to become a foreman for another spread. Some months pass. When he orders a shipment of cattle from his wife's ranch, the foreman discovers a pure white steer in the shipment with an unusual brand—a cross in the center of a heart. Before their marriage the cross and heart was a mark Santa left whenever she wanted to meet Webb secretly. Webb returns home to find that he is not only the father of a son but that his wife is at least willing to share the management of the ranch. One of the better scenes of the story occurs when Santa slips out to the cattle pen in the dark of night, ropes, throws, ties and brands the steer herself.

O. Henry's "The Marquis and Miss Sally" makes use of a woman in the disguise of a cowboy. When a couple of drifters come to the Diamond-Cross cow camp, one, with delicate features, short brown hair and smooth face, hires on as a puncher. The other, one with red hair, broad shoulders and plain face, hires on as cook. Immediately the camp dubs them Miss Sally and The Marquis. The two become good friends. The Marquis makes a good puncher in spite of the fact that he is reserved and takes no part in the roughhousing of the camp. Miss Sally proves dependable and the boss offers him the job of bookkeeper for the ranch. Along with his promotion Miss Sally asks for a house because he intends to marry soon. Later in the evening when a politician comes by campaigning for votes, the men decide to put on a mock wedding between the Marquis and Miss Sally. By that time, O. Henry's surprise ending is revealed. The Marquis confesses to Miss Sally that she is a girl. Because her father dies and because she often helped him with the cattle, she decides to be a cowboy. Miss Sally had guessed the Marquis' identity long before and what the hands think is a mock wedding turns out to be a real one.

Bertha Muzzy Sinclair, who wrote under the name of B. M. Bower is best remembered for her ranch adventure novels about Chip and the Flying U Ranch. Eugene Manlove Rhodes said that she was one who wrote "stories where people on paper act like people and horses do. . . ."[4] Another of her novels, *Rim O' the World*, published in 1919, presents a memorable ranch heroine, Belle Lorrigan. Belle is a city girl, a singer on the stage, who comes out west to the end of the train line to get away from something. What she is running from the reader never knows, and the people of the Rim (including her husband), in true western fashion, never ask. The first person Belle meets is Tom Lorrigan, arrogant and misunderstood owner of the Lorrigan ranch. He promptly asks Belle to marry him. Belle doesn't hesitate a minute, especially after Tom explains how it is in the West:

> Yuh, needn't be afraid uh me. We're rough enough and tough enough, and we maybe shoot each other now and again, but we ain't like city folks. We don't double-cross women. Not ever.

Belle takes to ranch living in Idaho like a duck takes to water. She refuses to ride horses but chooses instead to tear across the prairie in a buckboard pulled by two pinto broncs, Rosa and Subrosa. The horses are demons and must be roped and tied to get their collars on. Belle is described as a "golden-curled, pink-cheeked, honeythroated Amazon" who can shoot better than a man and sing an almost endless repertoire of songs. In one of the more touching scenes in the novel, the heroine sings Highland ballads to a seriously ill Scottish woman.

Belle's three sons are raised with a loose rein. They adore and respect their mother. She teaches them city manners but nothing of city life. Belle smokes cigarettes with the sons one minute and then whips out a six-shooter and plugs a hole in one son's hat to remind him to remove it in her presence the next time.

In one scene when the sheriff arrives to check the brands on some green hides, Belle buckles on her cartridge belt and won't allow the sheriff off his horse. If he does not leave, she plans to put a bullet in him "about six inches above the knee." When the sheriff keeps talking, Belle insists that if he does not hush, she will shoot his front tooth out.

The story abounds in melodramatic dialogue. The plot is at times amusing and at others fast paced, offering some unusual twists. A good family gets involved with rustling, for instance. The author gives some insights into what ranch people think about other ranch people. In spite of some good deeds by the Lorrigans, the town thinks ill of the family. The women hate Belle and refuse to visit her. Even in the face of loneliness, the heroine keeps busy with the ranch and her family. The reader understands why and forgives. On the other hand, Mrs. Sinclair shows the other ranchers' side of the story. Through Belle and her son, the viewpoints of the Rim are somewhat reconciled. It is a good and satisfying story and offers a look into the rancher's philosophy that a cattleman and his wife have rights on the range that do not exist in polite society.

Frantz and Choate write of Mrs. Sinclair in *The American Cowboy*:

> Mrs. Sinclair . . . had what so many cowboy writers lack, a real background of life among the bowlegged brethern. Born in Minnesota, she was reared in Montana, where she rode the range and fraternized with the men on horseback. From *Chip of the Flying U*, her first, down through a number of sequels, she wrote in a playful, humorous vein. She did not try to pontificate about the epic role of the cowboy,

> and she had no pretenses to history as such, but she was faithful to the Western historical milieu which she knew first hand.[5]

Perhaps the most famous novel dealing with a ranch woman is Emerson Hough's *North of 36* published in 1923. Although considered dated and in many ways laughable by modern standards, the novel contains a heroine, Taisie Lockhart, and hero, Dan McMasters, worthy of the best tale about the West.

Taisie is the orphaned daughter of Texas cattleman Colonel Lockhart. Her mother passed on when Taisie was seven. Consequently, her upbringing was up to the Colonel. He raised her in true ranch tradition. She is a superb horsewoman. Mounted on her incomparable Blancocito, a horse which even the seasoned hands have a hard time with, Taisie, dressed like a man and wearing her hair in two braids like an Indian, oversees the ranch in what she believes is a man's way. Her job is made considerably easier by adoring ranch hands who have known her since childhood. When Taisie discovers that she is broke, yet overrun with cattle for which there is no market, Dan McMasters, captain of the Texas Rangers, sheriff of Gonzales, U. S. Marshal and owner of the Del Sol spread, moseys by with news that there is a northern market for cattle. Taisie intends to be the first woman to drive a herd north.

With a swift gathering of her belongings including a trunk of scrip and a servant or two, Taisie is off up the trail. But, alas, the reader is doomed to disappointment in Taisie's trail behavior. She sobs a good part of the time. She would not, as the saying goes, do to ride the river with because she falls off her horse into the river and has to be rescued. She loses, with regularity, her trunk of scrip. Taisie is, of course, falling for McMasters, who pretends to fall in with the villains on the trail. Finally the plot is untangled and the two ride off into the sunset.

Douglas Branch in *The Cowboy and His Interpreters* points out that Taisie's ethical code has much in common with the "Middle-Western housewife, with only sparks of the freedom of the range-days of Texas." Branch believes the ethical defect is

Hough's: "He cannot describe the night-life of Abilene without squirming."[6]

Another who wrote about the West was Eugene Manlove Rhodes. Critics are quick to note that the stories of Rhodes are dated and lack good mechanics and that his narratives are difficult to follow. All agree, however, that his characterizations and dialogue are true to the men and women of the cattle ranges. His wit and charm, his feeling for the landscape and the peculiar code of the cattleman, and even his women are true to life, as he lived it and knew it as a working cowhand during troubled times in Tularosa, New Mexico, and later as he reflected about it on a farm in New York.

In one of Rhodes most famous stories, "Paso Por Aqui" (1926) a nurse says these words: "Your precious New Mexico! Sand!" she said. "Sand, snakes, scorpions; wind, dust, glare and heat; lonely, desolate and forlorn!" The woman speaker is an Eastern woman and Rhodes never hesitated to put unkind words about the West in the mouths of "foreigners." It helped to show them up for what they were. In contrast a ranch woman, Eva Scales, in "Maid Most Dear" (1930) speaks these lines about the same desert country: "I've lived here all my life. Except for a few trips to Silver City and El Paso, I've never been out of these hills." Her head lifted, her eyes lingered on the long horizons, lovingly. "If it is any better outside, I'm willing to be cheated." Not only does Eva love the land but she is also a brave and daring heroine who rides unafraid into a shooting match involving a lynch mob to help rescue Eddie and Skid, the heroes of the story.

Women in other Rhodes' stories are just as capable. In "Beyond the Desert" (1914) Bennie May Morgan meets MacGregor, a rider for Clay Mundy, under a rim of rock during a storm. "Get down unless you are afraid of hurting your reputation, that is," she says. She teases MacGregor when he guesses she is going to meet Clay Mundy, a rancher who is in a cattle war against her father. "You have come to plead with me for your friend—your employer to ask me to spare his youth and innocence—to demand of me, as the phrase goes, if my intentions are honorable. Is that it?" It turns out that MacGregor pays with his own life in order to spare her from a mock wedding with Mundy.

In "The Desire of the Moth" (1902) Stella Vorhis is the heroine who lives with her father on the Jornado del Muerto. The landscape is desolate but Stella "was one who found dear and beautiful this gray land, silent and ensunned." John Wesley Pringle, an old family friend, lovingly chides her for her forwardness when she lays "her hand across his gnarled brown fingers with an unconscious caress." He removes her hand and tells her, "Kindly keep your hands to yourself, young woman."

Minnie in "The Bird in the Bush" (1917) enjoys a similar open, friendly relationship of equals with Andy. She often rides out to hunt deer with the hero. Sometimes Minnie's friend, Jane, comes along. Andy explains: "Sometimes they brought Minnie's ma along for chaperone, sometimes not. It didn't make no difference. Them girls didn't need no chaperone, not much anyway."

Bernard DeVoto in "The Novelist of the Cattle Kingdom" finds fault with the women in Rhodes' stories. He complains that Rhodes never tells what they look like and insists that they are "incredible, self-conscious."[7] Another critic, W. H. Hutchinson, says that the women are "infrangibly virginal."[8] What both critics say is partially true—that the women are approached with reverence. It is also true, however, that they are very approachable. The women ride out alone, speaking frankly on equal terms with men. They seem very sure of themselves. The fault is less with the heroines and more with how the cowboy reacts. Rhodes himself said that while women were set on a pedestal it often annoyed the women. His women are few and vague, as Rhodes put it, "because they are just so in my memories. Conscientious realist. Yessir."[9]

The ranch women of Zane Grey's novels are very much alike. In fact, readers may have Grey to thank more than any other novelist for creating the stereotype by which all western women could be judged. The wife, Lucinda, in *30,000 On The Hoof* (1940) may be considered typical. Lucinda comes to the West from Missouri to marry her childhood sweetheart, Logan. She is to be, as he puts it, not only his wife, but his partner in the cattle business. After spending a page or two in telling about Lucinda's brand new, tight jeans, Grey is off and running with his tale of frontier hardship. Lucinda makes a hand, endures loneliness and privation in order to help Logan become a cattle baron. When the war takes two sons and wrecks the family cattle business, it is Lucinda who takes over and restores her husband and family to health and prosperity.

Another angle which Grey liked to feature in his stories was comparing eastern and western girls. The *Hash Knife Outfit* (1929) features Gloriana from the East and Molly from the West. The two girls ride with Stone, a hunted man, into the wilds of Arizona. Gloriana forgets to wear a hat or boots and comes dressed in a thin dress. "You'll have to ride as you are," says Stone. "Strikes me the Lord made you wonderful to look at, but left out any brains." The Easterner has trouble with her horse. She observes her friend: "The ease with which Molly mounted her horse, a wicked animal, was not lost upon Gloriana, nor the way she controlled him."

When the group stops for water, Molly refuses: "You see, out heah we train ourselves to do without water an' food. Like Indians, you know." While Molly spends much time toting and fetching, Gloriana spends time trying to keep her torn dress on her body.

Grey suffered the critic's disfavor for some years. It should be noted, however, that now Grey, like Louis L'Amour, has a share of doctoral students studying his novels. Grey's western women are all good, clean girls, but the author, in spending a fair amount of time in telling about tight levis and torn dresses, underscores their earthiness.

Some novelists have been concerned with the effect of cattle country on outsiders, particularly on women from the strongholds of gentility such as Virginia. While contrasting weather, terrain, and philosophy most authors indicate that for all its faults the West is preferable to the East.

Molly, Owen Wister's heroine in *The Virginian* (1902), learns to adjust to the West. Molly is a schoolteacher and only at the end of the story does she become a ranch wife. She has a high-toned, Vermont background, which she rejects, and a firm determination to do what she believes is right, which she retains. For starters she leaves a suitor whom she does not love and goes to Bear Creek, Wyoming, to teach school.

When Molly arrives, she manages to take a good many things in stride, horses among them. She learns to shoot and manage for herself as long as she is well supervised. Trampas, the villian, comments: "Riding and shooting and kissing the kids... That's a heap too pussy-kitten for me."

What Molly can't quite get the hang of is the code of the West and the philosophy accompanying the Virginian's words, "When you call me that, smile!" Nor would she have approved of the Virginian's singing, "If you go to monkey with my Looloo girl,/ I'll tell you what I'll do;/ I'll carve your heart with my razor, and/ I'll shoot you with my pistol too." Toward the end of the novel, however, Molly gains some understanding about how the range is different from Vermont, and she quits applying eastern solutions to western problems. She is even able to overcome her horror at the Virginian's attending to the business of eliminating Trampas on her wedding day. Molly eventually comes to have a deep love for the wild Wyoming land and because of her sincere affection for the West, the reader may forgive all her shortcomings.

Giant, by Edna Ferber, (1952) contains another heroine who comes to love ranch living. Virginia-born Leslie Benedict's concerns are not only the heat and emptiness but also the Texas attitude toward Mexicans. She works out her own methods of dealing with each. Luz, her sister-in-law, represents the outspoken, capable, hardened, no-nonsense ranch woman of early times. Miss Ferber only touches on Luz's independent single-mindedness, kills her off early, and never really develops her character. She obviously would have been too much for Leslie to cope with, but there might have been some interesting clashes between old Virginia and old Texas if Luz had lived. As Jordan, Leslie's husband, put it, "Luz is used to being the point. She'll have to have time to get used to being the drag." Women like Luz were not meant to ride drag and it seems just as well that she met her death on horseback.

There were those who found no pleasure in ranch life, who never adjusted or fit into the western scheme of things. In telling of such women, novelists characterize yet another type woman found in cattle country.

Dorothy Scarborough's novel *The Wind*, published in 1925, treats the effects of West Texas terrain and weather on a gentle Virginia-reared heroine, Letty Mason. When Letty's mother dies, she goes to live in Sweetwater, Texas, with her rancher-cousin Beverly Mason. On the train Letty makes the acquaintance of Wirt Roddy, who is attracted to her and tells her how hard the West is on women.

Letty is first overwhelmed by the empty spaces and next by the forwardness of Lige and Sourdough, who have been sent to meet her. Although they are good and honorable men and treat her with the courtesy and kindness of the range, it is not Virginia-proper courtesy and the heroine is frightened by them. Letty, however, is not as much disturbed by rough ways of cattle people as she is by the endless, lonesome space and the incessant, dry wind. She says to Lige, "I wonder if I'll ever have the courage to go horseback riding out there." Lige assures her that she will and that she will come to love all the beautiful things his own eyes see on the prairie. Lige then tells her tales of buffalo and cattle drives and of Cynthia Ann Parker and of the women who conquered the range frontier. With pride he tells Letty that the women were:

> . . . dead-game sports an' they stood the gaff. They didn't whine nor make life harder for their men. Of course, when you come down to brass tacks, the whole thing depended on the women folks. The women . . . could shoulder rifles and stave off Indians side by side with their husbands. And work—my stars, how they did work! Raised big families, did every lick of work, even to spinning and weaving. I take my hat off to the women of the West!

After hearing Lige's impassioned tribute to the Western woman, Letty feels unworthy. Letty is confronted with a flesh-and-blood example of a vibrant range woman in Cora, her cousin Beverly's wife. Cora is the real heroine of *The Wind.* Even Letty admits that the "West must be a bearable place, after all, if it could produce such a magnificent creature as she was." Cora was "like nature herself, contemptuous of weaklings and impatient and disregardful of others less capable than herself." And Cora expects Letty to make a hand. She is not considerate of the Virginia girl's gentle upbringing.

Cora eventually becomes jealous of the men's attentions to an outsider who insists on remaining helpless. Although sometimes coarse, loud and rude because she is jealous of Letty, Cora defends her way of life by telling Letty in no uncertain terms that when she met Bev she found him dying of consumption, nursed him back to health, made up his mind about marrying her, and helped him start his ranch. Cora declares her love for Bev, and it is in terms of Texas weather and landscape. She says:

> I love him like a cyclone and I love him, too, the way the prairie feels when it's still and calm at night, when the wind don't blow an' the spring flowers are in bloom and the stars shine soft.

She concludes, "There ain't any way of loving that I don't love Bev!"

Finally Cora's harsh treatment and Letty's hysterical fear of a windstorm drive her to marry Lige. The couple make their home on the prairie where the wind begins the final erosion of Letty's mind. She leads a dual existence, remembering Virginia while trying to cope with Lige and the tortures of the prairie. Letty finally asks Lige to let her leave. After Lige points out that Cora always stood by Bev and that Letty is a quitter—the worst sin a Westerner can commit—he rides off to get drunk, leaving Letty to face herself and the wind. While Lige is in town, Wirt Roddy, whom Letty met on the train, shows up at the ranch. Wirt abuses Letty and tries to take her away. She comes to her senses, refuses, and shoots him. The novel ends as Letty tries without success to cover Wirt's body with sand that the wind keeps blowing away. *The Wind* is a good novel and moves swiftly. The wind and Letty's behavior, however, are depressing.

Another heroine, Lutie Cameron in Conrad Richter's *Sea of Grass*, first serialized in *The Saturday Evening Post* in October and November of 1936, is just as depressed by the prairie landscape when she arrives to marry Colonel Brewton, but she has a better grip on her nerves and finds other ways—just as unsettling to the reader—to make her way out of the grassy troubles that threaten to drown her.

The men of Salt Fork, New Mexico, fall all over themselves trying to please Lutie. Lutie, early on spies a flashy piece of manhood, Brice Chamberlain, who later brings her to some grief.

When Lutie, beautiful and charming, first viewed the grassland "dipping and pitching endlessly like a parched sea," she "stopped as if she had run into barbed wire." She sets about changing the ranch atmosphere of drabness and monotony by filling the house with furniture and people. She does not, however, accept serenely the things she cannot change. Lutie pretends to plant trees for shade but Hal, the Colonel's nephew, sees clearly her reasons:

> Once or twice I drove her, and the moment we passed out through the dense wall of cottonwoods and tamarisks, she chatted incessantly, her sensitive face turned away from the wide sea of grass as if it were the plague, so that I swore she never saw the road runner racing with the carriage wheel or the antelope moving among the cattle. And I thought that at last I had begun to understand the reason for her wall of cottonwoods and tamarisks, which had not been planted for summer shade at all.

When constant entertaining and the birth of three children fail to settle Lutie into the routine of ranch life, she seeks diversion elsewhere. The town gossips take note of the fact that Lutie's third child, Brock, looks a lot like Brice Chamberlain. Finally, unable to endure the conditions of ranch living, Lutie decides to leave. She says to Hal, "I'm going where there's life, Hal. I'm going to balls and theaters and shaded streets and up-to-date stores and where every day people drive in the parks."

She pretends that her reason for leaving is Colonel Brewton's unfair treatment of nesters, but Hal takes notice that Brice Chamberlain plans to leave on the same train and would have done so had Colonel Brewton not been there on guard.

After some years have passed, during which the sea of grass is taken up by settlers, the old order is changed, and the Brewton children grow to young adulthood, Lutie returns. She comes at a time when Brock is pursuing a reckless life. He is killed and Lutie returns to the Colonel's ranch to make her peace with him. One of the town citizens remarks "It takes spunk to go to the old Colonel now . . . but then she always had it." Even the Colonel is willing to forget and forgive. He tells Hal, "It was a hard thing for a lady to go through. But she's one in a thousand, Hal. No one else will ever be like her." The reader is inclined to agree.

J. Frank Dobie said in *Life and Literature of the Southwest* that "Lutie, wife of the owner of the grass, is perhaps the most successful creation of a ranch wife that fiction has so far achieved." In spite of the fact that Lutie could never be coaxed to a roundup, that she could never come to any terms with the landscape, and that she returned after the children were grown and when her youth was gone, Dobie may be right. She is, by far, the best example of the effects of the Southwest on women "outsiders."

Arizona cattle country offers another locale as hard on women as Texas and New Mexico. Cattle baron Buck Johnson advertises in a Kansas City newspaper for a wife to come and share the vastness he loves in the story "The Rawhide" from Stewart Edward White's *Arizona Nights* (1937). With no thought for his wife's feelings, Buck brings her home to the ranch were, he assumes, she is completely happy. Estrella, his wife, is overwhelmed by all the nothing the desert has so much of. She becomes fascinated with the constricting properties of green rawhide and spends her many idle moments choking potatoes, gourds, and young cottonwood trees. Finally in desperation Estrella runs away with one of the ranch hands. When Buck catches up with the pair, he binds the couple together, kills a beef and covers them with the green hide and leaves them in the sun to think things over. White's story is bitter and, in spite of Buck's acknowledgment that he has not been fair to Estrella or considered how hard the desert was on her, without a satisfying ending. The story is effective in evoking the feeling of lonely ranch life where people lived out their lives without friends or neighbors knowing that they even existed much less how they felt.

Running away with ranch hands seems to be as good a solution as any for women who could not adjust to ranch life. Mae Horgan in *Jubal Troop* by Paul Wellman (1953) deliberately baits the hero in spite of the fact that Jubal tries hard to stay out of her way. Mae "had married Shep Horgan to escape the monotony of rural Indiana; she succeeded only in exchanging it for the deadlier monotony of the Dakota plains." She becomes "bored to a state of frenzy" and decides Shep's ranch hand, Jubal, can help her overcome her trying existence. Shep finds out about the two and feels honor bound to shoot it out with Jubal. In the end Shep is killed, Mae concocts a story about how Shep was defending her honor and a lynch mob goes after Jubal. Wellman apparently has little sympathy for Mae who uses men to get her what she wants. She is strong willed and scheming.

There were women who found it hard, even impossible, to adjust to ranch life but who stayed with it just the same. Probably many ranch wives found themselves in the same predicament of hating ranch living and yet, because of a sense of loyalty and duty to family and home, unable and unwilling to escape. It bears repeating that since ranchers and their families either lived so far away from civilization or else their duties on the range kept them from town contact, they often passed their days without anyone knowing much about how they lived or what their troubles were.

Matthilda Zachary in Alan LeMay's *The Unforgiven* (1957) must stay on a ranch far from civilization because she has a secret to keep. Her adopted daughter Rachel is an Indian. Knowing that the daughter will be ostracized, rejected, and even in some danger because of the hatred for Indians during that troubled frontier period, Matthilda, her daughter and her sons keep to themselves, fearing both races. The mother feels this way about the country:

> Matthilda Zachary would have hated and feared the prairie if no Indian had ever ridden it. The galling month-long winds, dust, mud, harshness—all this Matthilda could have forgiven. But she could not forgive what seemed to her the prairie's vast malignance, as boundless as its emptiness, and as mighty as its storms. . . . . For all its birdsongs, its flowers, and its wind-turned grass, the prairie kept changing into a horrid maw, that could swallow the labors of whole lifetimes in one savage night.

Eventually Rachel's heritage is revealed and trouble develops with both Indian and white. After an Indian attack in which Rachel does her part in defending the homestead, the novel ends on a note of hope that life may eventually work out for the family. One son notes that life for both women has been hard: "Maybe they got too much practice in facing up to the worst out there."

"I hate this place! It's nothing but wind and cold weather and dust and drought! And empty spaces." The dialogue tells what Martha thinks of ranch life in *Sam Chance* by Benjamin Capps (1965). She appears only briefly in the novel and if she adapts stoically, she never reconciles herself to life on the range. The loneliness is overwhelming. When her first baby is born she sobs: "I want to see my mother! I want to take my baby . . . and show her to my mother! I can't even . . . make her understand . . . what a grandma is!" Martha continues: "I want to go to church sometimes . . . and sing with other people! I want to see. . . Fort Griffin and Wichita . . . and places you see! I ought . . . to see some place . . . one time a year."

Chance devotes all his energies to ranching and is stunned when Martha dies at the early age of forty-two. She requests burial back in Tennessee, her girlhood home. Her son remarks in disbelief:

> "It's mother I don't understand." Then for a moment the boy, perhaps for the last time in his life, was a child again as he said, "I don't see why . . . she would ask to be buried so far away from home."

One of the most interesting types of modern ranch literature is the western parody in which writers gather up all the stock-in-trade situations, characters and clichés and present them in laughable style. They are important to the folklore of the West and of ranch life. The authors have come full circle back to the magazine and popular pulp material and created something unique from the standard situations involving shoot-outs, cattle drives, stampedes and over-wrought women.

Although Paul Patterson claims that he made no conscious effort to parody western life, he succeeds admirably in a book entitled *Sam McGoo and Texas Too* (1947). The author accomplishes his humor in the outrageous style of Davy Crockett's almanacs. The book is filled with typical cow-camp humor—boisterous and ridiculous.

Patterson begins by telling how the family in the story came West. They are forced to leave Rhode Island because Papa is a Rhode Island Red—a Communist. Papa is labeled communist because he thinks capitalism lets the rich have the capital and the poor have the "ism." The author explains, "The best cure for communism, naturally, is a nice big chunk of filthy capital, so the minute Papa got hold of that capital he was cured of communism." The family flees west with much of Providence in hot pursuit. After the family arrives it is Mama who takes the lead. When Indians threaten, it is Mama and the gun, Old Long Tom, together against the foe: "Mama fought silently, calmly. She let Long Tom do all the talking." All she had to show for her trouble was a charley horse in her trigger finger.

Papa is unable to make a living at the Horsehead Crossing on the Pecos, and since the couple cannot raise anything in the alkali, they raise children. Mama makes the living too. She shoes horses for a big cattle outfit. Some other comments about ranch females include: "Women seldom, if ever, wore evening gowns—too expensive. They were always getting their skirts tangled and mangled in their spurs." And this comment: "Willie never knew the secure comfort of a cradle. During his colicky spells his mother would take him up on a bad bucking horse and spur the critter in the shoulders." When Mama got lonesome and wanted a change of scenery, Papa called her to the dugout door where she "could stand and watch county after county blow by."

The hero of the story is the baby of the family, Gizbo. In telling of his courtship of a New England girl, Gizbo has something laughable to say concerning eastern women about whom Westerners have their own notions. When Gizbo meets his lady friend through a lonely hearts club she is "decked out in fancy, back-east riding clothes." The hero asks if she can ride and is surprised: "She went aboard like a western bronc skinner and helped me to scramble up behind the saddle." Later the horse throws Gizbo who tries to look graceful while he is falling in front of the lady. He finds landing difficult because, as he says, "one spur was hooked in the seat of my California pants and the other was fastened in the armhole of my beaded buckskin vest."

Gizbo tries hard to protect his eastern butterfly, Visalia, because he has taken a correspondence course in lovemaking and the course assured him that women want and need to be protected and dominated. The hero keeps fainting as they fall into one catastrophe after another. Gizbo explains:

> In these fiction romances they just ride along not noticing anything but each other's eyes, and reach their destinations just the same. It's not so in real life love—especially while crossing the serrated alkali flats of the Rawhide Country. If a feller didn't unlock his eyes, now and then, and glance at the road, he'd wind up in the bottom of a thirty-foot washout.

When Visalia falls into the water trying to get a closer look at a coyote, Gizbo tries to save her. Since he cannot swim, she saves him. (For four straight years she has been the intercollegiate swimming champion of New England!) When a villain enters the scene, Gizbo again goes forward to save the girl he loves or, as he puts it, "to fall beneath the lightning guns, or the iron shod hooves of his horse." Gizbo is knocked cold by the hooves of the horse and not the gun or the villain, but the heroine needs no protection. She gets the drop on the villain (she was also intercollegiate pistol champ) and ties him up.

Patterson wrote the book while serving with the army in Africa. His only purpose he said was to bring "his old Pecos life alive again."[10] The Pecos life not only lives, it roars in his funny book.

Other funny stories have grown out of traditional western situations. Roy Chanslor's *The Ballad of Cat Ballou* (1956) is one of them.

Cat, "nemesis of the hated Purple Valley Cattlemen's Association, avenger of the dispossessed," a Jezebel to some, a symbol of adventure and freedom to "desperate women" and "hopeless spinsters" is straight out of a dime novel. Born during a thunderstorm under the omen of a burning spruce tree, Cat later keeps company with Clay Boone and Kid Sheleen, the killer with the ice-blue eyes. Cat is a romping, stomping rancher's daughter and her antics are second only to those of Kid Sheleen, the drunken, used-to-be gunfighter. The novel has been made into a movie which won an Oscar for Lee Marvin, although Marvin himself thought the horse should have shared the prize.

Another rambunctious heroine appears in Robert Flynn's *North to Yesterday*, a novel about men who make a cattle drive north to a town that used to be called Trails' End, some ten years after the trail is closed. The difficulties imposed by a closed trail, such as fences and towns, make for moments of high comedy. The story is, as well, about traditions—range traditions—where there is no range. No matter that the group could have crossed the river over a bridge, the crew fords the river and drowns a hand. No matter that the horses get stolen, the men will herd on foot. No matter that only one farmer-turned-cowboy owns a gun, he will use it in defense of the herd when he isn't busy shooting part of the herd. Tradition must be maintained, even when the untraditional, anti-heroine turns up wandering by the river with an illegitimate baby in her arms.

The men are determined to cherish and protect her in spite of the fact that to do so is like trying to cherish and protect a bobcat. Covina lets the men know early that she will not help the cook and intends to herd cattle. When Covina begins to swear again, Lampassas tells her how things must be even if she does have a "stray" baby:

> "I'm a man," explained Lampassas. "And a man that works with cows all day has a right to cuss now and then."
> "I'm a woman, and I'm just as good as any goddam man and I've got the same goddam rights."
> "No goddam woman has the right to cuss," Lampassas said.
> "I can do anything any goddam man can do," Covina said.
> "You think you're pretty mean, don't you?" Lampassas said. "Well, I've seen wilder heifers than you milked in a gourd."

It turns out, however, that no one has met up with a heifer as wild as Covina. She holds up her end of the herding, uses her head, sees with unclouded vision and puts the others in her debt. Before the group reaches the end of the trail the men respect Covina more than any respectable woman they ever met. She is one of the most memorable females of western literature and she becomes so without a horse.

Robert Flynn explains his novel and he explains something about folklore as well. He believes that life, like the cattle drive in *North to Yesterday*, is a quest. Everyone goes armed with their own traditions which either hold up or do not hold up. Often people find that they have a new set of traditions at the end of the quest.[11]

There are two ranch women in Richard Condon's spoof *A Talent for Loving* (1961). While many of the standard western clichés are reversed, none is funnier than when the Indians rescue the whites from a cavalry massacre. One female, Marilyn Ridgeway, is a naturalist interested in cattle raising. Her motto is, "I care not who writes my nation's hymns if I may breed its beef." She frolics with the Blackfeet, Comanches and Mescaleros. When Marilyn meets Jim, the hero, he encourages her to get her college degree. He says, "You got to learn all you can. I don't know nothin'."

Evalina is the other vigorous virgin who learns of an old Aztec curse placed upon the women in her family which says that after her first kiss she will be possessed with a talent for loving. While all the other women in the family are embarrassed by the curse, Evalina is delighted.

There are so many novels which depict ranch life either seriously or laughably that it is possible to mention only a few representative ones. There is also nonfiction written by women on ranches and their accounts prove in fact what novelists proposed in fiction. Mary Taylor Bunton remembered how it was to trail a herd in *A Bride on the Old Chisholm Trail.* Mary Kidder Rak's *A Cowman's Wife* tells with charm and humor how ranch life was for a woman in the Chiricahua Mountains of southeast Arizona. *Interwoven* relates the story of two West Texas ranching families, the Matthews and the Reynolds, whose lives were intertwined through marriage and business partnerships. The biography is by Sally Reynolds Matthews. One of the most entertaining factual accounts of New Mexico ranch life is Agnes Morley Cleaveland's *No Life For A Lady.* Thanks to Mrs. Cleaveland's style the book reads more like a novel; she tells of the hardships of the range, of horses, of bear hunts, of the unchaperoned pleasures of ranch children and of a woman's usefulness in cow country. Eulalia Bourne in *Woman in Levis* writes in a humorous vein about her life as an independent cattlewoman and teacher in Arizona. She is especially good at revealing what men think of a woman who is also a rancher. *Hell on Women and Horses* by Alice Marriott destroys the myth of the title of the book by discovering in the lives of real ranch women that range life may have been hell on the horses, but the ladies had a pretty good time. *This I Can Leave You* contains the recollections of a Texas ranch wife, Mamie Burns, while she lived on the Pitchfork Ranch. *Heart-Diamond* by Kathy Greenwood gives in rich detail her life growing up on a small ranch in Southeastern New Mexico.

In the twenty-first century, books will provide most of the information about ranch life, cowgirls and cowboys. As marketing changes, as ranches adjust to new demands on the kinds and quality of cattle, as caretaker roles change on the range, as the range itself alters, information about life on the cattle ranches of the past, of which this era is now becoming a part, will come from books. There is still more research and collecting to be done.

12

Pauline Out West: the Cowgirl in the Movies

Roy Rogers and Dale Evans are smiling bravely at each other as they buckle on their silverplated holsters over their embroidered britches. Dale speaks: "Roy, the rustlers are stealing all of my cattle. The well is dry. The creek is poisoned. Mama is dead and Papa is captured. Hadn't we better ride fast?" "Why yes, Dale. We sure ought to, but do you think we could sing just one more verse of 'My Adobe Hacienda' before we go?"

The movie conversation is, of course, imaginary but the plot, songs included, is not stretching the truth too far from what the golden era of grade B westerns were really like. Thousands of youngsters in the 1930s and 1940s spent many a Saturday afternoon taking a deep seat and a short rein to watch Roy and Dale and Gene and Lash and a score of others act out what surely must have been the way it really was for stouthearted cowboys and cowgirls on the range.

If ever a medium exploited the western myth, it was the movies. Because westerns tended to lump all frontier women together whether they were saloon girls, cavalry colonel's daughters, school marms, Indian maidens, or prospectors' daughters, it was easy to toss cowgirls in the heap with the rest. If they could ride a horse, they qualified as western. Consequently the movies left such a tangled web that it will not soon be straightened out and maybe never.

Serials, short one-or two-reel movies, were popular with early filmmakers. Western heroines, whether cowgirls or not, were among the first on screens and made an impression on the minds of the public about what life was like for a woman in the West during pioneer times.

The first serials, *What Happened to Mary* in 1912 by the Edison Company and *The Adventures of Kathlyn* in 1913 by the Selig Company, proved that women were worth watching. Then in 1914, *The Hazards of Helen*, produced by the Kalem Company, featured a "girl telegrapher who kept the railroad running regardless of the obstacles placed in the path." The role was played first by Helen Holmes whose specialty was western films. Later Helen Holmes was replaced by Helen Gibson, a real western woman who had ridden with the Miller Brothers' 101 Show. In 1911, the 101 Show closed in Venice, California, leaving the riders stranded and unemployed. Some, including Helen Gibson, found work in pictures. The pay was eight dollars a week. Helen rode her horse to work each day from Venice to Topango Canyon, where scenes for western movies were shot.[1]

The action of the serials was pure dime novel stuff and the heroines performed in a variety of situations, many of them supposedly in the West.[2] Such titles as *The Fighting Trail*, with Carol Holloway; *The Terror of the Range*, played by Betty Compson; *The Riddle Rider*, featuring Ellen Sedwick wearing men's bib overalls; *The Way of a Man*, written by Emerson Hough and starring Ellene Ray; and *The Vanishing Rider* with Ethlyne Clair, all attest to the popularity of western women.[3]

Texas Guinan was another early filmmaker. She worked for the Bulls Eye Corporation. Texas began life in 1883 as Mary Louise Cecilia on the Guinan ranch near Waco, Texas. Her parents planned a musical career for her, but she left home to ride broncs in a circus. The ability to handle horses eventually led to a Hollywood job. Sometimes referred to as "the female Bill Hart," Texas was in demand as a female gunslinger.[4] According to author Paul Sann, she was "one of the most authentic lady gunslingers on the celluloid prairie. In those days she had a mop of black hair menacing enough to scare off the villain even without a six-shooter."[5]

Texas Guinan's own personality did more than a little to twist the cowgirl image, distorting Texas cowgirls in particular.

After her film career Mary Louise made it big in nightclubs in the 1920s with her famous greeting, "Hello Sucker." It was said that she did everything from wearing peach satin pajamas, reading Dostoevski by the "light of twenty-two onyx lamps and fourteen candelabra," to running a thrift store for the poor.[6] As one reporter put it, "Her attack on life is frontal. She has no more repressions or reflections than a plate of corned beef. She is just a square meal for men's need to be dazzled."[7] Texas' scrapes with the law during Prohibition were well publicized. Once she sang this song after returning from a session with a judge:

> Judge Thomas said, "Tex, do you sell booze?" I said, "Please, don't be silly. I swear to you my cellar's filled with chocolate and vanilly."[8]

The *New York Telegram* of August 6, 1928, reported on one of Texas' trips to court. She wore the following:

> One black straw hat. One rope of pearls. She said they were pearls. One lace-edged black veil, last used at Valentino's funeral. One black dress, the hem trimmed with thingummies. One pair of silk stockings, both without holes. One pair of patent leather slippers, with rhinestone buckles extending almost to the knees. One pair of white doeskin gloves, very refined. One diamond ring weighing three-and-a-half pounds. She once hooked a five-pounder, but it got away.

In spite of Texas Guinan's boisterous reputation in both films and nightclubs, most critics declared that the public liked her honesty and style.[9]

Bertha Blancett worked for the Bison Moving Picture Company as a stunt girl.[10] Prairie Lillie Allen supplied stock for motion pictures.[11] In 1916, Mildred Douglas and Dorothy Morrell wintered in Los Angeles and performed as extras in pictures, riding or walking through western scenes. They were paid ten dollars a day and received a box lunch at noon consisting of fried chicken, sandwiches and fruit. "It was," Mildred said, "like being on a picnic."[12]

The women of the earliest western movies were not usually designated as cowgirls but rather fell into the category of western heroines. The ladies wore long dresses and sunbonnets, and were depicted as pioneers. According to movie historians George Fennin and William Everson, the heroine was shown as a "full-fledged companion of the pioneer, certainly his equal, and occasionally possessed of an inner strength that made her his superior."[13]

As soon as the heroine was established on a ranch, strange things began to happen. Sometimes the movies took two steps backward by reducing her to a fainting, helpless, hand-wringer constantly in need of rescue or smelling salts. A kiss might have revived her, but the hero's kisses were saved for the horses. Cowgirls in some movies before the twenties were usually daughters or nieces keeping house for the men folks. Mothers were almost nonexistent, and presumed dead. About the only reference to Mama is when Daddy occasionally murmurs, "Ah, if only your mother were here." Generally, it was easier with the mother out of the way for the villain to force his attentions on the heroine, steal her land and cattle, and fistfight the hero. That the heroine is daddy's girl explains her expert horsemanship and her love of the out-of-doors.[14] In other words, western movie women were much like the early dime novel heroines or those found in the tales of Cooper, except that the ladies were doing their fainting out on the lone prairie rather than in the forest.

There were plenty of movies in which cowgirls did get in on the action. In *Frontier Days in the Early West* (1910) a woman dresses like a man and rides her own horse in a race. Two sisters in *Western Girls* (1912) disguise themselves in cowboy clothes, capture some stage robbers, and bring them at gunpoint to the sheriff.[15] In *Billy the Kid* (1911) a girl dressed as a man escapes from bandits without any assistance from the hero.[16] In 1918, Blanch Bates in *The Border Legion*, based on Zane Grey's novel, was featured in wild rides across rugged country; she shot a man during a struggle.[17] Women were sometimes allowed to ride for the posse as in *The Smuggler's Daughter* (1912)[18] and in *The Half-Breed's Plan* (1911).[19]

In *Rowdy Ann* (1919) the main character played by Fay Tincher is sent away from the family ranch to college to be educated. She wears her six-guns to class and comedy prevails throughout the film. Myrtle Steadman rides in roundups in *The Law and the Outlaws* (1913).[20] In 1915 *Bronco Billy's Sentence* featured Virginia Ames shooting with a lever-action rifle. When Billy hides in Miss Ames' ranch house she appears to be helpless in a physical struggle. After he kisses her and tries to run away, the heroine, however, proves she is not afraid when she can get her hands on a rifle. Before Anderson can escape she takes aim and hits the hero square in the head. She aims to kill and that she does not quite succeed is the fault of the script.[21]

One of the best cowgirl-in-action heroines was Ruth Delaney in *The Prairie Pirate.* When the Mexican bandit, Aguilar, rides up to the ranch house with evil in his eye, Ruth, clad in dress and cape, sees the danger. To bar the door, she begins throwing the furniture around much as if she had hold of a wild steer. Grabbing her trusty pistol the heroine begins to pick off Aguilar's men one by one. Just when things are going her way the script calls for her to hide in the cellar beneath the floor. Aguilar soon discovers her hiding place and peers down. He thinks about going after Ruth but considering the toll she has taken on his men, the bandit reconsiders for awhile. Besides, it is dark down there. The scene changes. Ruth's brother returns home. Something is mighty wrong. Examining the ground near the house, the brother discovers cigarette butts. Knowing that his sister would never take up nasty habits, the hero immediately suspects foul play. He eventually discovers his sister's body in the cellar. A note says, "Bandits coming. I won't let them take me." Making good that famous threat to save the last bullet for herself in order to avoid a fate worse than death, the heroine has killed herself.[22]

Cowgirls continued as plot motivators into the 1920s, when William S. Hart thrilled moviegoers. Hart specialized in roles in which he played the good bad man whose regeneration was often accomplished through the love of a good woman.[23] Hart's women, however, were usually different from the conventional heroine who had to be rescued from another man in the name of virtue. Many of the women in Hart's films were seductive villainesses and "his relations with them were a working arrangement involving money and sex, no questions asked, no answers given." When Hart occasionally encountered a virtuous lady, he either ran from her or "accomplished seduction, followed by remorse and a tragic death of atonement."[24]

Other ladies were taking part in some of the action as evidenced in a series of movies made by Ruth Mix in the twenties. The first film, *That Girl Oklahoma*, and those which followed featured "elaborate stunt work and trick riding."[25] Other cowgirls such as Ruth Roach appeared as extras in movies made at the 101 Ranch during the same era. *Trail Dust* was completely filmed on the 101 and parts of *North of 36* were filmed there.[26]

In the 1930s movie heroines really began to catch up with the Amazons of dime novels. The ladies became "more self-reliant, more athletic, and even sexier."[27] Occasionally a heroine was even given a part more important than the hero's. *The Singing Cowgirl* starring Dorothy Page was such a film. One of the first nude scenes appeared in *To The Last Man*. Esther Ralston not only took her clothes off but she fought the villain in behalf of the hero. Such films as *Gun Fire* and *When a Man's a Man* featured love triangles— something new for westerns.

While western wardrobes in the thirties were usually authentic, the costumes were noticeably formfitting and the camera moved in for tight closeups when the cowgirls mounted their horses. Fenin and Everson found that the only "inaccurate costuming" was in the use of Angora chaps. As an example, they point out that comics such as Jack Benny in *Buck Benny Rides Again* wore Angora chaps. The experts conclude that the furry leggings were used for a slapstick effect and that "the appearance of an actor in these chaps always brought forth gales of laughter from the supporting cast." Fenin and Everson are mistaken about the Angora chaps. Cattlemen and cattlewomen, particularly in the cold Northwest, and cowboys and cowgirls in Wild West shows and rodeo wore Angora chaps and they did not wear them for any comic effect. Working ranch people wore them for protection and warmth. Rodeo performers may have used them as part of a costume, but they were an authentic piece of costuming, not merely cute ornamentation. Perhaps Hollywood found the chaps amusing, and Jack Benny in Angora was a howl because a dude was wearing them, but, if chaps became associated with laughter, it was because Hollywood influenced our thinking on the subject.

In the 1940s and the 1950s, which may be considered the modern era of western heroines, three kinds of women appeared: women who take it all off, women who keep it all on, and singing girl pards.

Jane Russell in *The Outlaw* had the most to show by taking her clothes off, and with Jane around, the heroes wasted no more time kissing horses. The plot eventually boils down to a poker game, the winner of which gets his choice of Rio (the heroine) or the horse. The winner takes the horse. The heroine is certainly not a cowgirl, but critics of the film pointed out that "the logical conclusion is drawn that in the West a woman was an enjoyable luxury, but a horse was an absolute necessity."[28] *Duel in the Sun* featured a "torrid love affair between lecherous Gregory Peck and sensual half-breed Jennifer Jones against an epic background of empire building."[29] *Man Without a Star*, filmed in the 1950s, made use of bathtub scenes. While none of these movies used cowgirl heroines, the films nevertheless added some new dimensions to the personalities of traditional heroines. Short skirts, bare legs, unbuttoned flimsy blouses and men's pants at least a size too small said a good deal more than words about what western heroines had become, on the screen at least.

There were films in which the heroine left all her clothes on. Such films as *Fort Apache*, *Rio Grande*, and *She Wore A Yellow Ribbon* featured women in traditional long skirts and high-necked bodices, and, according to the critics, they enjoyed great popularity.[30] While dressed and undressed heroines who were rarely cowgirls appeared in western films of the 1940s and 1950s, the hard-riding, gun-toting, lariat-swinging girl pard managed to capture the attention of a portion of the movie-going public, although the group was primarily Saturday afternoon kid gangs. The best example of the movie pard was Roy Rogers' friend, Dale Evans. Dale was pretty, honest, quick on the draw, helpful, and in addition she could sing a mean duet with Roy.

A 1970s movie proves that the girl sport did not completely disappear from films with the social changes of the sixties. *J. W. Coop* has some good moments about modern rodeo. Big Marge appears briefly, one long pigtail trailing down her back, freckles on her nose, offering the hero a bear hug. Although she sports a vocabulary of curse words which is some concession to modern filmmaking, Marge is similar to dime novel sports. She is one of the boys, offers no threat to the hippie heroine but is her friend. She is large of body and heart. To modern viewers her presence is comic. Similarly, Kim Darby in *True Grit* is a pard-type who is able to fend for herself among outlaws or with John Wayne and Glen Campbell.

The western heroine's role in movies from the past to the present is often confusing. One critic says that the heroine is depicted either as the "weak and defenseless female, without any personality of her own, essentially dependent on the hero," or as "the titillatingly sexual and aggressive heroine."[31] The visual medium which might have done the most *for* the cowgirl did not seem to know what to do *with* her. Some of the blame probably can be placed on such people as the editors, screenplay writers, camera men, and even makeup men and their personal biases toward western women. Directors, actresses, and costume designers should probably bear the heaviest blame.

Directors of westerns seemed to have strong ideas about the West. John Ford, for instance, is accused of depicting the West not as it was but as it should have been. Heroines of such Ford movies as *Rio Grande*, *She Wore a Yellow Ribbon*, and *Fort Apache* are wearers of long dresses and behave like ladies because, apparently, that is the way John Ford directed their part. Costumes are picturesque. Joanne Dru in *She Wore a Yellow Ribbon* is pictured sitting sidesaddle and wearing a soldier's cap and coat. Supposedly that is the way women who lived in army camps dressed.[32] Once when asked if Ford agreed with the speech in *Liberty Valance* in which the editor declares,

"When the legend becomes a fact, print the legend," the filmmaker replied that he would, if it was good for the country.[33] Cecil B. DeMille, who was considered a showman, directed *The Plainsman*, a highly romanticized version of the life of Wild Bill Hickok. Gary Cooper played Hickok and Jean Arthur played Calamity Jane. The picture abounds in DeMille's "weakness for fancy dress and corny lines."[34] Jean Arthur gets more than her share of the corn as she pops a whip and strikes manly poses with her hands on her hips.

The actresses themselves no doubt added their own bit of confusion to the image of western women primarily because they were trained in a certain way of standing, walking and behaving on the screen. For instance in *An Arizona Wooing*, a 1915 silent movie starring Tom Mix, the heroine, played by Jean Dixon, uses all the poses taught in acting schools. She flutters her eyelashes, stands with one toe on point and lifts her hands to her face. The heroine dresses authentically and rides astride, attempting to help the hero when he is captured and tied up by a Mexican. About the most she manages is to pull on the bandit's sleeve, bat her eyes in wide alarm, and mouth what appears to be "Oo, Oo."[35]

Another aspect of the acting problem was that no female star of any stature ever made westerns her special field. The names of John Wayne, Gary Cooper, and Jimmy Stewart are generally linked to western pictures, but only Maureen O'Hara's name turns up more than a few times in major western pictures. Everyone from Majorie Main to Marilyn Monroe seems to have been qualified to star in westerns.

Still another reason for the distorted view of western women may be attributed to costume designers. In *North of 36*, which contained a real ranch heroine if there ever was one, Taisie Lockhart was played by a "delicately coiffured leading lady who brought into each scene suggestions of a Connecticut riding academy."[36] A critic for the *New York Times* was concerned because "one minute she is wearing rough, checkcloth knickerbockers and in the next she appears in billowing finery."[37]

It is difficult, perhaps impossible, to know why directors or actresses, or costume designers were bent on turning ranch women into something a little more refined, a little more agreeable to their idea of how western heroines behaved and dressed. Why real life heroic females who could ride, rope, punch cattle, make beds, cook meals, and birth babies have never found much acceptance as movie heroines is perhaps a question that puzzles only Westerners. But it is somewhat like a rank stranger telling you that he does not care for your favorite Aunt Bessie, that she is crude, sort of plain and a little embarrassing. With a little makeup and a change of clothes, however, and a little care about her tongue and her manners, she might learn to pass for any ordinary person.

One adequate picture of a ranch woman appeared in the 1958 film *The Big Country*, directed by William Wyler and starring Gregory Peck, Charlton Heston, Carroll Baker, and Jean Simmons. Carroll Baker plays the spoiled daughter of a wealthy Texas rancher (Charles Bickford). She brings her eastern dude fiancé, Gregory Peck, home to the ranch and immediately begins to think Peck is more of a dude than she bargained for when he refuses to stop the ranchhands from playfully roughing him up. Charlton Heston, who plays the foreman, and Peck, the antitraditional hero, work things out in an all-night fistfight in which neither wins. Since Miss Baker does not see the fight she begins to think less and less of Peck.

Meanwhile a supporting plot develops. Miss Baker's closest friend, Jean Simmons, is the owner of another ranch on which there is a hole of water called the Big Muddy. Both ranches, along with a third ranch owned by Burl Ives, have always used Big Muddy. Miss Baker's father tries to convince Miss Simmons that she should sell the water hole to him so that he can cut out the third party's use of it. Miss Simmons seeks the counsel of Peck who decides to buy it himself assuring that all three ranches may water their herds there. After a lot of ridin', shootin', and fistfightin', Peck also gets Miss Simmons.

Both women in the film are effective. They are dressed appropriately in ankle-length buckskin, boots, and hats. Their mannerisms are believable. They ride well enough. Even Miss

Simmon's English accent is not offensive. There were, after all, Englishwomen on the lone prairie in pioneer times. Most important of all they are vigorous, active women capable of managing their own affairs. They speak up to the men and their opinions are sometimes listened to. Miss Baker and Miss Simmons come close to the genuine article in spite of the fact that the film was not widely acclaimed by critics.[38]

There are other worthy western films but *The Big Country* seems about as good a film as any to compare and contrast with early westerns, to offer some conclusions about Hollywood's part in the folklore of the West and the reasons some embrace the lore and some reject it. Early films were primarily action and adventure. No viewer was required to think too deeply about the whys or wherefores—why the cowgirl in the film had just had her hair waved at the beauty parlour and wherefore did she get that awful habit of batting her eyes at the hero. Most theatergoers were watching the heroine shoot, rope, faint, run, scream, cry, or ride, ride, ride. Hollywood declared that was the way women in the West behaved. If they were not exactly right, neither were they entirely wrong. Not many real life cowgirls would mind being remembered that way. Maybe the early movies were not as bad as all that.

A heroine in a film such as *The Big Country* differs drastically in some ways from early western girls and in some ways not at all. The heroine rides, looks after the cattle, worries about the water holes, and oversees the ranch—many of the same tasks performed by her earlier celluloid sisters. The contemporary film actress, however, has one extra and important qualification. She *thinks.* The emphasis is not only on action but also on what the heroine thinks about the action. She is concerned with questions of right and wrong, of good and bad, of the codes which men in her part of the world uphold, and of how she figures into the scheme of things. The switch from action to thought, or better yet a combination of action and thought, may yet bring about more satisfying westerns.

One final opinion. Perhaps Hollywood's greatest sin is confusing ranch women with other frontier-pioneer types. When, occasionally, a viewer can cut out a cowgirl from the rest of the herd, she does not always come off too badly. Rather the cowboy image suffered the most. Cowboys rarely got thrown in with the bunch, but remained a distinct movie type. One thing at least may be said for filmed cattlewomen when you could find them: They all had better sense than to kiss horses.

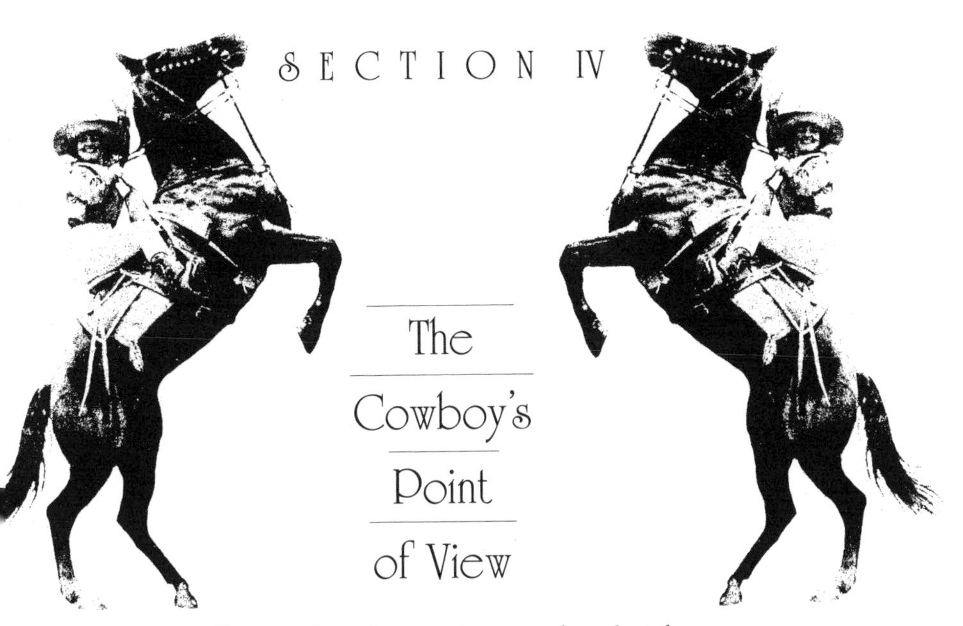

SECTION IV

The Cowboy's Point of View

No appraisal of women in general or of cattle women in particular would be complete without the man's point of view. In his songs and in his jokes and funny stories the cowboy tells it like it is—or like it isn't, depending on your point of view. What cowmen expressed about the women also added dimension and substance to the cowgirl heroine. The vote is not in yet on whether men did the cowgirl any favors.

13

My Love is a Rider

The songs the cowboys sang on the trail, around the campfire, with the herd, and later into a microphone or on records told a lot about their life—what they wore, what they did, what tickled them and made them laugh, what made them sad, what constituted bravery or cowardice. The songs which spoke of women proved that there were all kinds of heifers on the range and that cowboys knew them all.

Whether the girls approved or not cowboys were often likely to describe the fair sex in terms of cows. In Larry Chittenden's "Cowboy's Christmas Ball" the singer calls "Lock horns ter all them heifers and rustle them like men;/ Saloot yer lovely critters; now swing and let 'em go."[1] In another dance song:

> She ranges in the Live Oak branch;
> The purtiest heifer at the ranch;
> With hazel eyes an' golden hair
> An try to steal 'er if you dare.[2]

Some girls were pretty like Miss Mollie: "She was a lovely western girl, as lovely as could be;/ She was so tall, so handsome, so charming, and so fair."[3]

"The Colorado Trail" declares:

> Eyes like the morning star,
> Cheek like a rose,
> Laura was a pretty girl,
> God almighty knows.[4]

Not all cowboys were as kind, however. Lackey Bill says of a Texas girl: "She was a handsome figure though not so very tall;/ Her hair was red as blazes—I hate it worst of all."[5] Certain habits were noticed in songs. One rancher points out, perhaps with admiration, that "She loved her red liquor which served a man so."[6]

Horses often got top billing in a song. "Speckles" is really about a horse, but the cowboy pauses a moment to describe Mollie: "Old Speckles was saddled, I grabbed my gun, picked Mollie up as I passed;/ With the grit of her kind she hung on behind and never a question asked."[7] "A Cowboy's Prize" sings of another named Mollie. The fellow says that there "never was no gal like Mollie," that she was "hottern a hot tamale." True as steel and a real beauty is this prize. It turns out, however, that Mollie is a horse the man won in a raffle.[8]

Occasionally cowgirls get equal time with horses. Some girls can ride broncs "slick en keerless/ as everybody knows."[9] In "The Santa Fe Trail" one cowboy sees a girl on horseback he will never forget:

> I seen her ride down the arroyo,
> Way back on the Arkansas sands;
> She had smiles like an acre of sunflowers
> And a quirt in her little brown hand.
> She mounted her pinto so airy,
> She rode like she carried the mail;
> And her eyes near set fire to the prairie,
> Longside of the Santa Fe Trail.[10]

"Arizona Boys and Girls" sings of how you can tell a good girl. In addition to dipping snuff, a good girl has no trimming, or laces, and no nonsense. She wears a "long-eared" bonnet and "She'll marry you if you are broke or if you have the tin."[11]

While cowboys seemed to have various opinions in their descriptions of range women, all agreed about unfaithful females. In "The Trail to Mexico" a puncher goes home to find that his sweetheart has married. He swears he will go back West "Where the girls are few and the boys are true/ And a false hearted love I never knew," and where the "girls are good day after day and do not live just for pay."[12]

Many other men found, however, that the range had very nearly cornered the market on infidelity. One tries to marry a rich rancher's daughter. She is "pretty, tall and handsome, both neat and very fair." When her intended crosses the plains she sends him a letter saying she has married someone else.[13] Another loved a brown-eyed girl by the last name of Lee in Bell County, Texas. The mother objects and emphasizes her dislike by aiming a six-shooter at the cowboy. He ends the song,

> I pressed her to my aching heart
> And kissed her a last farewell,
> And prayed a permanent prayer to God
> To send her Ma to hell.[14]

A drover from Midland falls in love with a "good woman's daughter upon the north side" in "The Lovesick Cowboy." When she finds another he says, "Don't depend on a woman—you're beat if you do."[15] Yet another puts it in stronger language:

> Now I've got no use for women,
> A true one may seldom be found.
> They use a man for his money;
> When it's gone they turn him down.
> They're all alike at the bottom;
> Selfish and grasping for all,
> They'll stay with a man while he's winning,
> And laugh in his face at his fall.[16]

Even some eastern girls prove untrue when they get to the West. In "The Peeler's Lament" the man asks an eastern girl to marry him. She says she has always "craved for a hell-roarin life." He lifts "her into the right stirrup astride,/ And we doubled that horse to parson's warm side."[17] The marriage does not last long.

Mexican women, another group about whom cowboys sing, often do not fare too well in the end, but at least they are all faithful and helpful.

A Texan by the name of Mustang Gray once had reason to be grateful for the help of a señorita when he was captured and held prisoner in Monterrey. The song tells:

> A señorita loved him,
> And followed by his side;
> She opened the gates and gave to him
> Her father's steed to ride.
>
> God bless the señorita,
> The belle of Monterrey,
> She opened wide the prison door,
> And let him ride away.[18]

There are other versions of the song, but all feature an "Anglo-American who provokes the undying love of a Mexican maiden who will deny her ties of family, country and even her religion, if need be, to serve her cowboy hero."[19]

"Lasca," a poem composed by Frank Desprez, describes another Mexican beauty who saves the life of her lover by throwing her body on top of his during a stampede. The maiden's charms are many:

> Lasca used to ride
> On a mouse-gray mustang close to my side,
> With a blue serape and bright-belled spur;
> I laughed with joy as I looked at her!
> Little she knew of books or of creeds;
> An Ave Maria sufficed her needs.

Lasca is killed in the stampede and her cowboy remembers fondly "She would hunger that I might eat,/ Would take the bitter and leave me the sweet."[20]

Two songs mention women outlaws of the West. Both songs are claimed by Jack Thorp, collector and author of many cowboy songs. The first ditty tells a story about the Overland Stage as it stops to pick up a woman passenger. Thorp notices that the lady is "bridle-wise," that she is slim and girlish, that she has the devil in her eyes because she wears her shawl "Spanish-wise." She makes a man want to protect her. Later however, the female passenger pulls out a Winchester and robs the stage. She cuts a horse loose from the team and gallops away.[21] Although the stage robber is not named, Thorp calls several names in "Women Outlaws." He mentions Bronco Sue, probably Bronco Sue Yonker who once lived near Tularosa, New Mexico. It is said that Sue raised fine horses, swore expertly and passed "pleasant moments with the cowboys in roundup camps."[22] Belle Starr, Shudders, Pike Kate, Altar Doane, Calamity Jane, Sister Cummings and Rose of Cimmaron complete the roll. Rose, no doubt, was the same Rose who rode with the Doolin gang in Oklahoma and who loved Bitter Creek Newcomb. Thorp obviously admired the women outlaws:

> Hunted by many a posse,
> Always on the run,
> Every man's hand against them,
> They fought, and often won.
>
> With a price upon each head,
> They'd have to fight and stand,
> And die as game as any man
> With a gun in either hand.[23]

While many cowboy songs favor cows and horses over women, moan about the unfaithful Anglo-Saxon girls, or take only passing notice of prairie lasses in general, there are a few songs in which ranch women are the main order of business. "The Little Cowgirl" by Jack Thorp tells of a young woman's life on the range. She says that her family came to the ranch in a wagon, that they brought all their stock and horses with them, and that, as she puts it, "We was all raised with cattle/, So I guess it's in our blood." The girl loves dances and to hear her dad play "Turkey in the Straw." Although her family is not stylish, they own a good ranch and a horse pasture that "runs clear down to the branch." She is contented and feels fortunate to have hinges on the door, a pair of shop-made boots, and some silver-mounted spurs. Life on the range could not be any better for the cowgirl:

I've got a young cow-puncher roped,
I've got him on my string,
En everything is lovely,
We'll be married in the spring.[24]

The heroine in "Fair Lady of the Plains" is a capable ranch woman ready and able to fight. Her husband tells how she helped him herd cattle "through hard, stormy rains" and how she spent all one season at the roundup. He adds, "She would drink with me from the cold, bitter cup." The woman's husband taught her to "use a six-shooter in both of her hands" and never to run "as long as loads lasted in either gun." In the spring the wife goes along to help with a herd of wild steers. When Indians attack she wakes up "the battle to fight." Amid pouring rain, lightning and thunder the wife takes a bullet in the brain and is killed.[25]

The "Pecos River Queen" supposedly grew out of an incident about a woman on the range by the name of Patty Moorhead. Jack Thorp said he heard about Patty from Roy Bean and composed the song about her. As he tells it:

She's known by all the cowboys on the Pecos River wide;
They know full well that she can shoot, that she can rope and ride;
She goes to every round-up, every cow-work without fail.
Looking out for all her cattle branded "walking hog on rail."

She made her start in cattle, yes, made it with her rope;
Can tie down e'ry maverick 'fore it can strike a lope;
She can rope and tie and brand as quick as any man;
She's voted by all cowboys as A1 top cow-hand.

When a puncher tells Patty he would risk anything for her sake, she invites him to ride his horse over the high railroad bridge on the Pecos River as she does. The suitor refuses and so Patty is left without a mate.[26]

Most lovers of cowboy songs are familiar with the sad "Little Joe the Wrangler." I asked one retired puncher-friend what he thought about the song. He replied that he used to cry every time he heard it.[27] Asked if he had ever heard "Little Joe the Wrangler's Sister Nell," the man said "No, but if it's any sadder than Little Joe, I don't want to hear it." I allowed as how it was sadder and spared him the pain. The sequel to "Little Joe" tells of how his twin sister Nell rode up to the herd looking for her lost brother. She was a "slender little figure dressed in grey," and ready for herding cattle:

> An old slouch hat with a hole on top was perched
> upon her head,
> She'd a pair of rawhide chaps, well greased and worn,
> And an old twin rig all scratched and scarred
> from workin' in the brush,
> And a slick mague tied to her saddle horn.

Although Joe failed to mention a twin in his song, she repeats the story which Joe has already told about how Papa took another wife after Mama died and that "She beat us and abused us, and she starved us most the time." The drovers decide which is the best way to tell Nell of Joe's death. Next morning Nell is on the job:

> "I'll wrangle in the mornin' boys," she says as she turns in.
> "I'll have the horses at the wagon 'fore it's day."
> As the mornin' star was risin' I saw the kid roll out,
> Saddle up the grey night horse and ride away.[28]

When Nell sees Joe's horse with the herd she knows he is dead.

"Little Joe the Wrangler's Sister Nell" probably was written long after "Little Joe." The song does not seem to be widely known. As one authority, Katie Lee, puts it, Nell "sure knew a bunch more about working cattle than her twin brother."[29]

Miss Pompey Stiles is another cowgirl worth knowing. She appears prominently in "The Dying Desperado." Pomp's boyfriend describes her:

> She's a shore plumb good-un, you don't meet 'em every day.
> Could spin the longest windy, could rope the biggest steer,
> And ride the wildest bronco that stands upon its ear.
>
> She ain't much on the figger and don't give a damn for styles,
> Her father was a hog-thief; and her brother was doin' well
> 'Till he went to liftin' cattle, and was caught and sent to hell.[30]

The cowboy knew Pompey well enough to want to marry her. She had saved his life once in a dance hall by shooting out the light so that he could escape. Later in the song, when the hero is made sheriff, his first duty is to shoot Bill Trencher in the head when he finds Pompey in Bill's arms. Pompey is a little dismayed: "Pomp sort of jumped aside and made a little frown./ You shot too high that time. Aim a little further down."

There are other rambunctious females in cowboy songs. One appears in a paraphrased and probably expurgated version of "My Love Is A Rider." First sung about a cowboy, the song is filled with "lusty sexual symbolism . . . that pictures the cowboy as a potent lover who woos a maiden by jumping in the saddle, riding the bronco, swinging the rawhide."[31] When the cowboy uses the woman as the object of the song (sometimes Belle Starr's name is mentioned) then the woman becomes the lusty sexual symbol. The first verses are as follow:

> My love is a rider, wild broncos she breaks,
> Though she promised to quit it, just for my sake.
> She ties up one foot and the saddle puts on.
> With a swing and a jump she is mounted and gone.
>
> The first time I met her, 'twas early one spring,
> Riding a bronco, a high-headed thing.
> She tipped me a wink as she gayly did go,
> For she wished me to look at her bucking bronco.[32]

If there are a few songs which hint about a cowgirl's sex life, are there not some out and out bawdy ballads? Certainly, but few are printed in collections because not many folks are willing to sing such songs in front of a mixed herd. The songs generally remain back of the chutes after Jack Daniels has been consulted.

And what kinds of women did the cowboy prefer? Ramon F. Adams declares that "He wanted her feminine with frills and fluffs all over. He had no use for them he-women. . . ."[33] For Jack Thorp the ideal of womanhood on the range "was to be found somewhere between those who toted a stiletto . . . and those who carried a bustle and a Bible."[34]

Beverly Stoeltje, an authority on women on the frontier, notes both Adams' and Thorp's kinds of women and one other type. She says:

> The symbolic transformation of images of women that took place on the frontier involved the following initial images (1) the refined lady symbolizing "true womanhood,". . . [Adams' kind of woman] (2) the "backwoods belle". . . who could accomplish fantastic deeds involving strength and capability and who had the ability to establish informal elements of institutionalization, in particular the family; [Thorp's kind of woman] and (3) the bad woman outside the boundaries of society. . . .[35]

A glance at women such as the one who had "eyes like a morning star, cheeks like a rose" in "The Colorado Trail," or rambunctious Pompey Stiles in "The Dying Desperado," or the woman who committed robbery in "The Overland Stage" attest to the fact that cowboys recognized all three groups in their songs.

Very little has been said about the sources, authors, variants, and dates of cowboy songs. No attempt has been made to include modern songs such as "Ride 'Em Cowboy" or "Rodeo Cowboy" or songs of the commercial era of Tin Pan Alley. Such reveal little about ranch women. Controversy rages anyway in this era of debunking the cowboy and his life: Who really wrote some of the ballads? Did some balladeers really know anything of western life? Are not some of the songs too artistic to be considered seriously as coming from the range? And did cowboys ever actually sing very much anyway? All are questions better left to others. It needs only to be pointed out that the songs of or about the range have contributed to the folklore of the cowgirl and reinforce the idea that women on the cattle frontier could ride, rope, herd, and generally make a hand. And many men of songs leave the impression that it was safer to let the ladies have a mighty loose rein!

14

No Laughing Matter: Ranch Women in the Humor of the West

Bill was sweating over the forge trying to get some horseshoes ready when his wife walked up. She watched him cuss and hammer awhile. When he put down a hot shoe, she walked over to it, picked it up and immediately flung it to the ground.

"Honey," inquired Bill. "Did you burn yourself?"

"No," she said, in tears. "It jest don't take me long to look at a horseshoe."[1]

While women on the cattle ranges were held in high regard by their men, they were often the object of jokes, stories and yarns, and none of them gentle. And yet, anyone who has even a passing acquaintance with ranch women knows that many of them are charming, intelligent, attractive creatures. While they may, to hear the men tell it, seem to have bad cases of Stupid and Thick Head, ranch ladies surely have not cornered the market on those traits, and they probably have no more drips and rejects in their ranks than women in other walks of life.

If the joke and yarn tellers make it appear that ranch women like the women in Tennyson's "Locksley Hall" are held something better than a dog, a little dearer than a horse, then there must be a reason, possibly something passed down for several generations. A look at the stereotypes of American frontier humor shows where the modern ranch woman has been pastured.

As early as the 1830s the region of the old Southwest which included Alabama, Tennessee, Mississippi and parts of Missouri, Arkansas and Louisiana, abounded in tall tales and funny stories. The stories were so exaggerated and outrageous that magazines and newspapers began to publish some of the better yarns. Borrowing partly from the style of such works as *The Travels of Baron Munchausen* and from the style of witty eighteenth-century essayists such as Addison, Steele and Goldsmith, the authors of frontier humor had only to look around them at the backwoodsmen and their way of life for a supply of stories. Frontier women figured prominently in some of the material. The ladies are strange and wondrous creatures.

Solomon Franklin Smith in his story "The Consolate Widow," published in 1868 in *Theatrical Management in the West*, depicts one frontier woman in the "Nation" as accepting tragedy in a stoic, detached way, just one more calamity in a calamity-filled existence. Smith describes a crowd gathered around a dead man who in a "quarter race for a gallon of whiskey" ran against a building full speed and wedged his head between the ends of two logs. Smith inquires if the doctor has been sent for and if the wife has been notified. He asks how the woman is going to feel when she learns of her husband's death. The wife, who has been sitting on the ground during the whole episode "smoking composedly," says, "it's too bad he lost the race and the whiskey."[2]

Smith continues: "You madam: You the wife of this man who has been so untimely cut off?" Then with logic that made sense to her even if to no one else, she replied:

> "Yes, and what about it?" said she. "Untimely cut off? His throat's cut, that's all, by that 'tarnal sharp end of a log; and as for its being untimely, I don't know but it's as well now as any time—he warn't much account, no how!"[3]

George Washington Harris' famous character Sut Lovingood, who appears in *Sut Lovingoods Yarn: Spun by a "Nat'ral Durn'd Fool"* published in 1867, had a lot to tell about frontier women—none of it too nice and a lot of it bawdy. Instead of saying that Mrs. Yardley of "Mrs. Yardley's Quilting" is a dirty old woman, he says instead:

> Ole Missus Yardley wer a great noticer ove littil things, that nobody else ever seed. She'd say right in the middil ove sumbody's serious talk. "Law sakes! thar goes that yaller slut ove a hen, a flingin straws over her shoulder."[4]

Mrs. Yardley's daughter was a lot like her. She was a rambunctious girl and did not care for fancy dressing.

While Sal did not care for the "fashun plates," another backwoods woman, appearing in William C. Hall's *Polly Peablossom's Wedding* published in 1851, did care. Her name was Miss Sally Hooter. Sally had seen pictures of a bustle and decided to make herself one out of a sausage. When the family attends a "meetin" the spirit begins to take hold of everyone including Sally. She rolls and hollers with the rest until the sausage works loose down around her ankles. Sally's spirit rises considerably when she thinks she is being bitten by a snake.[5]

Professional humorists were not the only ones who noticed the peculiarities of frontier women. Mrs. Frances Trollope in *Domestic Manners of the Americans* noted that pioneer wives were worse off than English peasants and lived in an atmosphere of "indecent poverty." Their manner of addressing children by their Christian names or calling them "honey" Mrs. Trollope found uncouth.[6]

Randolph B. Marcy in his book *Thirty Years of Army Life on the Border*, written in 1866, declared that the manners of the settlers on the borders of Arkansas and Texas were "eminently peculiar, and very different from those of any other people" he had met. He attributes the peculiarities of women to living so far from civilization.[7]

While men such as Smith, Harris, Hall and Marcy found a good deal to laugh about in frontier females, nowhere are the peculiarities of the backwoods belle more pronounced than in the almanacs of Davy Crockett published from 1835 to 1856. According to Mody C. Boatright, Davy's scalding humor came about because sophisticated travelers thought pioneers were hardly human. When pioneer women did not compare favorably with their eastern sisters, the backwoodsmen enjoyed taking down their city opponents by poking such fun at their own women in such an outrageous way that they made the city fellows look ridiculous. The backwoodsman accomplished his burlesque by the process of turning things upside down:

> By a process of inversion in which he was adept, ugliness, uncouthness, and "unladylike" strength and demeanor were so exaggerated that they could not be taken seriously. Thus he created a laugh and showed contempt for leisure-class standards of femininity.[8]

Crockett's pioneer women emerged most awesomely put together. Almost any woman who was anyone was mutilated in some way. Sally Ann Thunder Crockett was missing the thumb and forefinger of one hand because a catfish she was skinning alive bit it off. Bets Undergrove was missing an eye. Jerusha Stubbs also had only one eye "but it was pretty enough for two" and it had one advantage "where folks must rise early and she could wake up in half the time the others could."[9]

If mutilation was not enough to distinguish the backwoods belle, her size was. The bride of Luke Logroller was "six feet high in her stocking feet; that is, she would have been only she'd got no stockings." Nance Bowers "war seven feet tall out of her stockings and hair comb." If the ladies were not tall, they were likely to be "pretty thick through." One fellow's girl friend was so big that when he courted her, he took along a piece of chalk. He hugged her as far as he could reach. Then he would mark the place with chalk and hug her a little further. Once, it was said, he met his rival halfway round.[10]

The garb of the pioneer woman was noticeable as well. Like any woman of fashion, she liked lots of fur, particularly bearskin petticoats. Mrs. Crockett made eight hundred petticoats in two years and then "sallied out in the fall to sell them." Two ladies named Zipporina and Jerusha were fond of fur. Zipporina liked to wear a bearskin shawl. Jerusha leaned to wolf hide. She made herself a shift of wolf hide which she acquired by killing the wolf with her peg leg. One lady made herself a rattlesnake garter and another made a petticoat from scalps taken from the Alamo.[11]

Pioneer women were not merely ornamental. They were accomplished. One of Davy's acquaintances could neither sing nor play the piano but she could "outscream a catamount and jump over her own shadow; she had good strong horse sense and knew a woodchuck from a skunk." Luke Logroller's wife-to-be was a fine wrestler. Luke and the lady wrestled for the entertainment of friends while they awaited the arrival of the parson to marry them. The narrator declared, "and I wish I may be flung myself if she didn't fling him three times hand running." Various other females could "laugh the bark off a pine tree," "sing a wolf to sleep," fight duels with thunderbolts, and wrestle alligators.[12]

The belles of Crockett's almanacs were helpful. Sally Ann, Davy's wife, used to patch the seat of her husband's pants with foxskin and when Davy wanted to sharpen his thumbnail, she turned the grindstone. Sal even made eggnog at Easter for Davy in spite of the fact that she had to milk a wild buffalo and dare an eagle's aerie for eggs.[13]

Neither were frontier women of the woods afraid. Indians who were foolish enough to approach any of Crockett's women quickly came to grief. Granny Crockett, who was 120 years old and had a cough so loud it caused the cider barrels to roll around in the cellar, once went to the woods to find hickory limbs to chew for her cough. When an Indian surprised her she coughed on him and he rolled "as if struck by the bare foot of a earthquake." After Granny walked on home the Indian "died of the full-gallop consumption."

To enhance all their many endearing qualities, backwoods belles were practical and logical thinkers—at least by their own standards. Florinda Furry often went to Sunday meetin' with her rooster in her pocket just in case there was a cock fight after services. Katy Whippoween raised a passel of children with hardly any expense. She cut down her husband's clothes for the oldest boy, and the oldest boy's outfit for the next, and so on down the line until she came to the youngest. When she was without clothing for him "she covered him with glue and feathers and sent him on to school."[14]

In later times, the wondrously endowed Sluefoot Sue shared many characteristics of her pioneer sisters. Pecos Bill first encountered Sue riding a catfish "big as a whale." Bill fell for Sue and wanted to marry up but she would not consent until Bill let her ride Lightning, Bill's horse. Bill knew how dangerous such a ride would be but Sue stubbornly insisted. Bill never got to marry Sue because Lightning pitched her clear to the moon and there she stayed.[15]

In another version, Sue's dress had a spring-steel bustle which kept bouncing her up to the moon. High Pockets, Bill's friend, says, "Better shoot her before she starves to death. It would be a kindness, Bill." Bill decides instead to lasso her and Sue gets mad because she is shamed in front of her wedding guests.

Bill insists, "But I tried to tell you."

With true frontier logic Sue replies, "Yes, but you didn't stop me! I'm not gettin' hitched with you, Pecos Bill. A man who'd do a thing like that to his bride can't be trusted."[16]

The rambunctious, grotesquely costumed, mutilated, bold females of frontier times have never quite disappeared from the humor of the West. The women have made the transition to modern times without any loss of their brand of logic, practicality and helpfulness.

One of the best sources of western humor about ranch women is the cartoons of Ace Reid. Ace's cartoons appear in the ranching sections of western papers, in farm and ranch magazines, on calendars, and in paperback volumes called *Cowpokes.* Ace grew up on a ranch in Electra, Texas, and his main characters, Jake and Zeb, are right out of the cowlot. Fred Gipson thought Ace's cartoons true to a modern cowboy's life. He said: "I never look at one of his Cowpoke drawings without roaring with laughter and, at the same time, feeling an urge to weep. They're so darn true!"[17]

The ranch women of modern cartoons are reminiscent of Crockett's mutilated women. Ace Reid's cattlewomen are often portrayed with long noses and stringy hair. While the backwoodsman bragged about the heft of his woman, the cowboy cartoonist depicts his woman so skinny that only the direction of her feet give a clue about which is the front and which is the back of her. The women of Davy's almanacs were grotesquely costumed and so are Reid's women. They wear dresses made from flour sacks, aprons, baggy stockings and lace-up shoes. One cartoon depicts a wife who, like Sally Hooter in "Polly Peablossom's Wedding" and like Crockett's fur-covered females, wants to be a fashion plate. She is dressed in a plaid coat, flowered dress, and outdated hat. Looking at a large stack of flour sacked in colorful prints, she eyes the one on the very bottom: "I'll take this one. It's such a nice print."

The women of Reid's cartoons are plain, work-worn and stupid, and they have learned to suffer terribly and loudly. One cartoon shows a ranch wife standing at the clothesline complaining that she never gets to go anywhere. The cowboy answers, "Whatta you mean I never take you anywhere? Only last week I took you to a grocery store and twice to funerals." While standing beside an outside washtub and washboard, another ranch wife, holding one child as another clings to her skirts, tells the insurance man, "Yes, Mister, I do need some life insurance 'cause I sure ain't doin' much livin' now."

Like Sally Ann Crockett, Ace Reid's women are accomplished and helpful. A cartoon shows the wife coming from the corral as her husband says, "There goes Maw. She's number one at that place. She's first to get up, first to fix breakfast, first to milk and first to go to bed." Still another shows smoke coming from the back of the house as the wife speaks: "No, Paw, I ain't burning your dinner. I'm ironing and only scorchin' your shirt." In another scene a cowboy fans himself while his wife changes the tire on the pickup. "Liz," he says, "I wish you'd hurry a little. I'm gettin' hot out here." As another cartoon cowboy runs a wild cow he says, "Yep, she's gonna make a good milk cow . . . for my wife!"[18]

Another cartoonist whose style and view of ranch women is almost identical to Ace Reid's is Lex Graham. One of his best cartoons features the helpful wife. It shows both husband and wife riding after a steer. The husband ropes the steer and the wife, with a satisfied smile, ropes the hind legs of her husband's horse.[19]

While the cartoons of Ace Reid and Lex Graham give visual proof of the staying power of women in western humor, contemporary stories and tales also attest to the influence of early western humor. The helpful wife appears in this tale:

> Mary was newly married to a rancher and anxious to be of help to him. As they rode over the grasslands hazing the cattle at a gentle pace toward home, the young bride thought about how little she knew of cows. Well, she could learn. In fact she was about to get her first lesson.
>
> "Stay here by the gate, Mary," said Henry, her husband. "I'm going to take the cows into another pasture. I don't want the bull in with them yet. See the bull, Mary? He's over yonder. He's a dandy. Best I ever had. You don't have to do anything. The men and I will take care of it. You just stand there and rest and watch awhile. You're doin' fine, Mary. Now, just stay still."
>
> With his instructions carefully given, the husband rode quietly and slowly back to the herd and the hands took their positions, some with the cows, all with their eyes on the bull across the way.
>
> Things went well for a time. Then the bull caught the scent of the cows. With his nose in the air, the lord and master bellowed a time or two and brought the cows to a halt. With a determination that only several seasoned cowhands and a secure fence would stop, the bull headed for the gate—the gate by which sweet Mary stood.
>
> The hands turned toward the gate. It was wide open! Mary had opened the gap and walked her horse through to nibble some green grass on the other side. She glanced up just in time to see the bull making straight for her. Mary might be green, but she had distinctly heard her husband say that he did not want

> that bull in with the cows. Mary grabbed the end of the gate and hastily secured the barbed wires. Thinking how pleased everyone would be, Mary was surprised to hear her husband and all the boys screaming, "No, no, no. It's too late now. Let him through. Don't try to stop him now."
>
> The wife was even more astounded when she looked up just in time to see the bull run right over the gate leaving his bullish credentials impaled on the barbed wire.
>
> For what seemed like a long time, the husband stomped the ground and swore and stomped some more. Mary understood how awful he felt, and she was beginning to catch on that somehow she was the reason for his tirade. Mary broke down and cried until she was making more noise than her husband could stand.
>
> "But Henry," she wailed. "I was only trying to help. Can't you even say thank you?"
>
> Completely baffled, Henry sputtered and spewed and finally mumbled, head hanging low, "Why yes, Mary. Thank you kindly for castrating my ten thousand-dollar bull."[20]

Like the consolate widow in Solomon Franklin Smith's story who saw with a clear vision and logic which escaped everyone but herself, many cattlewomen are possessed of the same clearsightedness. Stella Polk of Mason, Texas, a storyteller and author of books about her life in Mason County, remembered these stories testifying to the logic of some ranch females.

> Uncle Pac and his wife Aunt Hanna had a little feist dog. They thought he was tops until Uncle Pac caught him sucking eggs. About a week later Uncle Pac caught Aunt Hannah switching the feist. "What are you whipping the dog for?" he wanted to know.
> "I'm switching him for sucking those eggs," she said.
> "But that was a week ago."
> "Oh," said Aunt Hannah, "But I mentioned it to him!"

Dora and Flossie were close neighbors. Dora who lived nearest the road, was notoriously filthy. Flossie, who lived half a mile away, was meticulously clean. The telephone system came through. When the builders asked for land easements, the pioneers gladly gave them. That is, all but Flossie. Under no circumstances would she allow a wire to be strung from Dora's house to hers. Pressed for a reason, she gave it. "That Dora," she said, "has bed bugs. Now you string that line from her house to mine and them bugs will form a black line, a walking that wire from her house to mine!"[21]

Still another example of cowgirl logic occurred near Saginaw, Texas: When the cowboys who were fixing to work cattle came up short-handed, the foreman reluctantly asked the wife of one of the men if she could vaccinate. The woman said she could. The plan was to separate the heifers from the steers, vaccinate the heifers with Abortus (a serum which helped prevent abortions) and to vaccinate both heifers and steers for black leg.

The lady was more than a little jumpy, but she filled two needles with Abortus and Black Leg serum and took her place along with the men who were going to dehorn, gotch ears, daub wounds, brand, and castrate. Everyone fell to work at once and it was all the woman could do just to keep filling needles and shoving them in. She did not have time to pay attention to what her fellow workers were doing. They finished one bunch and the foreman called a break. "That's all the steers, now let's get the heifers."

"The heifers?" asked the lady. "I thought we just worked the heifers."

The foreman walked over, looked at the two needles, and saw right away that the woman had vaccinated all the steers with Abortus.

> "Now," said her husband, red with embarrassment. "Look what you done. What you got to say for yourself?"
>
> "Well," she replied with her head down. "When I get done, ain't no steers goin' to lose no calves, and ain't no heifers gonna get black leg in this herd."[22]

But if women on ranches are without a man's logic or reason, they have other endearing qualities. Stella Polk's friends were, like the women of the almanacs, practical thinkers:

> In those days when neighbors butchered together, Cora had been up since before dawn in order to be ready for the neighbors who would meet at her house to cut up the butchered beef.
>
> Since the day was hot and there was no ice then, the women worked with all haste, even after their men had retired to the long gallery to smoke and talk. Mid-afternoon came before the women got the kitchen washed up. Just as they started to move out into the shaded yard, one of them pointed to a huge dish pan of beef they had overlooked. Cora had had it. She simply picked up the pan of beef, walked to the kitchen window and threw the beef to the hogs wandering around outside. Then she turned to the ladies. "Now we can talk," she said.

Ranch women are also brave even if they are poor, defenseless women all alone like Stella Polk's "Grandama." As with Crockett's women, the Indians get the worst of it.

> When Uncle Alf and his wife, called Grandama, were young, Uncle Alf had to be away from home one night. His wife had barred the cabin door and set their two babies on the floor when she heard an owl hoot. Thinking to save their chickens, she got the old long-barreled shotgun and stepped outside.
>
> The owl hooted again, this time on a false note, and Uncle Alf's wife darted back into the cabin. She barely had time to bar the door when Indians sur-

> rounded the cabin, yelling and pounding on the door. What was she to do? She noticed the big pot of water boiling on the fireplace hook. She got the boiling water and hurried upstairs. Leaning far out the window over the front door, she carefully threw it all over the howling Indians.
>
> Now the Indians had something to howl for as they ran away screaming.
>
> Telling this story after she really was old, Grandama invariably would break out in tears. "Just think," she would sob, "there I was a lone, helpless woman with two babies and all those Indians."[23]

Most important of all, ranchers' wives like the woman Captain Marcy encountered accepted life as it was and were patient—most of the time. James Bratcher of El Paso remembered a story told to him by Roy Stubbs of Wimberley, Texas.

Roy explained to his wife before he married her that he would probably be trading horses "till Kingdom come." She knew it and said it would be fine with her:

> And she never said anything, except this one time. Things were awful dry and horses, good polo types, could be got cheap. I just couldn't turn 'em down at what they were going for around the country. The Army buyers would be at Marble Falls that spring, and I had maybe 150 prospects to try on them. I was paying pasturage from Blanco to Junction, and still not passing up a good one when he came cheap. But money was getting thin. One day she said:
>
> "Roy, before we married you told me you were going to trade horses just like always, and I said I'd never say anything. And I haven't. But, Roy, you want all the horses."[24]

The caricatures of ranch women may be grotesque and outrageous but the women who are the subjects of the humor often laugh louder than anyone else because of a certain grain of truth embodied in such stories, and because it is laughter within a closed circle where only veterans of ranch life dare speak so boldly. An outsider could get himself killed for telling the same stories.

The West, particularly the states of the Great Plains, remains figuratively and literally closer to the frontier than other areas and has been guilty, among other things, of clinging to a kind of frontier mentality, a naïvete, a lack of sophistication in its manners, its writing, its philosophy, its education. Songs and humorous stories about cowgirls and ranch females reflect that old-fashioned, even backward attitude, as some would see it. The West, however, has come of age and behaves and thinks much like the rest of the look-alike world. Not many songs or funny stories center on cowgirls in the latter part of the twentieth century. "Ditties" and dirty jokes about cowgirls are in limited circulation with the emphasis on sexual prowess or, worse still, lack of it. But even in these days, it pays to be careful about the crowd. Modern cowgirls are capable of defending their reputations and themselves. Story tellers better be prepared to retreat, run, fight, or change their tune.

Conclusion

The final chapter of a book is generally reserved to tell the reader: This is the end of the story. There isn't any more. Happily such is not the case in this book. If cowgirls have a past which can be traced from ranch life to rodeo, through books, movies, songs, jokes and stories, then they also have a future. If nothing else, females in the West, in the United States and even in other parts of the world, keep showing up in jeans, boots and hats to remind us that cowgirls, genuine or imitation, are among us.

Some females still run ranches, ride in rodeos, take care of families, and at the same time snap out broncs, ship cattle, breed horses. The late twentieth-century cowgirl is much alive and shows every indication of riding not into the sunset but of thundering over the hill right into the twenty-first century, scholar-posse, observer, and admirer right behind.

Because the past is not far behind us, because there were many left to testify, and because there were good records and even pictures available, it has been possible to watch the cowgirl grow up. Observers saw the legend as it was forged, noticed the process, participated in the debunking if they wanted to, watched the progression into myth, and stood in wonder at what cowgirls have become.

Underlying everything else in *The Cowgirls* has been the intention of tracing cowgirls from women who merely lived in the West and were by accident drawn into ranch life to those who, through show business and other means, imitated the life. Through written and visual portrayal, all were eventually hybridized into something real yet unreal. By giving them the name embraced by an adoring world—cowgirls—many were caught in a wide loop, fake and imaginary included.

It is obvious to even the casual reader that what began without clear and precise definition moved into a general and loose identification. Without apology, this book meandered all over the western landscape, sometimes ahorseback and sometimes afoot and often by the word—spoken, written and sung—which is the process of folklore. Those who have read for pleasure are probably more satisfied. Others may tend to say, "Yes, but. . . ."

To analyze what has happened to cowgirls, we must analyze what has happened to the cowboys. Among cowboys, as a stereotype of western-frontier-heroic-men, observers, historians, and writers have discovered sub-groups. There were trail drivers, ranch owners, cooks, side-kicks, ranch hands, husbands, fathers, foremen, drunks, dudes, preachers, and cowboys strong, weak, sad, pitiful, mean, funny, gay, horny, honest, loyal, brave, singing, unworthy and worthy—but cowboys all. The reading public has not always been happy with the exposure of the last types but generally novelists and film makers, the real taste makers whether for good or bad, delivered their observations in the form of satire or parody, accompanied by large doses of humor easily swallowed but never completely digested enough to be satisfying. The problem is that audiences often think the characters are not based on reality but merely contrived to make us laugh; in other words, cowboys exist to entertain us.

One cowboy group will illustrate the point—cowboy singers. How we laugh or get angry with the distorters, the interpreters who fed us as little children at the Saturday matinee on the idea that some cowboys could sing as well as they could ride. Roy and Gene, of course. There is, however, a whole body of cowboy ballads dating to the late nineteenth century which proves beyond a shadow of a doubt that some, if only a few, really were musical, poetic in a folksy, earthy kind of way, and that their music borrowed and adapted from earlier forms of some other frontier. The songs, incidentally, reveal much not only about a cowboy's life but also about his aspirations, his dreams, his philosophy, and, yes, about cowgirls. Maybe the only phony idea in the movies was that cowboys sang "Happy Trails to You" at the same time they rode. If you analyze it, "Happy Trails" isn't much worse a song than "Ridin' Old

Paint." Neither of them are great songs, but one is considered authentic, and one is supposed to be fake.

I use Gene and Roy as an illustration because the debunking generation which appeared in the 1950s and 1960s continues today to treat western movies and their heroes and heroines with contempt, saying that the movie portrayals have done much to injure the "real" cowboy image. What the critics are saying is that real cowboys, real men, did not feel, and if they did they did not sing sissy songs about their horses or their women. I say no.

If the cowboy suffers a wide interpretation, cowgirls have suffered the same fate. And from the same sources—dime novels, sensationalizing reports, novels, nonfiction studies, reminiscences, films, song and jokes, tales. Still, there is often a grain of truth, another angle we can't afford to miss. All have been thoroughly given their opinion in the book without much explanation or analysis.

Cowgirls are finding their time and place today and refuse to stay in the past. Just as there are all kinds of cowboys, so there are all kinds of cowgirls, liberated as well as lesbian. We may watch the cowgirl split into a hundred parts, just as the cowboy was split. But we can still say, there goes a cowgirl.

The Cowgirls stops in the past but leaves the gate open to the future. For most of us, cowgirls exist in memory—a figure on horseback. Whether the public believes fact or fantasy about the cowgirl heroine is not too important. She remains our foremost genuine American heroine, internationally adored. She is part of our heritage, and every generation from the West or not has a right to claim her. Mounted on a splendid horse she helped conquer the West, and she conquered some hearts as well. She rides the range today reminding us of a distant time and place. Because she is a horsewoman, she always seems a little above us, someone to look up to, someone moving elusively away. We can command her to rise from the mists of the past and become what the cowboy saw alongside the Santa Fe Trail:

I saw her ride down the arroyo
Wayback on the Arkansas sand,
With a smile like an acre of sunflowers
And a little brown quirt in her hand.
She mounted her pinto so airy
And rode like she carried the mail.
Her eyes nigh set fire to the prairie
Way out on the Santa Fe Trail,
Yo ho, way out on the Santa Fe Trail.

Afterword

Though millions of words have been written and said about the cowboy over the last hundred years—often mistakenly proclaiming him dead—the cowgirl has been overlooked at one extreme, overdrawn at the other, misinterpreted and misunderstood. As Joyce Roach's book illustrates, the cowgirl has never truly been defined. No simple definition will fit.

The Cowgirl Hall of Fame in Hereford, for example, honors a wide assortment of Western women, ranging from the ranchwomen who were and are the true cowgirls to the Indian woman Sacajawea, who helped guide the Lewis and Clark expedition in the Northwest.

Growing up on a West Texas ranch, I always took the term *cowgirl* literally, meaning a girl or woman who worked with cattle—you could include horses—the same way I took the term *cowboy* literally. There was honor in being called *cowboy*, an honor not bestowed lightly. It was never bestowed on me, not by anyone who ever watched me at work in the saddle. Any coffeepot polisher from town could go out to the country and became a *ranchhand* overnight, but it took years and a lot of skill to earn the title *cowboy*.

Cowgirl could mean no less, it seemed to me.

It never occurred to me that there could ever be such a thing as an urban cowboy. I still, thank goodness, have heard nothing about urban *cowgirls*.

I can't say that I ever knew very many women who at the time were truly called cowgirls except in a rodeo context. As a boy I saw the late Tad Lucas trick-riding in the Midland rodeo. She was all that Joyce Roach says she was: a thrilling performer, a superb horsewoman. I remember some rodeos that had special women's events. One of the real heart-stopping moments I ever had as a rodeo spectator was at Pecos one year, when they featured women's calf roping. The cowgirl missed her first loop and flipped it back over her head while she shook down her second rope. Every cowboy in the arena and every person in the grandstands saw something that she didn't: the loop settled over a post or a stay in the arena fence, even as she spurred full-tilt away from it with the rope still firmly tied to the saddlehorn. A collective gasp went up from an audience expecting to see her horse flip over backward and possibly crush her to death when she hit the end of the rope.

It didn't happen. That post came up out of the ground slick as a pickle out of a jar. I don't remember if she ever caught the calf or not. I was too busy catching my breath to care one way or the other.

My mother might have been classified as a cowgirl, if you wanted to stretch a point. She had grown up on her grandfather's ranch north of the Red River in Oklahoma. As a girl she rode horses and helped work cattle. My father was a working cowboy, and she rode horseback with him for a time after they were married. As the children came along, however, she shifted her attention from horses and cattle to home and family. Only once or twice did I ever see her on a horse while we boys were growing up. I had to accept her credentials as a cowgirl purely on faith, for I did not see them demonstrated except in a few old black-and-white photographs from earlier times. She was a dutiful ranch wife, focusing her energies on the cookstove and sewing machine, the mop and the broom, and on seeing that we did all the schoolwork required of us.

In later years, after we were all grown and gone from home and she and Dad bought a small ranch of their own, she returned to riding horseback now and then, or to driving the pickup to help Dad while *he* rode the horse. She helped him feed, and she helped him treat the hurt and sick animals around the barn. The cowgirl work she did was of a practical nature, not for public entertainment.

My father's mother had essayed much the same role in an earlier generation. As the wife of a ranch foreman it was her great "privilege" to cook for anywhere from one to a dozen cowboys every day, the number varying according to the kind of cattle work being done at the time. She was not a cowgirl in the conventional sense, but she was a vital part of the ranch operation. She was not paid for it, either. It was simply expected of her because she was the foreman's wife.

It seems to me that was the basic role of most of the ranchwomen I knew in my growing-up years. They cooked for cowboy crews and sometimes helped around the fringes of the cattle work, things like opening gates or standing in a gate to keep an animal either in or out. They sometimes drove the pickup while their husbands poured feed out over the tailgate, or in some lamentable instances poured the feed while their husbands drove. The ones I knew didn't often ride out with a roundup crew, though it would probably have exerted a worthwhile civilizing influence on the cowboys' vocabularies if they had.

This is not to say by any means that it never happened. I have known of some women, usually ranchmen's daughters or wives, who did or still do just everything the cowboys do, who ride with their menfolk and hold up their end of the cow work like the top hands of old. In fact, there may be more of it today than in the past for the simple reason that labor costs and shortages of skilled ranch labor have left most cattle operations short-handed. By necessity if not always by choice, ranchmen enlist the active help of their wives and daughters for jobs they used to hire men to do.

Moreover, for several reasons the bigger ranches today have a larger percentage of stable family men in their cowboy force, in contrast to the mostly-bachelor crews they used to have in the good old-bad old days when skilled cowboys used to haunt saddle shops, hotel lobbies and street corners, looking for a job. Thus, more women are exposed to the likelihood of being asked to help fathers, brothers and spouses with their outdoor work.

Another recent book, *Heart-Diamond*, by Kathy Greenwood, details her and and her mother's labors on the Greenwood family ranch in Eastern New Mexico.

More than a few women today are noted as breakers and trainers of horses. Fern Sawyer of Belen, New Mexico, was one of the best cutting horse trainers and riders who ever graced a contest arena, and it is worth a special trip to watch Mrs. Buster Welch of Sweetwater, Texas, put a cutting horse through its paces.

Mrs. Roach speaks of the organization of the Girls' Rodeo Association in San Angelo, Texas, in 1949. I can vouch for that because I was there as a livestock reporter for the San Angelo *Standard-Times*, writing up the meeting. I also reported on a few of the all-girl rodeos that enjoyed strong popularity around that time. They were a novelty, but most novelties have a short lifespan. That one did. Before long, the only rodeo event left for the girls and women was barrel racing, unless you count the rodeo queen contests which value *glow* more than *go*.

My definition of the term *cowgirl* is probably too narrow. Joyce Roach certainly suggests that it is. Reading her book may have given you one of your own. Even if not, you probably have a greater appreciation for the part women played in what used to be considered a man's work, though it really wasn't, not for very long, anyway.

Elmer Kelton
San Angelo, Texas
April, 1990

Notes

THROUGH A GLASS DARKLY

1. Larry McMurtry, *In a Narrow Grave: Essays on Texas* (Austin: Encino Press, 1968), 148.

2. "Cowgirls," *Texas Monthly* (November 1987), 110.

3. Dixon Wecter, *The Hero in America* (Ann Arbor: University of Michigan Press, 1960), 342.

4. Agnes Morley Cleaveland, *No Life For A Lady* (Boston: Houghton Mifflin, 1941), 22.

5. T. H. Kerttula, "There Was No Christmas," *True West* (December 1963), 20.

6. Emily Porter, *Memory Cups of Panhandle Pioneers* (Clarendon, Texas: Clarendon Press, 1945), 194.

7. Emily Jones Shelton, "Lizzie E. Johnson: A Cattle Queen of Texas," *Southwestern Historical Quarterly* (January 1947), 355-62.

8. J. Frank Dobie, *The Mustangs* (Boston: Little Brown and Co., 1952), 43.

9. William Forrest Sprague, *Women of the West.* (Boston: Christopher Publishing Co., 1940), 176-77.

10. T. A. Larson, "Dolls, Vassals and Drudges: Pioneer Women in the West," *Western Historical Quarterly* (January 1972), 28.

11. Sprague, 211.

12. C. L. Sonnichsen, *From Hopalong to Hud: Thoughts on Western Fiction.* (College Station: Texas A&M University Press, 1978), 3

HAIRPINS ON THE TRAIL

1. Isabella Bird, *A Lady's Life in the Rocky Mountains* (Norman: University of Oklahoma Press, 1960), 129.

2. J. Marvin Hunter, ed., *The Trail Drivers of Texas* (Nashville, Tennessee: Cokesbury Press, 1925), 769 for Belcher, 885 for Slaughter, 298 for Burks. For other information about Burks see also C. L. Douglas, *Cattle Kings of Texas* (Ft. Worth: Branch and Smith, 1939),

188; *Cotulla Record*, December 8, 1972; January 5, 19, 26, February 2, 9, 16, 1973; all reprinted from 1931 *Record*; T. U. Taylor, *The Chisholm Trail and Other Routes* (San Antonio: Naylor Publishers, 1936), 162–64.

3. Mary Taylor Bunton, *A Bride on the Old Chisholm Trail* (San Antonio: Naylor Publishers, 1939), 19–65.

4. T. U. Taylor, *The Chisholm Trail* (San Antonio: Naylor Co., 1936) 171-72 for Bunton; 157–62 for Cluck.

5. Ibid., 167–68.

6. Shelton, "Lizzie E. Johnson," 351-66.

7. *Austin American–Statesman*, "Lizzie E. Johnson," April 25, 1926.

8. Shelton, "Lizzie E. Johnson," 357.

9. Ibid., 362.

10. Douglas, *Cattle Kings of Texas*, 185-88.

11. J. J. Waggoner, *History of the Cattle Industry in Southern Arizona* (Tucson: University of Arizona, 1952), 33.

12. Pearl Foster O'Donnell, *Trek to Texas: 1870-1880* (Ft. Worth: Branch Smith Co., 1966), 130-32. Some of O'Donnell's information comes from "Kate Medlin Story," *Los Angeles Sunday Times* (January 6, 1907).

13. The details of Margaret Borland's life are found in a file under her name in the Texas State Archives, Austin, Texas.

14. Hunter, *Trail Drivers*, 75-77.

15. "Cowboy Jo was a Woman," *Denver Rocky Mountain News* (March 13, 1904) magazine insert. See also James Horan, *Desperate Women* (New York: Putnam's Sons, 1952), 305.

AMAZONS ON THE RANGE

1. Philip Ashton Rollins, *The Cowboy* (New York: Charles Scribner's Sons, 1922), 35.

2. "From Cowboy to Owner and Operator of Vast Domain Marked Life of Charlie Hart," *Clovis News Journal* (May 29, 1938).

3. Thelma Crosby and Eve Ball, *Bob Crosby, World Champion Cowboy* (Clarendon, Texas: Clarendon Press, 1966), 36-37.

4. J. Evetts Haley, *Charles Goodnight: Cowman and Plainsman* (New York: Houghton, Mifflin, 1936), 262.

5. Phoebe Kerrick Warner, "Molly Ann Goodnight," unpublished manuscript. Panhandle-Plains Museum, Canyon, Texas.

6. Ibid.

7. C. May Cohea, "Pioneer Women," unpublished manuscript. Panhandle–Plains Museum, Canyon, Texas.

8. For more on Molly Goodnight see also True Burton, *A History of the JA Ranch* (New York: Argonaut Press, 1966).

9. Mrs. George Kitt, "Mrs. John Slaughter," from notes made in an interview, No. 56312-3, Arizona Pioneer Historical Society Library, Tucson, Arizona. See also "Noted Pioneer Woman is Dead," *Arizona Daily Star* (April 3, 1941).

10. Frank Alkire, *The Little Lady of the Triangle Bar*, 1942. No. A415. Arizona Pioneer Historical Society Library, Tucson, Arizona. See also *Arizona Republic* (January 31, 1950).

11. Kerttula, 20–21, 47.

12. Jo Jeffers, "Ranch Wife," *Arizona Highways* 38 (September 1962): 4.

13. Laura V. Hamner, *Light n' Hitch* (Dallas: American Guild Press, 1958), 156–65.

14. S. Omar Barker, "Mrs. Mountaineer," *New Mexico* (May, 1946), 23, 43.

15. Jackie DeSpain, interview by Mrs. Lillie Fox, April 23, 1966, Panhandle-Plains Museum, Canyon, Texas.

16. Mary Haughian, letter to author, Terry, Montana, July 10, 1972. Mary is Susan's daughter-in-law. See also Helena Huntington Smith, "Montana's Favorite Redhead," *Colliers* (August 2 1952), 19-22.

17. "Women Become Cowboys Out in the West," *Boston Evening Record* (October 2, 1901). See also "Women Who Have Shown Rare Pluck," *Denver Times* (September 8, 1901).

18. "Girl Who Has Made Success in Managing Cattle Ranch," *The Denver Post* (Sunday, May 4, 1902).

19. "Texas Girl Captures Lion with Lasso," undated, unnamed newspaper article from the Western History Collection, Denver Public Library.

20. Mary Stuart Abbott and Tana Mac, "Child of the Open Range," *Frontier Times* (December-January 1964), 20-22.

21. Florence Fenley, *Oldtimers: Their Own Stories* (Uvalde, Texas: Hornby Press, 1939), 156.

22. Lily Klasner, *My Girlhood Among Outlaws*, ed. Eve Ball, (Tucson: University of Arizona Press, 1972), 48-49.

23. William Roscoe "Mrs. William Jackson ('Kittie' White) 1882—," *Pioneer Cattlemen of Arizona* (Phoenix: McGrew Commercial Printery, 1951), 32.

24. "An Interesting Interview with Sharlot M. Hall, Arizona's Poet and Prescott's Pride," *Yavapai Magazine* (October 1924) typescript in the Sharlot M. Hall file, Arizona Historical Society, Tucson, Arizona.

25. James L. Watson, "Sharlot Hall: Arizona's Pioneer Lady of Literature," *Journal of the West* (October, 1965), 539-52.

26. "A Daring Western Woman: Texas Girl Who Acts as Cattle Guard," *Denver Times* (Feb. 17, 1901), 30.

27. C. P Westermeier, *Trailing the Cowboy*, (Caldwell, Idaho: Caxton Printers, 1950), quoting "Texas Cattle Girls," Kansas Cowboy (Dodge City, Kansas) (February 28, 1885), 326.

28. Westermeier, *Trailing the Cowboy*, quoting Great West (Denver, Colorado) (July 12, 1884), 325.

29. "'Miss Million' Manages Her Own Ranch: Was A Poor School Teacher in the East, Went West and is Now Famous and Wealthy," *Denver Times* (Sunday, November 4, 1902).

LAY THAT PISTOL DOWN, BABE

1. Eugene Manlove Rhodes, "Beyond the Desert" from *The Best Novels of Eugene Manlove Rhodes*, ed. Frank Dearing (Boston: Houghton Mifflin, 1949), 459.

2. From the files of Mody C. Boatright, University of Texas.

3. Paul Patterson, letter to author, Crane, Texas, March 11, 1972.

4. Adelle Harrell, "Bob Crabb, Ranchman on Shoe-Bar Ranch," July 3, 1939. Unpublished manuscript, Panhandle–Plains Museum, Canyon, Texas, 1-2.

5. C. W. Hurd, "Women Who Helped Make the West Wild," *Bent County Democrat* (Las Animas County) (July 15, 1938) Western History Collection, Denver Public Library.

6. Westermeier, *Trailing the Cowboy*, quoting "A Romantic Young Woman in the Role of a Drover," *Cherokee County Republican* (Columbus, Kansas) (January 26, 1877), 324.

7. "Frontier Sketches," *The Denver Field and Farm* (April 29, 1911).

8. F. Newton Reynolds, "Pioneering in the West," as related by Newt Bowers. Unpublished manuscript, Panhandle–Plains Museum, Canyon, Texas.

9. Fenley, *Oldtimers*, 64.

10. Ann Bassett Willis, "Queen Ann of Brown's Park," *The Colorado Magazine* (April 1952), 91-92.

11. Klasner, *My Girlhood Among Outlaws*, 34-35.

12. Coleman Evans papers, Diary, Part 5, Box 1, No. 0692E, Arizona Pioneers Historical Society Library, Tucson, Arizona.

13. "Women Who Have Shown Rare Pluck," *Denver Times*, Sept. 8, 1901.

14. Harriett Farnsworth, *Remnants of the Old West* (San Antonio: Naylor, 1965), 92-93.

15. "Women Who Have Shown Rare Pluck," *Denver Times*, Sept. 8, 1901.

16. Hobart Huson, *A History of Refugio County* (Woodsboro, Texas: Rooke Foundation, 1955), 203.

17. O. W. Nolen, "Banquete's Gun-toting Woman Horse Trader," *Corpus Christi Caller* (March 4, 1937).

18. Ibid.

19. Jesse Robinson file, Texas State Archives, Austin, Texas.

20. Huson, *A History of Refugio County*, 203.

21. "Banquet[t]e Home of Gun-toting Woman," *San Antonio Express*, Feb. 11, 1934.

22. Colonel Henry Perkins, Mercedes, Texas, "Sallie Skull," *Frontier Times* 6 (November 1928), 79.

23. "Banquet[t]e Home of Gun-toting Woman."

24. Huson, *A History of Refugio County*, 203-06.

25. Ibid.

26. Perkins, "Sallie Skull," 79.

27. Jesse Robinson File, Texas State Archives.

28. J. Frank Dobie, *Some Part of Myself* (Boston: Little and Brown, 1967), 98.

29. Perkins, "Sallie Skull," 79.

30. Dee Woods, "The Enigma of Juana Mestena," *Frontier Times* (February-March, 1966), 34.

31. Huson, *A History of Refugio County*, 203. Author's note: Shortly after the publication of the first edition of *The Cowgirls* in 1977, a gentleman from Arlington, Texas called, saying he was a distant kinsman of Sally Skull. His first name was Robert, his last name is forgotten. He said that according to family stories, Sally was caught stealing horses from a herd in Mexico and was shot. Although Robert said he would send written confirmation, I have never heard from him again.

32. Fenley, *Oldtimers*, 135-36.

33. Nolen, "Banquete's Gun-toting Woman."

34. A synthesis of previously given sources appears in author's "Horse Trader," *The Women Who Made The West* (Garden City, New York: Doubleday and Company, 1980), 178-186. Sally Skull also appears as a character in the musical folk drama, *Texanna*. Her philosophy expressed in the song, "Ride, Sally, Ride" is that horses were the most important thing in a western woman's life. The musical was produced in Texas during the Sesquicentennial in 1986. Sally Skull's name is spelled in various ways; it is also Sallie Skull, Sallie Scull, or Sally Scull.

INTO THEIR OWN HANDS

1. E. E. Townsend, Alpine, Texas, unpublished reminiscenses, from the files of Mody C. Boatright.

2. O. L. Shipman, *Taming the Big Bend* (Austin: Von Boeckmann-Jones, 1926), 101-03.

3. Dobie, *Some Part of Myself*, 176.

4. Hallie Stillwell, letter to author, Alpine, Texas, March 12, 1971.

5. E. E. Towsend, Boatright files.

6. Shipman, *Taming the Big Bend*, 101-04.

7. Dobie, *Some Part of Myself*, 177.

8. Willis, "Queen Ann," 82.

9. "Jury Unable to Decide if 'Queen Ann[e]' is Guilty," *Denver Post* (August 13, 1911). See also "Stories of Brown's Park and Its Glamorous Queen," *Steamboat Pilot* (April 20, 1939).

10. Willis, "Queen Ann," (July 1952): 225-35.

11. Mary Ann Kane, "Woman Rancher, Alleged Rustler, Dead," *Denver Post* (August 20, 1956).

12. Willis, "Queen Ann," (July, 1952), 219-24.

13. Willis, "Queen Ann," (January, 1953), 62-63.

14. Grace Ernestine Ray, *Wily Women of the West* (San Antonio: Naylor Co., 1972), 49.

15. Willis, "Queen Ann," (October, 1952), 285-87.

16. "Throng Courtroom For Queen Ann[e] Case," *Craig Empire* (August 16, 1913).

17. John Rolfe Burroughs, *Where The Old West Stayed Young* (New York: William Morrow and Co., 1962), 314-16.

18. Kane, "Woman Rancher, Alleged Rustler, Dead."

19. William A. Keleher, *Violence In Lincoln County* (Albuquerque: University of New Mexico Press, 1957), 159. In conversations with Maurice Fulton, author of *History of the Lincoln County War*, Mrs. McSween said it was an organ, not a piano which she owned. It was of a size that two men could move it. Information from "Sue McSween, Miscellaneous Notes," made by Robert Mullin who edited Fulton's book. Mr. Mullin sent me his notes on Susan along with a letter on November 8, 1973. Hereafter referred to as Mullin Notes.

20. Maurice G. Fulton, *History of the Lincoln County War* (Tucson: University of Arizona Press, 1968), 265-67.

21. Eve Ball, *Ma'am Jones of the Pecos* (Tucson: University of Arizona Press, 1969), 137-38. Further information from Eve Ball, in a letter to author, Ruidosa, New Mexico, May 17, 1973. Also Keleher, *Violence in Lincoln County*, 238.

22. "Funeral of Mrs. S. E. Barber Held at White Oaks Wednesday," *Carrizozo Outlook* (January 9, 1931).

23. Mullin Notes.

24. Mullin Notes. Also, although it may have not been widely known at the time or even had anything to do with Chisum's reputation as a woman-avoider as Mullin says, John had a Negro slave by whom he had two daughters. The family lived near Roanoke, Texas, and John cared for them generously and visited them whenever he could. Descendants of Chisum live today on the land willed to them by their famous ancestor. Harwood Hinton, editor of *Arizona and the West*, Tucson, Arizona, has made an extensive study of the family and shared this information with me during a conversation in August 1973.

25. Susan Barber, letter to Maurice Fulton, October 2, 1929, University of Arizona Library, Special Collections.

26. Article quoted in Keleher's *Violence in Lincoln County*, 160.

27. Mullin Notes.

28. Roy Harman and Clara Snow, joint letter to author, Carrizozo New Mexico, November 18, 1973.

29. Lacy Simms, letter to author, Alamogordo, New Mexico, December 4, 1973.

30. Simms letter.

31. Harman-Snow letter.

32. Mullin Notes.

33. Harman-Snow letter.

34. Eve Ball, letter to author, Ruidosa, New Mexico, May 17, 1973 .

35. Harman-Snow letter.

36. Barber letter to Fulton, January 28, 1926.

37. Barber letter to Fulton, August 1, 1930.

38. Barber letter to Fulton, June 13, 1926.

39. Barber letters to Fulton, June 13, November 22, January 28, 1926, July 2, 1928, and August 1, 1930.

40. James Padgitt, "The City Slicker," *West Texas Historical Association Yearbook* (October 1954), 61-70.

41. Padgitt, "Colonel William H. Day: Texas Ranchman," *Southwestern Historical Quarterly* (April 1950), 354-59.

42. Padgitt, "Early Day Coleman," *West Texas Historical Association Yearbook* (October 1952), 84.

43. Padgitt, "Colonel William H. Day," 365-66.

44. Padgitt, "Mrs. Mabel Day and the Fence Cutters," *West Texas Historical Association Yearbook* (October 1950), 55-57.

45. Ibid., 59.

46. Ibid.

47. Ibid., 60-67.

48. Ibid.

49. Padgitt, "Captain Joseph C. Lea, the Father of Roswell," *West Texas Historical Association Yearbook* (October 1959), 61-63. See also Padgitt, "Early History of New Mexico Military Institute," *West Texas Historical Association Yearbook* (October 1958).

Author's note: James Padgitt is Mrs. Mabel Day Lea's grandson.

THE LADY RUSTLERS

1. Virginia Cole Trenholm and Maurine Carley, *Wyoming Pageant* (Casper, Wyoming: Prairie Publishing Co., 1946), 207.

2. Hurd, "Women Who Helped Make The West Wild."

3. "Cattle Queen of Wyoming Must Serve Sentence," *Denver Post* (October 23, 1921).

4. Ray, *Wily Women of the West*, 33-36.

5. Raymond Hatfield Gardner, *The Old Wild West: The Adventures of Arizona Bill* (San Antonio: Naylor and Co., 1944), 239.

6. *Western Farm Life*, "Grace Newton," September 15, 1937, 12.

7. Gardner, *The Old Wild West*, 239.

8. Evett Dumas Nix, *Oklahombres* (Printed in U. S. A., 1929), 147-49.

9. Westermeier, *Trailing The Cowboy*, quoting "A Female Cow Boy," *Texas Live Stock Journal* (April 21, 1883), 325.

10. Ramon F. Adams, *Burrs Under the Saddle*, (Norman: University of Oklahoma Press, 1964), 277.

11. Nix, *Oklahombres*, 133.

12. Horan, *Desperate Women*, 246-248.

13. Zoe A. Tilghman, *Marshal of the Last Frontier* (Los Angeles, California: Arthur Clark, 1949), 206.

14. Horan, *Desperate Women*, 247.

15. Nix, *Oklahombres*, 224.

16. Horan, *Desperate Women*, 253-55.

17. Nix, *Oklahombres*, 228-29.

18. Horan, *Desperate Women*, 262-63. See also Zoe A. Tilghman, "I Knew 'Rose of the Cimarron,'" *True West* (May-June, 1958), 21. Mrs. Tilghman says Rose married Charles Noble in 1897. When Noble died, Rose married "an old friend" and moved to Stillwater, Oklahoma. She died there in 1956.

19. Ray, *Wily Women of the West*, 25-27.

20. Mari Sandoz, *The Cattlemen* (New York: Hastings House, 1958), 341.

21. E. B. Dykes Beachy, "The Saga of Cattle Kate," *Frontier Times* (February-March, 1964), 23.

22. Hurd, "Women Who Helped Make West Wild."

23. *Fort Smith Elevator*, "Cattle Kate" (March 1, 1889).

24. Forbes Parkhill, *The Wildest of the West* (New York: Henry Holt and Co., 1951), 31.

25. Ray, *Wily Women of the West*, 22.

26. Beachy, "Saga of Cattle Kate," 23.

27. Beachy says that Averill set Kate up in her own place about a mile from his place, "Saga of Cattle Kate," 23.

28. Ray, *Wily Women of the West*, quoting Ramon F. Adams, 23.

29. Ray, *Wily Women of the West*, quoting a letter from Agnes Wright Spring, 23. For more about Cattle Kate see also Horan, *Desperate Women*, 230.

30. From Mody C. Boatright's file on frontier women. The story was from his unpublished and unfinished essay on women dressed up like men.

OUT OF THE CHUTES: THE EARLY YEARS

1. Mody C. Boatright, "The American Rodeo," *American Quarterly* (Summer 1964), 198.

2. Don Russell, *The Lives and Legends of Buffalo Bill* (Norman, Oklahoma: University of Oklahoma Press), 1965, 291-95.

3. Mary Lucille Deaton, "The History of the Rodeo" (Master's Thesis, University of Texas, 1952), 16.

4. Russell, *Lives and Legends*, 314-30.

5. Don Russell, *The Wild West* (Fort Worth, Texas: Amon Carter Museum of Western Art, 1970), 105.

6. Russell, *Lives and Legends*, 315-76.

7. Russell, *The Wild West*, 50-52.

8. Russell, *Lives and Legends*, 446.

9. Foghorn Clancy, *My Fifty Years in Rodeo* (San Antonio, Texas: Naylor and Co., 1952), 26.

10. Westermeier, *Trailing the Cowboy*, 344.

11. Russell, *The Wild West*, 59.

12. Westermeier, *Man, Beast, Dust: The Story of Rodeo* (World Press, 1947), 35-36.

13. Milt Hinkle, "Cowgirls—Rodeo's Sugar and Spice," *Frontier Times* (October-November, 1971), 40.

14. Warren Richardson, "History of First Frontier Days Celebration," *Annals of Wyoming* (1947), 42-43.

15. Lee Ryland, "Skirts, Powder Puffs and Rodeos," *Big West* (April 1968), 8-9. See also Deaton, "History of the Rodeo," 96.

16. Westermeier, *Man, Beast, Dust*, 83.

17. Hinkle, "Cowgirls," 40.

18. Robert D. Hanesworth, *Daddy of 'Em All* (Cheyenne: Flintlock Publishing Co., 1967), 35-48.

19. Clancy, *Fifty Years in Rodeo*, 26.

20. Cheyenne Frontier Days programs called them cowgirls in 1897.

21. Typed interview with Stephens from a tape recording taken December 27, 1952 and belonging to Mody C. Boatright. Stephens was an old-time puncher remembered for "Night Herding Song," published in Lomax's collection in 1910.

22. Fred Gipson in *Fabulous Empire* (Boston: Houghton Mifflin 1946), 235-7, makes no mention of Lucille but tells only about Will Rogers roping a steer that got into the stands. Tom Mix is mentioned in Russell's *The Wild West*, 80.

23. Louise Cheney, "Lucile [sic.] Mulhall, Fabulous Cowgirl," *Real West* (March 1969), 13-15, 58, 59, 73. See also Ryland, "Skirts, Powder Puffs and Rodeos," 10, Westermeier, *Man, Beast, Dust*, 84, Hinkle "Cowgirls," 40-42, and Russell, *The Wild West*, 79-80.

24. Mildred Chrisman, letter to author, March 12, 1972.

25. Ruth Roach, later Mrs. Fred Salmon, interview with author, at the Salmon ranch, Nocona, Texas. March 19, 1972.

26. Russell, *The Wild West*, 78-83. See also Gipson's *Fabulous Empire* for more about the 101 Ranch.

27. Ellsworth Collings and Alma Miller England, *The 101 Ranch* (Norman, Oklahoma: University of Oklahoma Press, 1938), 166.

28. Russell, *The Wild West*, 82.

29. Cleo Tom Terry and Osie Wilson, *The Rawhide Tree: The Story of Florence Reynolds in Rodeo* (Clarendon, Texas: Clarendon Press, 1957), 51.

30. Dee Brown, *The Gentle Tamers* (Lincoln, Nebraska: University of Nebraska Press, 1968, paperback), 189.

31. Clancy, *Fifty Years in Rodeo*, 26.

32. Russell, *The Wild West*, 82.

33. Terry and Wilson, *The Rawhide Tree*, 50-51.

34. Russell, *The Wild West*, 91.

35. Ibid., 85-106.

36. Westermeier, *Man, Beast, Dust*, 46.

37. Hinkle, "Cowgirl's," 40.

38. Westermeier, *Man, Beast, Dust*, 48-49.

39. Clancy, *Fifty Years in Rodeo*, 67-68.

40. Velda Tindall Smith and Charlie Smith, interview with author, March 9, 1972 at the Smith's Kennedale, Texas ranch. Both knew Fox and rodeoed with her during their careers.

41. Clancy, *Fifty Years in Rodeo*, 135. See also Hinkle, "Cowgirls," 42.

42. Westermeier, *Man, Beast, Dust*, 319.

43. Clancy, *Fifty Years in Rodeo*, 76.

44. Russell, *The Wild West*, 108.

45. Crosby and Ball, *Bob Crosby*, 84. See also Westermeier, *Man, Beast. Dust*, 128.

46. Mildred Douglas Chrisman, letter to author, March 31, 1972.

47. Mabel Strickland, now Mrs. Sam Woodward, letter to author, Buckeye, Arizona, April 3, 1972.

48. Other information taken from Mabel Strickland's correspondences on February 4, May 15, July 7, 1971 and March 2, 1972 to author. See also Willard H. Porter, "The American Rodeo," *The American West* (July 1971), 40-47, for mention of Mabel Strickland in rodeo.

OUT OF THE CHUTES: THE LATER YEARS

1. Russell, *The Wild West*, 106.

2. Crosby and Ball, *Bob Crosby*, 77-80.

3. Ruth Roach Salmon, interview with author, March 19, 1972. For more about Ruth see also *The Nocona News* (January 21, 1949).

4. Lorene Bowman, "Famed Wild West Showgirl Now Nocona Ranch Woman," *Wichita Falls Times* (March 30, 1958).

5. Information from the Palladium program belonging to Ruth Roach Salmon.

6. Vera McGinnis Farra, letter to author, Oklahoma, May 12, 1972.

7. Mildred Douglas Chrisman letter to author, Arixona, March 31, 1972.

8. Sally Gray, "Florence Hughes Randolph," *Quarter Horse Journal* (March 1971), 42-44, 50, 52, 54, and (April 1971), 124-126, 140, 142, 144. Florence died in late April of 1971.

9. Tad Lucas, interview with author, May 21, 1970, Fort Worth, Texas, and from many visits and phone calls since then.

10. Crosby and Ball, *Bob Crosby*, 90.

11. Juanita Gray McCracken, interview with author, Kennedale, Texas, March 19, 1972.

12. Velda and Charlie Smith, interview with author, Kennedale, Texas, March 9, 1972, and from many visits and phone calls since then.

13. Gray, "Florence Hughes Randolph," *Quarter Horse Journal* (April, 1971), 126.

14. Crosby and Ball, *Bob Crosby*, 156-157.

15. Boatright, "The American Rodeo," 202. Additional information about rodeo is found in Kristine Fredriksson, *American Rodeo: From Buffalo Bill to Big Business* (College Station: Texas A&M Press, 1985).

WITH QUIRT AND SPUR

1. Information on this and all other events was obtained from taped interviews with Tad Lucas, Velda and Charlie Smith, and from notes made while visiting Juanita and Jack McCracken, from scrapbooks and souvenir programs, unless otherwise stated.

2. See also Hinkle, "Cowgirls," 40.

3. Mabel Strickland Woodward, letter to author, Arizona, July 7, 1971. Velda and Charlie Smith also remembered the incident. When I asked Tad why she didn't tell me the story, she said it was because it sounded so unlikely, she was afraid I wouldn't believe her.

4. Clancy, *Fifty Years in Rodeo*, 168.

5. This story seems to circulate wherever rodeo people gather and remember old times.

6. Gray, "Florence Hughes Randolph," 50.

7. Ibid., 52.

8. Farra letter.

9. Westermeier, *Man, Beast, Dust*, 99-129.

10. Ibid., 120.

11. Hanesworth, *Daddy of 'Em All*, 147.

12. Deaton, "History of Rodeo," 65-66.

13. "Local Rancher, Rodeo Performer, Jackie Worthington Dies Saturday," *Jacksboro Gazette News* (September 28, 1987).

14. For a description of modern cowgirl participation see "Cowgirls," *Texas Monthly* (November 1987).

I SEE BY YOUR OUTFIT

1. Cheney, "Lucile [sic]. Mulhall," 13. See also Russell, *The Wild West*, 73.

2. Russell, *Lives and Legends*, 466-67. See also "The Princess Passes," *Hoofs and Horns* (February 1941).

3. Cheney, "Lucile [sic] Mulhall," 59.

4. Ryland, "Skirts, Powder-Puffs and Rodeos," 11.

5. Hanesworth, *Daddy of 'Em All*, 35.

6. Russell, *The Wild West*, 23.

7. Tad Lucas, taped interview with author, Fort Worth, Texas, May 21, 1970.

8. Terry and Wilson, *The Rawhide Tree*, 76.

9. Hanesworth, *Daddy of 'Em All*, p. 91.

10. For drawings of Mexican charros and rancheros wearing the type clothing copied by the cowgirls see José Cisneros, *Riders of the Border: A Selection of Thirty Drawings* (El Paso, Texas: Texas Western Press, 1971), 36, 50.

11. Westermeier, *Man, Beast, Dust*, 72.

12. Guy Logsdon, "The Rodeo Cowboy" (Paper read before American Folklore Society, Atlanta, Georgia, November 9, 1969).

13. Brown, *The Gentle Tamers*, 109-10.

14. Bird, *A Lady's Life*, 10.

15. Hallie Stillwell, letter to author, Alpine, Texas, March 12, 1971.

16. See chapter on gunwomen.

17. Crosby and Ball, *Bob Crosby*, 36.

18. Cleaveland, *No Life For a Lady*, 242.

19. Collings and England, *The 101 Ranch*, 166.

20. C. L. Sonnichsen, *Cowboys and Cattle Kings* (Norman: University of Oklahoma Press, 1950), 31.

WILD, WILD WOMEN

1. Ned Taylor, *Rough Rider Weekly*, "King of the Wild West's Nerve; or, Stella in the Saddle" (New York: Street and Smith, 1906), 27.

2. Joe Frantz and Julian Ernest Choate, Jr., *The American Cowboy* (Norman: University of Oklahoma Press, 1955), 145.

3. Edmund Pearson, *Dime Novels, or, Following an Old Trail in Popular Literature* (Boston: Little, Brown and Co., 1929), 37.

4. Henry Nash Smith, *Virgin Land* (New York: Vintage Books, paperback, 1950), 129-31.

5. Titles of only a few dime novels such as *Ang'l of the Range; Backwoods Belle; Baleful Beauty of Brimstone; The Beautiful Amazon of Hidden Valley; Belle of the Border; Bessie the Stock Tender's Daughter; Blackfoot Queen; Border Huntress; Camille the Card Queen; Chip, the Girl Sport; Dainty Dot of Gold Gulch; Daisy Dare, the Sport from Denver; The Fair Huntress of the South-West; Fandango Queen;*

Frontier Angel; Flower of the Prairie; Girl Mustang Rider; Hunted Maid of Taos; Jack, the Girl Shot; Keetsea, the Queen of the Plains; Lillie, the Reckless Rider; Mad Madge, the Outlaw Queen; Masked Woman of the Colorado Canyon; Outlaw Queen; Rose of Wyoming; Stella Delorme's Comanche Lover; and *Wilda the Brand-Burner's Daughter* indicate to what extent women were involved in the action. Titles taken at random from list of titles in Albert Johannsen, *The House of Beadle and Adams and Its Dime and Nickel Novel* (Norman: University of Oklahoma Press, 1950).

6. Smith, *Virgin Land*, 134.

7. Douglas Branch, *The Cowboy and His Interpreters* (New York: Cooper Square Publishers, Inc., 1961), 181.

8. Smith, *Virgin Land*, 134.

9. Waldo E. Koop, letter to author, Tucson, Arizona, June 26, 1972. Mr. Koop, an authority on Rowdy Joe Lowe and Rowdy Kate found that Kate was very ladylike in most of her actions. She probably suffered from Rowdy Joe's reputation more than from her own.

10. Smith, *Virgin Land*, 129.

11. Brown, *The Gentle Tamers*, 59-65.

12. Johanssen, *House of Beadle and Adams*, 301.

13. Smith, *Virgin Land*, 131.

14. Mrs. E. J. Guerin, *Mountain Charley or The Adventures of Mrs. E. J. Guerin, Who Was Thirteen Years in Male Attire*, eds. Fred Mazzula and William Kostka (New York: Ballantine Books, 1971), vii-xi. A first edition is in the DeGolyer Library, Dallas, Texas.

15. Smith, *Virgin Land*, 130.

16. Westermeier, *Trailing the Cowboy*, 323-27.

17. Quoted in "Arizona's Mollie Monroe Calamity's Counterpart," *Tucson Daily Citizen* (Friday, October 19, 1973).

18. "Our California Letter," *The Weekly Arizona Miner* (Prescott, Arizona) (January 30, 1880). For more about Mollie see also the Hayden File, Arizona Pioneer Historical Society Library, Tucson, Arizona.

19. Joseph E. Badger, Jr., *The Barranca Wolf; or, The Beautiful Decoy, A Romance of the Texas Border* (New York: Beadle and Adams), July 3, 1883, Half Dime Library, No. 310, 2.

20. E. L. Wheeler, *The Detective Queen; or, Denver Doll's Devices* (New York: M. J. Ivers and Co.), March 14, 1900, Deadwood Dick Library, 3.

21. Wheeler, *The Girl Sport; or, Jumbo Joe's Disguise* (New York: M. J Ivers and Co.), March 7, 1900, 4-7, 23.

22. Wheeler, *Deadwood Dick on Deck; or, Calamity Jane, The Heroine of Whoop-Up* (New York: M. J. Ivers and Company), June 21, 1899, 2-4, 24.

23. Wheeler, *Deadwood Dick in Leadville; or, A Strange Stroke for Liberty* (New York: M. J. Ivers and Company), August 16, 1899, 9-22.

24. George Waldo Browne, *The Tiger of Taos; or, Wild Kate, Dandy Rock's Angel* (New York: Beadle and Adams), June 17, 1879, Half Dime Library, 3-5.

25. J. Edward Leithead, "Arietta: Heroine of Wild West Trails," *Dime Novel Round-Up* (April 15, 1963), 32-36.

26. Leithead, "Ted Strong and His Rough Riders," Dime Novel Round–Up (June 15, 1961), 66-67.

27. Leithead, "Arietta," 33.

28. Leithead, "Ted Strong and His Rough Riders," 77.

29. Russell, *The Wild West*, 83.

30. Leithead, "Ted Strong," 78.

31. Frank Lockwood, *Pioneer Days in Arizona* (New York: 1932), 282.

32. Taylor, King of *Wild West's Nerve*, 2-24.

33. Wilson M. Hudson, Andy Adams: *Storyteller and Novelist of the Great Plains* (Austin: Steck Vaughn, 1970), 29.

34. True Grit Series was introduced by Henry T. Coates and Company in 1902. Information from Denis R. Rogers, "A Publication Pattern," *Dime Novel Round-Up* (September, 1972), 81.

35. Badger, *The Barranca Wolf*, 8.

36. Charles M. Harvey, "The Dime Novel in American Life," *Atlantic Monthly* (July 1907), 44.

37. William A. Settle, "The Dime Novel as an Historian's tool," *Dime Novel Round-Up* (September 1970), 95.

38. Merle Curti, "Dime Novels and the American Tradition," *Yale Review* (Summer, 1937), 761.

39. Harvey, "Dime Novel in American Life," p. 43.

A BOOK BY ITS COVER

1. W. H. Hutchinson, "Virgins, Villains, and Varmints," *The Rhodes Reader* (Norman: University of Oklahoma Press, 1957), introductory essay, xiii.

2. Ibid.

3. Helen Rogan, Review of *The Californios*, by Louis L'Amour. Time (April 29, 1974), 108.

4. Hutchinson, *A Bar Cross Man* (Norman: University of Oklahoma Press, 1956), 200.

5. Frantz and Choate, *The American Cowboy*, 175.

6. Branch, *The Cowboy and His Interpreters*, 205. Dr. Jim McNutt at the Institute of Texan Cultures, San Antonio, Texas, developed a permanent exhibit, Ranch Women: Roles, Images, Possibilities, and made a case that Amanda Burks, cattlewoman from Cotulla, Texas, was the model for Taisie Lockhart.

7. Bernard DeVoto, "The Novelist of the Cattle Kingdom," in May Rhodes, *The Hired Man on Horseback* (Boston: Houghton-Mifflin 1938).

8. Hutchinson, "Virgins, Villains and Varmints", xviii.

9. Hutchinson, *A Bar Cross Man*, 208

10. Paul Patterson, interview with author, Texas Folklore Society meeting, San Antonio, Texas, April, 1974.

11. Robert Flynn, interview with author, San Antonio, Texas, April 12, 1974.

PAULINE OUT WEST

1. Kalton C. Lahue, *Continued Next Week* (Norman: University of Oklahoma Press, 1964), 23-155.

2. Richard Griffith and Arthur Mayer, *The Movies* (New York: Bonanza Books, 1957), 87.

3. Titles from *Continued Next Week*, and from Raymond William Stedman, The Serials (Norman: University of Oklahoma Press, 1971).

4. Claire Eyrich, "Give the Little Girl —" *Fort Worth Star-Telegram* (May 18, 1969).

5. Paul Sann, *The Lawless Decade* (New York: Crown Publishers, 1957), 183.

6. Jerry Flemmons, "Suckers Were Just Buddies to Our Texas Guinan," *Fort Worth Star-Telegram* (May 16, 1969) Evening.

7. Willima Bolitho, "Two Stars," *Delineator* (January 1931), 15.

8. Sann, *Lawless Decade*, 183.

9. Bolitho, "Two Stars", 15.

10. Clancy, *Fifty Years in Rodeo*, 26.

11. Westermeier, *Man, Beast, Dust*, 48-49.

12. Mildred Douglas Chrisman, letter to author, Arizona, March 31, 1972.

13. George Fennin and William Everson, *The Westerns From Silents to Cinerama* (New York: Crown Publishers, 1962), 40-209.

14. Mody C. Boatright, "The Cowboy Enters the Movies," *The Sunny Slopes of Long Ago*, Texas Folklore Society Publication, 33 (Dallas: Southern Methodist University Press, 1966), 62-64.

15. *The Moving Picture World* (November 30, 1912), 209.

16. *The Moving Picture World* (August 5, 1911), 308.

17. *New York Times Film Review* 1913-1918 (New York: New York Times and Arno Press, 1970), 40.

18. *The Moving Picture World* (July 13, 1912), 176.

19. *The Moving Picture World* (February 18, 1911), 378.

20. *Catalog of Motion Pictures* Davenport: Eastin-Phelan Corp. (Spring-Summer, 1972).

21. *Bronco Billy's Sentence*, Blackhawk Films, Eastin-Phelan Corp., Davenport, Iowa.

22. *The Prairie Pirate*, Blackhawk Films, Eastin-Phelan Corp., Davenport, Iowa.

23. *New York Times Film Review* (New York: Arno Press, 1970), 21.

24. Griffith and Mayer, *The Movies*, 93.

25. Fennin and Everson, *From Silents to Cinerama*, 148.

26. Gipson, *Fabulous Empire*, 187.

27. Fennin and Everson, *From Silents to Cinerama*, 210.

28. *Ibid.*, 183-267.

29. Michael Parkinson and Clyde Jeavons, *A Pictorial History of Westerns* (New York: Hamlyn Publishers, 1972), 55.

30. Ibid., 58-61

31. Fennin and Everson, *From Silents to Cinerama*, 40-41.

32. Parkinson and Jeavons, *Pictorial History*, 151, 160.

33. Peter Bogdanovich, *John Ford* (Berkeley: University of California Press, 1968), 34.

34. Parkinson and Jeavons, *Pictorial History*, 37.

35. W. M. Selig, *An Arizona Wooing* (1915) Blackhawk Films, Eastin-Phelan Corp., Davenport, Iowa.

36. Fennin and Everson, *From Silents to Cinerama*, 234.

37. *New York Times Film Review*, 223.

38. Parkinson and Jeavons, *Pictorial History*, 73, 192.

MY LOVE IS A RIDER

1. N. Howard (Jack) Thorp, *Songs of the Cowboys*, eds. Austin and Alta Fife (New York: Clarkson N. Potter, 1960), 38.

2. John and Alan Lomax, *Cowboy Songs and Other Frontier Ballads* (New York: Macmillan, 1938), 241.

3. Ibid., 188.

4. Ibid., 7-8.

5. Ibid., 188.

6. Margaret Larkin, *Singing Cowboy* (New York: Oak Publications, 1963), 148-50.

7. Thorp, *Songs of Cowboys*, 164.

8. Ibid., 48-49.

9. Ibid., 91.

10. Lomax, *Cowboy Songs*, 308-11.

11. Thorp, *Songs of Cowboys*, 1-2.

12. Lomax, *Cowboy Songs*, 55.

13. Thorp, *Songs of Cowboys*, 134.

14. Larkin, *Singing Cowboy*, 72-74.

15. Lomax, *Cowboy Songs*, 269.

16. Ibid., 300.

17. Ibid., 189.

18. Thorp, *Songs of Cowboys*, 10. See also J. Frank Dobie, "Mustang Gray: Fact, Tradition, Song," *Tone the Bell Easy* (Austin: Texas Folklore Society, 1932), 109. Dobie says Maberry "Mustang" Gray was not a cowboy but a ruthless raider who preyed on Mexican ranches.

19. Ibid., 104.

20. Katie Lee, *Ten Thousand Goddam Cattle* (Flagstaff: Northland Press, 1976), 104-05, 207-08.

21. Thorp, *Songs of Cowboys*, 124-25.

22. C. L. Sonnichsen, *Tularosa* (New York: Devin Adair, 1961), 23.

23. Thorp, *Songs of Cowboys*, 170-71.

24. Ibid., 94-95.

25. Larkin, *Singing Cowboy*, 148-50.

26. Thorp, *Songs of Cowboys*, 126-27.

27. Paul Patterson, letter to author, Sierra Blanca, Texas, 1973.

28. Lee, *Ten Thousand Goddam Cattle*, 122-23.

29. Ibid., 211.

30. Lomax. *Cowboy Songs*, 223-24.

31. Richard M. Dorson, "A Theory for American Folklore Reviewed," *American Folklore of the Historian* (Chicago: University of Chicago Press, 1971), 68.

32. The version in which the man appears as the rider may be found in Jack Thorp's "Banjo In The Cow Camps," *Atlantic Monthly* (August 1940), 200. He says the song was expurgated before printing. Also called "Johnny Ringo" in Lee, *Ten Thousand Goddam Cattle*, 109.

33. Ramon F. Adams, *The Old-Time Cowhand* (New York: Collier Books, 1961), 337. Guy Logsdon, *The Whorehouse Bells Were Ringing*, (Chicago: University of Illinois Press, 1989) offers a collection of bawdy cowboy songs about the cowboy life, cowgirls included.

34. Thorp, *Songs of Cowboys*, 745.

35. Beverly J. Stoeltje, "A Helpmate for Man Indeed," *Journal of American Folklore* (January-March, 1975), 40.

NO LAUGHING MATTER

1. A story which circulates whenever cow people congregate.

2. Hennig Cohen and William B. Dillingham, *The Humor of the Old Southwest* (Boston: Houghton Mifflin, 1964), ix-x.

3. Ibid., 74.

4. Ibid., 181.

5. Ibid., 319-21.

6. Mody C. Boatright, *Folk Laughter on the American Frontier* (New York: Collier Books, 1961), 17-18.

7. Randolph B. Marcy, *Thirty Years of Army Life on the Border* (New York: Harper and Bros., 1866), 357.

8. Boatright, *Folk Laughter*, 44.

9. Ibid., 45-46.

10. Ibid., 43.

11. Ibid., 45-46.

12. Ibid.

13. Ibid., 53.

14. Ibid.

15. Leigh Peck, *Pecos Bill and Lightning* (Boston: Houghton Mifflin, 1940), 61-65.

16. Irwin Shapiro, *Pecos Bill and Other Tales* (New York: Golden Press, 1958), 17-18. See also Mody C. Boatright, *Tall Tales from Texas* (Dallas: Southwest Press, 1934).

17. Brochure provided by Ace Reid Enterprises, Box 868, Kerrville, Texas.

18. Ace Reid cartoons are found in *Cowpokes, More Cowpokes, and Draggin S Cartoons* (Kerrville, Texas: Ace Reid Enterprises).

19. Lex Graham cartoon books published under the title, *North Forty* (Wichita Falls, Texas).

20. A familiar, circulating tale.

21. Stella Polk, letter to author, Mason, Texas, March 1, 1973. The first story is also found in Stella Polk, *Mason and Mason County* (Austin: Pemberton Press, 1966).

22. Family story about Joyce Roach, Summer, 1975.

23. Polk letter. Outwitting Indians by pouring hot water or oil on them appears in many early accounts. I call it the "Three Little Pigs" motif.

24. James Bratcher, letter to author, Fort Worth, Texas, March 31, 1973.

BIBLIOGRAPHY

BOOKS

Adams, Ramon. *Burrs Under the Saddle*. Norman: University of Oklahoma Press, 1964.

———. *The Old Time Cowhand*. New York: Collier Books, 1961.

Ball, Eve. *Ma'am Jones of the Pecos*. Tucson: University of Arizona Press, 1969.

Bird, Isabella. *A Lady's Life in the Rocky Mountains*. Norman: University of Oklahoma Press, 1960.

Boatright, Mody C. *Folk Laughter on the American Frontier*. New York: Collier Books, 1961.

Branch, Douglas. *The Cowboy and His Interpreters*. New York: Cooper Square Publishers, 1961.

Brown, Dee. *The Gentle Tamers*. Lincoln: University of Nebraska Press, 1968.

Bunton, Mary Taylor. *A Bride on the Old Chisholm Trail*. San Antonio, 1939.

Burroughs, John Rolfe. *Where the Old West Stayed Young*. New York: William Morrow, 1962.

Burton, True. *A History of the JA Ranch* (New York: Argonaut Press, 1966).

Clancy, Foghorn. *My Fifty Years in Rodeo*. San Antonio: Naylor and Company, 1952.

Cleaveland, Agnes Morley, *No Life for a Lady*. Boston: Houghton Mifflin, 1941.

Collins, Ellsworth and Alma Miller England. *The 101 Ranch.* Norman: University of Oklahoma Press, 1938.

Crosby, Thelma, and Eve Ball. *Bob Crosby, World Champion Cowboy* (Clarendon, Texas: Clarendon Press, 1966).

Dobie, J. Frank. "Mustang Gray: Fact, Tradition, Song," *Tone the Bell Easy.* Austin: Texas Folklore Society, 1932.

———. *The Mustangs.* Boston: Little Brown and Co., 1952.

———. *Some Part of Myself.* Boston: Little Brown and Co., 1967.

Dorson, Richard M. "A Theory for American Folklore Reviewed," *American Folklore of the Historian.* Chicago: University of Chicago Press, 1971.

Douglas, C. L. *Cattle Kings of Texas.* Fort Worth: Branch Smith, 1939.

Farnsworth, Harriett. *Remnants of the Old West.* San Antonio: Naylor, 1965.

Fenley, Florence. *Oldtimers: Their Own Stories.* Uvalde, Texas: Hornby Press, 1939.

Frantz, Joe and Julian Ernest Choate, Jr. *The American Cowboy.* Norman: University of Oklahoma Press, 1956.

Fredriksson, Kristine. *American Rodeo: From Buffalo Bill to Big Business.* College Station: Texas A&M Press, 1985.

Fulton, Maurice G. *History of the Lincoln County War.* Tucson: University of Arizona Press, 1968.

Gardner, Raymond Hatfield. The Old West: *The Adventures of Arizona Bill.* San Antonio: Naylor and Co., 1944.

Gibson, Fred. *Fabulous Empire.* Boston: Houghton Mifflin, 1946.

Greenwood, Kathy. *Heart-Diamond.* Denton: University of North Texas Press, 1990.

Guerin, Mrs. E. J. *Mountain Charley or The Adventures of Mrs. E. J. Guerin, Who Was Thirteen Years in Male Attire.* ed. Fred Mazzula and William Kostka. New York: Ballantine Books, 1971.

Haley, J. Evetts. *Charles Goodnight: Cowman and Plainsman.* New York: Houghton, Mifflin, 1936.

Hamner, Laura V. *Light n' Hitch.* Dallas: American Guild Press, 1958.

Hanesworth, Robert D. *Daddy of 'Em All.* Cheyenne: Flintlock Publishing, 1967.

Horan, James D. *Desperate Women.* New York: G. P. Putnam, 1952.

Hudson, Wilson M. *Andy Adams: Storyteller and Novelist of the Great Plains.* Austin: Steck Vaughn, 1970.

Hunter, J. Marvin, ed. *The Trail Drivers of Texas.* Nashvile: Cokesbury Press, 1925.

Huson, Hobart. *A History of Refugio County.* Woodsboro, Texas: Rooke Foundation, 1955.

Hutchinson, W. H. *A Bar Cross Man.* Norman: University of Oklahoma Press, 1956.

———. "Virgins, Villains and Varmints," *The Rhodes Reader.* Norman: University of Oklahoma Press, 1957.

Keleher, William A. *Violence in Lincoln County.* Albuquerque: University of New Mexico Press, 1957.

Klasner, Lily. *My Girlhood Among Outlaws.* ed. Eve Ball. Tucson: University of Arizona Press, 1972.

Larkin, Margaret. *Singing Cowboy.* New York: Oak Publications, 1963.

Lee, Katie. *Ten Thousand Goddam Cattle.* Flagstaff: Northland Press, 1976.

Lockwood, Frank. *Pioneer Days in Arizona.* New York: Macmillan, 1932.

Logsdon, Guy. *The Whorehouse Bells Were Ringing.* Chicago: University of Illinois Press, 1989.

Lomax, John and Alan. *Cowboy Songs and Other Frontier Ballads.* New York: Macmillan, 1938.

Marcy, Randolph B. *Thirty Years of Army Life On the Border.* New York: Harper and Bros., 1886.

McMurtry, Larry. *In a Narrow Grave: Essays on Texas.* Austin: Encino Press, 1968.

Nix, Evett Dumas. *Oklahombres* (Printed in U. S. A., 1929)

O'Donnell, Pearl Foster. *Trek to Texas: 1870-1880.* Fort Worth: Branch Smith, 1966.

Parkhill, Forbes. *The Wildest of the West.* New York: Henry Holt and Co., 1951.

Peck, Leigh. *Pecos Bill and Lightning.* Boston: Houghton Mifflin, 1940.

Polk, Stella. *Mason and Mason County.* Austin: Pemberton Press, 1966.

Porter, Emily. *Memory Cups of Panhandle Pioneers.* Clarendon: Clarendon Press, 1945.

Ray, Grace Ernestine. *Wily Women of the West.* San Antonio: Naylor, 1972.

Rhodes, May. *Hired Man on Horseback.* Boston: Houghton Mifflin, 1938.

Rhodes, Eugene Manlove. "Beyond the Desert" from *The Best Novels of Eugene Manlove Rhodes.* ed. Frank Dearing. Boston: Houghton Mifflin, 1949.

Rollins, Philip Ashton. *The Cowboy.* New York: Charles Scribner's Sons, 1922.

Roscoe, William. "Mrs. William Jackson ('Kittie' White) 1882—," *Pioneer Cattlemen of Arizona.* Phoenix: McGrew Commercial Printery, 1951.

Russell, Don. *The Lives and Legends of Buffalo Bill.* Norman: University of Oklahoma Press, 1970.

———. *The Wild West.* Fort Worth: Amon Carter Museum of Western Art, 1970.

Sandoz, Mari. *The Cattlemen.* New York: Hastings House, 1958.

Sann, Paul. *The Lawless Decade.* New York: Crown Publishers, 1957.

Shapiro, Irwin. *Pecos Bill and Other Tales.* New York: Golden Press, 1958.

Shipman, O. L. *Taming the Big Bend.* Austin: Von Boeckmann-Jones, 1926.

Sonnichsen, C. L. *From Hopalong to Hud: Thoughts on Western Fiction.* College Station: Texas A&M University Press, 1978.

———. *Tularosa.* New York: Devin Adair, 1961.

Sprague, William Forrest. *Women of the West.* Boston: Christopher Publishing Co., 1940.

Smith, Henry Nash. *Virgin Land.* New York: Vintage Books, 1950.

Taylor, T. U. *The Chisholm Trail and Other Routes.* San Antonio: Naylor, 1936.

Terry, Cleo Tom and Osie Wilson. *The Rawhide Tree: The Story of Florence Reynolds in Rodeo.* Clarendon: Clarendon Press, 1957.

Thorp, N. Howard (Jack). *Songs of the Cowboys.* ed. Austin and Alta Fife. New York: Clarkson N. Potter, 1960.

Tilghman, Zoe A. *Marshal of the Last Frontier.* Los Angeles: Arthur Clark, 1949.

Trenholm, Virginia Cole and Maurine Carley. *Wyoming Pageant.* Casper: Prairie Publishing Co., 1946.

Waggoner, J. J. *History of the Cattle Industry in Southern Arizona.* Tucson: University of Arizona, 1952.

Wecter, Dixon. *The Hero in America.* Ann Arbor: University of Michigan Press, 1960.

Westermeier, C. P. *Man, Beast, Dust: The Story of Rodeo.* New York: World Press, 1947.

———. *Trailing the Cowboy.* Caldwell: Caxton Printers, 1950.

CARTOONS

Graham, Lex. *The North Forty.* Wichita Falls: Lex Graham.

Reid, Ace. *Cowpokes.* Kerrville: Ace Reid Enterprises.

DIME NOVEL

Badger, Joseph E., Jr. *The Barranca Wolf; or, The Beautiful Decoy, A Romance of the Texas Border.* Half Dime Library. New York: Beadle and Adams, July 3, 1883.

Brown, George Waldo. *The Tiger of Taos; or, Wild Kate, Dandy Rock's Angel.* Half Dime Library. New York: Beadle and Adams, June 17, 1879.

Curti, Merle. "Dime Novels and the American Tradition," *Yale Review*, Summer, 1937.

Harvey, Charles M. "The Dime Novel in American Life," *Atlantic Monthly*, July 1907.

Johannsen, Albert. *The House of Beadle and Adams and Its Dime and Nickel Novel.* Norman: University of Oklahoma Press, 1950.

Leithead, J. Edward. "Arietta: Heroine of Wild West Trails," *Dime Novel Round-Up*, April 15, 1963.

———. "Ted Strong and His Rough Riders," *Dime Novel Round-Up*, June 15, 1961.

Pearson, Edmund. *Dime Novels; or, Following an Old Trail in Popular Literature.* Boston: Little, Brown and Co., 1929.

Denis R. Rogers, "A Publication Pattern," *Dime Novel Round-Up.* September, 1972.

Settle, William A. "The Dime Novel as a Historian's Tool," *Dime Novel Round-up*, September, 1970.

Taylor, Ned. *Rough Rider Weekly.* "King of the Wild West's Nerve; or, Stella in the Saddle." New York: Street and Smith, 1906.

Wheeler, E. L. *Deadwood Dick on Deck; or, Calamity Jane, The Heroine of Whoop-Up.* New York: M. J. Ivers, June 21, 1889.

———. *Deadwood Dick in Leadville; or, a Strange Stroke for Liberty.* New York: M. J. Ivers, August 16, 1889.

———. *The Detective Queen; or Denver Doll's Devices.* New York: M. J. Ivers, March 4, 1900.

———. *The Girl Sport; or, Jumbo Joe's Disguise.* New York: M. J. Ivers, March 7, 1900.

EXHIBITS

Ranch Women: Roles, Images, Possibilities. Institute of Texan Cultures. San Antonio, Texas.

FILES

Boatright, Mody C. Loaned to the author; now, possibly located at The University of Texas, Austin, Texas.

Borland, Margaret. Texas State Archives. Austin, Texas.

Mullin, Robert. "Sue McSween, Miscellaneous Notes." New Mexico.

Robinson, Jesse. Texas State Archives. Austin, Texas.

Townsend, E. E. Loaned to the author; now, possibly located in Alpine, Texas, or at The University of Texas, Austin, Texas, as a part of Mody C. Boatright files.

FILMS

An Arizona Wooing. Blackhawk Films. Davenport: Eastin-Phelan Corp.

Boatright, Mody C. "The Cowboy Enters the Movies," *The Sunny Slopes of Long Ago.* Dallas: Southern Methodist University Press, 1966.

Bogdanovich, Peter. *John Ford.* Berkeley: University of California Press, 1968.

Bronco Billy's Sentence. Blackhawk Films. Davenport: Eastin-Phelan Corp.

Catalog of Motion Pictures. Davenport: Eastin-Phelan Corp. Spring-Summer, 1972.

Fenin, George and William Everson. *The Westerns from Silents to Cinerama.* New York: Crown Publishers, 1962.

Griffith, Richard and Arthur Mayer. *The Movies.* New York: Bonanza Books, 1957.

Lahue, Kalton C. *Continued Next Week.* Norman: University of Oklahoma Press, 1964.

The Moving Picture World. February 18, 1911, August 5, 1911, July 13, 1912, November 30, 1912.

New York Times Film Review. New York: Arno Press, 1970.

Parkinson, Michael and Clyde Jeavons. *A Pictorial History of Westerns.* New York: Hamlyn Publishers, 1972.

The Prairie Pirate. Blackhawk Films. Davenport: Eastin-Phelan Corp.

Stedman, Raymond William. *The Serials.* Norman: University of Oklahoma Press, 1971.

INTERVIEWS

Flynn, Robert. Interview with author. San Antonio, Texas, 1974.

Lucas, Tad. Interview with author. Fort Worth, Texas, 1971, 1972.

McCracken, Juanita Gray. Interview with author. Kennedale, Texas, 1972.

Patterson, Paul. Interview with author. Crane, Texas, 1974.

Roach, Ruth. Interview with author. Nocona, Texas, 1972.

Smith, Velda Tindall and Charlie Smith. Interview with author. Kennedale, Texas, 1972.

LETTERS

Barber, Susan McSween. Letters to Maurice Fulton, Jan. 28, June 13, Nov. 22, 1926; July 2, 1928; Oct. 2, 1929; Aug. 1, 1930. Special Collections, University of Arizona Library, 1928-1930.

Ball, Eve. Letter to the author. Ruidosa, New Mexico. 1973.

Bratcher, James. Letter to the author. Fort Worth, Texas, 1973.

Chrisman, Mildred. Letter to the author. Lawton, Oklahoma, 1972.

Farra, Vera McGinnis. Letter to the author. Oklahoma. May 12, 1972.

Harman, Roy and Clara Snow. Joint letter to the author. Carrizozo, New Mexico, 1973.

Haughian, Mary. Letter to the author. Terry, Montana, 1972.

Koop, Waldo. Letter to the author. Tucson, Arizona, 1972.

Patterson, Paul. Letter to the author. Crane, Texas, 1973.

Polk, Stella. Letter to the author. Mason, Texas, 1973.

Simms, Lacy. Letter to the author. Alamogordo, New Mexico, 1973.

Stillwell, Hallie. Letter to the author. Alpine, Texas, 1971.

Strickland, Mabel. Letters to the author. Buckeye, Arizona, 1971-72.

NEWSPAPERS

Arizona Daily Star. "Noted Pioneer Woman is Dead," April 3, 1941.

Austin American Statesman. "Lizzie E. Johnson," April 25, 1926.

Bent County Democrat. "Women Who Helped Make the West Wild," July 15, 1938.

Boston Sunday Post. George Brinton Beal, October 30, 1932.

Carrizozo Outlook. "Funeral of Mrs. S. E. Barber Held at White Oaks Wednesday," January 9, 1931.

Clovis News Journal. "From Cowboy to Owner and Operator of Vast Domain Marked Life of Charlie Hart," May 29, 1938.

Craig Empire. "Throng in Courtroom for Queen Anne Case," August 16, 1913.

Cotulla Record. "Amanda Burks," December 8, 1972; January 5, 19, 26, February 2, 9, 16, 1973.

The Denver Field and Farm. "Frontier Sketches," April 29, 1911.

Denver Post. "Cattle Queen of Wyoming Must Serve Sentence," October 23, 1921; "Girl Who Has Made Success in Managing Cattle Ranch," Sunday, May 4, 1902; "Jury Unable to Decide if Queen Ann[e] is Guilty," August 13, 1911; Kane, Mary Ann. "Woman Rancher, Alleged Rustler, Dead," August 20, 1956.

Denver Rocky Mountain News. "Cowboy Jo Was a Woman," March 13, 1904.

Denver Times. "Women Who Have Shown Rare Pluck," September 8, 1901.

Fort Smith Elevator. "Cattle Kate," March 1, 1889.

Fort Worth Star Telegram. Clair Eyrich, "Give the Little Girl . . ," May 18, 1969; Jerry Flemmons, "Suckers Were Just Buddies to Our Texas Guinan," May 16, 1969.

Jacksboro Gazette News. "Local Rancher, Rodeo Performer, Jackie Worthington Dies Saturday," September 28, 1987.

Los Angeles Sunday Times. "Kate Medlin Story," January 6, 1907.

New York Telegram. August 6, 1928.

San Antonio Express. "Banquet[t]e Home of Gun-toting Woman," February 11, 1934.

San Francisco Mail. "Mollie Monroe," May 27, 1877.

Steamboat Pilot. "Stories of Brown's Park and Its Glamorous Queen," April 20, 1939.

Tucson Daily Citizen. "Mollie Monroe Calamity"s Counterpart," October 19, 1973.

The Weekly Arizona Miner. "Our California Letter," January 30, 1880.

Western Farm Life. "Grace Newton," September 15, 1937.

Wichita Falls Times. "Famed Wild West Showgirl Now Nocona Ranch Woman," March 30, 1958

PERIODICALS

Abbott, Mary Stuart and Tana Mac, "Child of the Open Range," *Frontier Times*, December-January, 1964.

Barker, S. Omar. "Mrs. Mountaineer," *New Mexico*, May, 1946.

Beachy, E. B. Dykes. "The Saga of Cattle Kate," *Frontier Times*, February-March 1964.

Boatright, Mody, C. "The American Rodeo," *American Quarterly*, Summer 1964.

Bolitho, Willima. "Two Stars," *Delineator*, January 1931

Cheney, Louise. "Lucile Mulhall, Fabulous Cowgirl," *Real West*, March 1969.

Gray, Sally. "Florence Hughes Randolph," *Quarter Horse Journal*. March 1971, April 1971.

Hinkle, Milt. "Cowgirl—Rodeo's Sugar and Spice," *Frontier Times*, October-November 1971.

Jeffers, Jo. "Ranch Wife," *Arizona Highways* 38, September 1962.

Kertula, T. H. "There Was No Christmas," *True West*, December 1963.

Larson, T. A. "Dolls, Vassals and Drudges: Pioneer Women in the West," *Western Historical Quarterly*, January 1972.

Padgit, James. *West Texas Historical Association Yearbook*, "Captain Joseph C. Lea, the Father of Roswell," October 1959; "Colonel

William H. Day: Texas Ranchman," April 1950; "The City Slicker," October 1954; "Early Day Coleman," October 1952; "Early History of New Mexico Military Institute," October 1958; "Mrs. Mabel Day and the Fence Cutters," October 1958.

Perkins, Col. Henry. Mercedes, Texas, "Sallie Skull," *Frontier Times* 6, November 1928.

Porter, Willard H. "The American Rodeo," *The American West*, July 1971.

Richardson, Warren. "History of First Frontier Days Celebration," *Annals of Wyoming*, 1947.

Rogan, Helen. Review of *The Californios*, by Louis L'Amour. Time, April 29, 1974.

Ryland, Lee. "Skirts, Powder Puffs and Rodeos," *Big West*, April 1968.

Shelton, Emily Jones. "Lizzie E. Johnson: A Cattle Queen of Texas," *Southwestern Historical Quarterly*, January 1947.

Smith, Helena Huntington. "Montana's Favorite Redhead," *Colliers*, August 2 1952.

Stoeltje, Beverly J. "A Helpmate for Man Indeed," *Journal of American Folklore*, January-March 1975.

Texas Monthly. "Cowgirls," November 1978, October 1987.

Tilghman, Zoe. "I Knew Rose of Cimarron," *True West*, May-June 1958.

Texas Livestock Journal. "A Female Cow Boy," April 21, 1883.

Watson, James L. "Sharlot Hall: Arizona's Pioneer Lady of Literature," *Journal of the West*, October, 1965.

Willis, A. B. "Queen Ann of Brown's Park," *Colorado Magazine*, April, July, October 1952; January 1953.

Woods, Dee. "The Enigma of Juana Mestena," *Frontier Times*, February-March, 1966.

THESIS

Deaton, Mary Lucille. "The History of the Rodeo," University of Texas, 1952.

UNPUBLISHED MANUSCRIPTS

Alkire, Frank. "The Little Lady of the Triangle Bar," No. A415, Arizona Historical Society Library, Tucson, Arizona.

Cohea, C. May. "Pioneer Women," Panhandle-Plains Museum, Canyon, Texas.

DeSpain, Jackie. "Lillie Fox," Panhandle-Plains Museum, Canyon, Texas.

Evans, Coleman. Papers. Diary. No. 0692E, Arizona Historical Society Library, Tucson, Arizona.

Harrell, Adelle. "Bob Crabb, Ranchman on Shoe-Bar Ranch," Panhandle-Plains Museum, Canyon, Texas.

Kitt, Mrs. George. "Mrs. John Slaughter," No. 56312-3, Arizona Historical Society Library, Tucson, Arizona.

Reynolds, F. Newton. "Pioneering in the West." Panhandle-Plains Museum, Canyon, Texas.

Warner, Phoebe Kerrick. "Molly Ann Goodnight," Panhandle-Plains Museum, Canyon, Texas.

INDEX

About the Author

Joyce Roach's roots are in rural Texas. She has never gotten over it, nor is she trying. The rural past is the source of her best writing in non-fiction—*Eats: A Folk History of Texas Foods*—co-authored with Ernestine Sewell Linck; fiction, a short story—"Just As I Am" —Doubleday Anthology, *Women of the West*; children's stories—*A Horned Toad's Christmas;* musical folk-drama— *Texanna* and *Nancy MacIntyre, A Tale of the Prairies*, and humorous narrative —"A High Toned Woman"— from *Hoein' the Short Rows.* She speaks, sings, teaches and writes about the West and agrees with one of the lines from *The Cowgirls*—"If it's any better on the outside, I'm willing to be cheated."

Joyce Gibson Roach is a member of the Texas Institute of Letters and the Texas Folklore Society, a two-time winner of the Spur Award from Western Writers of America—one of them for *The Cowgirls*—and a recipient of the Carr P. Collins Award for nonfiction from the TIL.